T5-ASC-437

PREDICTING SUCCESS IN HIGHER-LEVEL POSITIONS

PREDICTING SUCCESS IN HIGHER-LEVEL POSITIONS

A Guide to the System for
Testing and
Evaluation of Potential

Melany E. Baehr

Quorum Books

NEW YORK · WESTPORT, CONNECTICUT · LONDON

658.3112
B13p

Library of Congress Cataloging-in-Publication Data

Baehr, Melany E.
    Predicting success in higher-level positions : a guide to the
System for Testing and Evaluation of Potential / Melany E. Baehr.
        p.   cm.
    Includes bibliographical references and index.
    ISBN 0–89930–626–8 (alk. paper)
    1. System for testing and evaluation of potential.   2. Employment
tests—Data bases.   3. Job analysis—Data bases.   4. Job
descriptions—Data bases.   5. Job evaluation—Data bases.
I. Title.
HF5549.5.E5B35   1992
658.3′112′011—dc20   91–22017

British Library Cataloguing in Publication Data is available.

Copyright © 1992 by Melany E. Baehr

All rights reserved. No portion of this book may be
reproduced, by any process or technique, without the
express written consent of the publisher.

Library of Congress Catalog Card Number: 91–22017
ISBN: 0–89930–626–8

First published in 1992

Quorum Books, One Madison Avenue, New York, NY 10010
An imprint of Greenwood Publishing Group, Inc.

Printed in the United States of America

The paper used in this book complies with the
Permanent Paper Standard issued by the National
Information Standards Organization (Z39.48–1984).

10 9 8 7 6 5 4 3 2 1

For my daughters
E. Alexandra Baehr and Karen E. Baehr,
in acknowledgment of their support
and understanding

University Libraries
Carnegie Mellon University
Pittsburgh, Pennsylvania 15213

Contents

Illustrations

TABLES

FIGURES

APPENDICES

Acknowledgments

The research underlying the System for Testing and Evaluation of Potential (STEP) program was initiated in the early 1970s at the Human Resources Center of The University of Chicago. The Human Resources Center was an interdisciplinary organization with faculty representatives from the behavioral sciences, education, and business administration. The STEP project was a group effort conducted primarily by the Human Resources Research and Development Division of the Center, with contributions from a number of the Center's other professional members.

I wish to express my gratitude to all of the Center's faculty and staff who contributed to the project. In particular, I am indebted to Dr. Wallace G. Lonergan, Director of the Center, for his support over the years and for his personal participation in the project. I am also deeply appreciative of the varied contributions of my long-time professional associate and Technical Editor, the late Frances M. Burns. I am indebted to the Center's Measurement Analysis and Research Laboratory for data processing and to the Laboratory's Director, Mr. Ernest C. Froemel, for his professional contribution to and continuing interest in the project.

An uneasy period in the history of the project came after the closing of the Human Resources Center in 1982, when the future of the accumulated data banks, psychological measurement instruments, and ongoing research studies was uncertain. The project's uninterrupted continuation was ensured through a grant provided by Mr. J. Patrick Rooney, Chief Executive Officer of the Golden Rule Insurance Company, to whom I tender my grateful thanks. The project was eventually continued under the jurisdiction of The University of Chicago's Office of Continuing Education with the understanding support of the Office's Director, Mr. Philip Nowlen.

The present publication was made possible through the support and services provided by London House. I am indebted to Dr. William Terris, Chairman; Dr. John Jones, Vice President, Research and Development; and to Dr. Donald Moretti, Director of the STEP program at London House for continuing the research underlying the program. Considerable strides have been made in improving and expanding the program and in streamlining its implementation in industrial organizations. The present publication is based on the results of an extensive statistical analysis of a considerably enlarged data base undertaken by Research Assistants in the Research and Development Division of London House. I wish to express my thanks for their services and, in particular, for the services of Mr. Ronald Prenta. Finally, I wish to express my appreciation to the clerical staff and the Office Manager, Lisa Hoffman, for the arduous retyping of chapters and tables.

Industrial-Organizational research is not possible without the cooperation of the companies and businesses that provide the employees whose test and inventory responses constitute the data base. Organizations contributed to the ongoing research in different ways. One group of organizations participated in selection test validation studies for specific occupational groups, conducted in accordance with federal guidelines on employee selection procedures. Another group of organizations provided the vast majority of middle-management and executive-level employees by sending participants to the Management Development Seminars (MDS) conducted by The University of Chicago in Vail, Colorado, from 1970 to 1986, inclusive. Most recently, data have been provided by the organizations that have implemented the program through London House.

I am grateful for the contribution of the many business and industrial organizations to the research effort and extend my thanks for their support. It is unfortunately not feasible to list all the organizations that have conducted cooperative research projects with the Human Resources Center, sent participants to the Management Development Seminar, or have contracts with London House. A partial list of major contributors is given in the following section.

The STEP program continues to be an integral part of the MDS curriculum and is the basis of the career counseling conferences conducted individually with all participants. I wish to thank Mr. Paul N. Pohlman, Director of the Seminars, for helping to make the data available for research purposes. I am also indebted to MDS faculty who conducted the career counseling conferences, in particular to Drs. Mihaly Csikszentmihalyi, David A. Kipper, and John Dreibelis of The University of Chicago and Dr. Donald M. Moretti of London House.

In a different context, I wish to thank and to acknowledge the contribution of Dr. Donald M. Moretti for coauthoring Chapter 7; and of Dr. Brian D. Steffy, Franklin and Marshall College, Lancaster, PA who is the senior author of Chapter 9.

Finally, the author takes full responsibility for the analyses and interpretations contained herein as well as for any omissions or misinterpretations she may have made.

Partial List of Organizations Contributing to the Data Base

Ace Hardware

Air Products and Chemicals, Inc.

Alabama Power and Light Company

Albertson's Inc.

American Cyanamid Company

American Hospital Association

Amoco Corporation

Armour Agricultural Chemical Company

AT&T Bell Laboratories

Avis

Bank Administration Institute

Bank of America

Bankers Trust Company

B.F. Goodrich Company

Blue Cross/Blue Shield of Delaware

Blue Cross/Blue Shield of Florida

Blue Cross/Blue Shield of Georgia

Borg Warner Acceptance Corporation

Brooklyn Union Gas Company

Burger King Corporation

Cargill, Inc., Nutrena Feed Division

Champlin Petroleum Company

Chicago, Milwaukee, St. Paul Pacific Railroad

Citicorp

Consolidated Rail Corporation

Continental Corporation

Control Data Corporation

Cooper Laboratories, Inc.

Coors Brewing Company

Country Companies

Digital Equipment Corporation

Dow Corning Corporation

Eastman Kodak Company

Ely Lilly International Corporation

Environmental Protection Agency

Equitable Life Assurance Society

Federal Reserve Bank of Atlanta

Federal Trade Commission

Filene's Basement

First Interstate Bank

First National Bank, Erie, PA

Formica Corporation

General Electric

General Motors Corporation

Golden Rule Insurance Company

Gould, Inc.

GTE

Gulf Oil Corporation

Herman Miller, Inc.

IBM Corporation

Illinois Department of Transportation

Internal Revenue Service, Field Audit Division, Chicago

Iowa Department of Transportation, Highway Division

Jet Propulsion Laboratory

John Hancock Mutual Life Insurance Company

John Sexton and Company

Kennecott Corporation

Lazarus Department Stores

Lukens Steel Company

Marathon Oil Company

Martin Marietta Energy Systems

Massachusetts Bay Transportation Authority

McGraw Edison Power Systems

Medtroic, Inc.

Mellon Bank

Mercury Marine Division, Brunswick

Michigan Hospital Service

Nalco Chemical Company

National Amusements

National Westminster Bank, Ltd.

New Brunswick Electric Power Commission

New Jersey Bell Telephone Company

North American Coal Company

Olin Corporation

Owens-Corning Fiberglass Corporation

Pacific Gas and Electric Company

Pearle Health Centers

Peoples Natural Gas

Portland General Electric Company

Provident Life and Accident Insurance Company

Quaker Oats Company

RCA

Reebok International, Ltd.

Rockwell International

Safeway Stores, Inc.

San Diego Gas and Electric Company

S.C. Johnson and Son

Security Pacific National Bank

Sherwin Williams Company

Silver Burdett Company

Southland Corporation

Sperry Univac

Standard Oil of Indiana

Stonhard, Inc.

Sun Company, Inc.

Supermarket Institute

Teachers Insurance & Annuity Associations

Tenneco

Timken Company

Union Carbide

Union Mutual Life Insurance

Union Pacific Railroad

United Airlines, Inc.

United States Department of Agriculture

United States Department of the Army

United States Department of Health and Human Services

United Way of America

U S Sprint

Washington State Auditors

Waverly Press

Wendy's International

Westinghouse Electric Corporation

Weyerhaeuser Paper Company

Winn-Dixie Supermarkets

Wisconsin Power and Light Company

PREDICTING SUCCESS IN HIGHER-LEVEL POSITIONS

1

Introduction: The Human Resource Management Function and an Overview of the System for Testing and Evaluation of Potential (STEP)

Today's business enterprises have to cope with unparalleled internal and external pressure in a constantly changing environment to maintain profitability, or even to ensure survival. In their speculations on management development in the 21st century, Porter and McKibbin (1988, p. 43) state that "*change* has indeed become (perversely) a steady fixture on the landscape of the 20th-century life." For example, changes can be seen in such diverse areas as foreign competition, technological change and obsolescence, unpredictable markets, social values, women in the work force, government control of wages and employment practices, and increasing numbers of mergers. The realization by higher management that economic survival and success require a relevantly qualified work force capable of adapting to new conditions leads to planning for that work force. Stated more generally, the human resource management system must serve the overall objectives and mission of the organization and thus be linked to the strategic business planning process.

The importance of an integrated, cost effective, and professionally sound system for human resource planning and development has long been recognized. McGregor (1960, p. 3) states, "One of the major tasks of management is to organize human effort in service of the economic objectives of the organization." More recently, a panel of resource executives saw systematic resource planning and its incorporation in the broader, strategic plans of the organization as vital to determining whether or not the organization gains the competitive edge (Panel Discussion, 1985).

How then can a human resource system play a significant role in implementing such diverse objectives as staffing for rapid expansion, successfully liquidating a failing subsidiary, or for moving from a corporate to an autonomous structure? Our research has shown (as discussed in later chapters) that while in the United States we tend to think of managerial potential as represented by the "entrepreneurial manager," such managers perform best in an expanding economy and that "regulatory and controlling" managers, who have entirely different patterns of abilities and behavior are likely to be more effective in a downsizing situation. Again, when an organization changes from corporate to autonomous management, as in the case of AT&T, different patterns of managerial skills are required, which may demand the reorganization of the entire management structure.

To be effective in helping to implement organizational objectives, a human resource system must fulfill at least two needs: (1) accurately forecasting the human resource requirements and (2) providing management with the tools and knowledge for sound personnel decisions. In general, businesses and their managers have been slower to accept and act on advances in the social sciences than on those in any other branch of science. Part of the reason for this is that managers feel that they have been familiar with the content of the social sciences, human nature, since their childhood as opposed to, say, the content of nuclear physics or microbiology. This leads managers to rely on what they perceive as their experience-based knowledge of human nature in personnel decision making. The writer, in the role of consultant in industrial organizations, has encountered managers who do seem to have developed considerable insight into human behavior. As a result of long years of watching successful and unsuccessful performers in particular positions, they can now make well-informed guesses as to which employee will be successful in those positions. This discerning ability, however, is likely to be specific to the positions and could not be effectively applied to organizational development programs for employees in different occupational specialties and levels of organizational functioning.

Another reason for managers' skepticism with respect to the social sciences, whose subject matter is that most complex of mechanisms, the human being, is that the social sciences are, indeed, less well developed than their physical counterparts. Vital areas of controversy in certain areas of the social sciences have resulted in a less well-accepted body of knowledge and in findings that are necessarily less precisely stated than those of the physical sciences. This situation, combined with management's strong desire for efficient human resource management tools has, in the past, led to a fair amount of quackery and the imposition of reportedly infallible systems on an unsuspecting business community. Fortunately, the Civil Rights Act of 1964 followed by the establishment of the Equal Employment Opportunity Commission in 1965 and the successive governmental guidelines, which prescribed requirements for demonstrating the validity of selection and promotion procedures, did much to remedy this situation. In later years, validation requirements, including the concept of the necessity for the job relatedness of personnel procedures, were well established through litigation and court action. Partially because of the enforcement of these requirements, industrial-organizational psychology has seen a period of considerable progress and growth in the past two decades and many behavioral scientists feel they can make a case to management that their discipline is now able to make a significant contribution to the achievement of the objectives of the business enterprise.

The System for Testing and Evaluation of Potential (STEP), developed and validated over the past twenty-five years at the Human Resources Center of The University of Chicago and later at London House, a Macmillan/McGraw-Hill company, is a human resource management system that can provide managers with objective and reliable information for a variety of human resource decisions including selection and placement, succession planning, and individual and organizational development.

RATIONALE FOR THE SYSTEM FOR TESTING AND EVALUATION OF POTENTIAL (STEP)

Whenever a personnel decision is to be made, psychologists and managers alike quite naturally think in terms of evaluating the qualifications of the individual candidates. Indeed, the measurement of human abilities and individual differences has been the natural milieu of the psychologist since Alfred Binet (1903) began his study of the learning problems of French schoolchildren. It should be noted, however, that the tests developed by Binet (later revised and translated versions are known in America as the Stanford Binet) were directed toward the measurement of a particular behavior outcome, achievement at school. Similarly, if they are to be useful in the industrial environment, evaluation procedures must be linked to the demands of the job or be shown able to predict performance of the important functions in the position as determined by job analysis.

There has been an increasing emphasis on job analysis in the successive governmental guidelines and in the 1978 "Uniform Guidelines on Employee Selection Procedures," which encourages multiunit as opposed to job-specific validations. Job analysis is now firmly established as a prerequisite of virtually all personnel procedures. STEP was planned as a job-analysis-based system. In addition, equal effort and similar techniques were employed to develop separate instruments to measure the demands of the job, and the abilities, skills, and attributes of the individual.

Two Interlocking Measurement Systems

The concept of relating systems for measuring the demands of the job and the qualifications of applicants is not a new one. No one has spoken more eloquently or forcefully of the need to relate systems dealing, respectively, with the world of work and the world of human abilities than has Dunnette (1976). Others have devised methods for accomplishing this link but these have usually been post hoc procedures applied to independently developed systems.

One typical example of these linking procedures is the considerable effort devoted to relating the measures from the well-known General Aptitude Test Battery (GATB) (Dvorak, 1956) with measures from the Position Analysis Questionnaire (PAQ) (McCormick, Jeanneret, & Mecham, 1969). In later studies (McCormick, DeNisi, & Shaw, 1979), the PAQ dimensions were related to commercially used tests. There were also attempts to relate the six categories of jobs in the classification system developed by Holland et al. (1970) to the Owens background data classification system (Neiner & Owens, 1985). To the knowledge of the writer, at the time of its development the STEP program was the first to be based on two measurement systems specifically developed for a higher-level population, with the major thrust of the basic research being to establish the relationships between them.

The Definition and Measurement of Potential

It has long been acknowledged that a critical input in almost any personnel decision, over and above more easily obtainable information about the candidate such as age, qualifications, and past performance, is an estimate of the potential for successful performance in the position(s) under consideration. Although the concept of "potential" is reasonably clear, its definition and measurement in the employment context has been somewhat elusive.

In the STEP program, potential is operationally defined in terms of its two interlocking measurement systems. Specifically, potential is an empirically derived estimate of the degree of "fit" between the requirements of the functions to be performed in the position and the abilities, skills, and attributes that the individual has at his or her command for their performance. Theoretically, it should be possible to assess an individual's potential for a variety of higher-level positions from the administration of a single test battery when the functions to be performed in the positions have been identified through job analysis. Since potential is specifically defined in terms of the functions that have to be performed in a given position, it follows that one cannot speak of "high-potential" individuals in a vacuum. An individual may have different potential for different types of positions or for the same type of position at different levels of functioning.

Severe damage can be done to the careers of individuals and to the organization's human resource by procedures for classifying individuals according to some poorly defined concept of "potential" or even of generalized "managerial potential." The labels attached to employees as a result of such procedures often dog their footsteps throughout their work life with the organization. It is not uncommon for supposedly infallible "high potentials" to find that they cannot perform effectively in a different functional department or in positions with increased responsibility. It is in such failure-prone situations that work "burnout" begins to appear and, depending on the organization's human resource policy, the afflicted individual may either be given extended leave and advice to seek help, put out to pasture in some nonsensitive position, or ruthlessly severed from the payroll. Just as bad, and more difficult to document, is the number of "low potentials" who are never given the opportunity to try out for other positions. The sad results of the procedures are the flawed careers of individuals and the irresponsible expenditure of the organization's human resource.

The Measurement of Acquired Job Skills

Since the estimates of potential are derived from measures of the individual's mental abilities, aptitudes, and basic behavior tendencies that are relatively permanent after maturity, it follows that some newly graduated M.B.A.'s may show excellent potential for an executive position but no one would seriously consider placing them there until they had acquired further maturity and proficiency in the relevant job skills. Job skill is, therefore, the flip side of potential. Potential is the individual's capability of performing in a position, the level of job skill is the individual's "job readiness" for placement in the position.

As in the case of the estimates of potential, in this job-analysis-based program the assessments of job skills are derived from the operational definition of the job obtained through a job analysis. Precisely the same instrument that is used in the job analysis is used, with a different response mode, by the individual for self-assessment, or by the supervisor for the assessment of the individual's proficiency in the identified important functions of the job. Details of this procedure and its applications for the diagnosing of training needs and for individual and organizational development are given in later chapters.

THE TARGET POPULATION

Since a prerequisite of the STEP program is the identification of the functions performed in the position(s) under consideration, it follows that it is applicable only to those positions for which this information is known or attainable.

Classification by Hierarchy and Level of Functioning

The STEP program was specifically developed for higher-level personnel who are incumbents in twelve occupational groups that occur in four, three-rung managerial hierarchies encountered in most business and industrial organizations. These are (1) the Line managerial hierarchy, starting with first- and second-line supervisors; (2) the Professional managerial hierarchy, starting with university-trained engineers, architects, and other hard-science professionals; (3) the traditional Sales managerial hierarchy, starting with sales representatives of industrial products; and (4) the Technical hierarchy, recently developed in response to the burgeoning high-technology organizations, starting with technical specialists such as programmers and computer analysts. The remaining eight key positions are the four middle-level managers and four executive managers of these personnel.

This rational classification system for higher-level employees was developed in response to research needs and has also proved useful for a number of practical personnel procedures. In the Hunter and Schmidt terminology (see Hunter, 1986), upward movement across the levels in any hierarchy indicates increasing "complexity" of the job, and membership in a hierarchy indicates "type" or occupational speciality. Figure 1.1 illustrates this classification system.

General Characteristics of the Target Population

The types of organizations that represent the four hierarchies, the typical educational qualifications of incumbents, and typical job titles found at all three of the levels in each hierarchy are shown in Figure 1.2.

Educational Qualifications

In the Line hierarchy, incumbents are generally not expected to have specific educational qualifications at the entry-level position. The average number of years of education at this level is generally one or two years beyond high school, very often at a junior college or trade school. Managers in the Line hierarchy often hold bachelor's degrees or beyond, reflecting the fact that middle managers in this hierarchy are often recruited at college campuses and placed directly in management training programs.

Entrants to the Professional and Technical hierarchies are generally required to hold at least bachelor's degrees in their areas of speciality. Master's or doctor's degrees are often held by their respective managers. Specific academic qualifications are generally not required for entry-level

Figure 1.1
Twelve Key Positions in Four, Three-Rung Managerial Hierarchies

Occupational Level	Line	Professional	Sales	Technical
I	Executives Vice Presidents General Managers	Executives Vice Presidents General Managers	Executives Vice Presidents General Managers	Executives Vice Presidents General Managers
II	Middle Managers of Line Personnel	Middle Managers of Professional Personnel	Middle Managers of Sales Personnel	Middle Managers of Technical Specialist Personnel
III	Supervisors 1st and 2nd Line	Non-Management Professionals Engineers Scientists Lawyers Architects	Sales Representatives	Technical Specialists Actuaries Accountants Analysts Programmers

Sales Representatives, although many hold degrees in the liberal arts and sciences, in marketing, or in areas related to the products sold. The latter often comes about as the result of professionals, such as practicing chemical engineers, switching careers to the sale of chemical products.

Average Annual Earnings

Data on the salary and total earnings were collected for all occupational groups for the period 1975 to 1987 and corrected for cost of living increases to the 1987 level. There is the expected rise in earnings from Level III to Level I. The greatest variability in the annual earnings of the different occupational specialities is at Level III, where entrants to the Professional and Technical hierarchies earn in the $65,000 to $55,000 range, respectively, as compared with $30,000 for entrants to the Sales hierarchy and only $26,000 for the lowest-earning first-line supervisory group. The earnings of the different occupational specialties even out at the middle-management level at an average of about $60,000 1987 dollars in each hierarchy. The concurrent average for top executives ranged from $79,000 to $88,000, with executives in the Line hierarchy having the highest average income.

Average Age

Data were also collected on the age of incumbents in the occupational groups. The youngest age group is entry-level Sales Representatives in

Figure 1.2
Characteristics of Incumbents in the Managerial Hierarchies

	Line	Professional	Sales	Technical
Typical Organizations	Manufacturing, Merchandising, Mining, Armed Services	Minerals & Chemicals, Aerospace, Pharmaceutical, Law offices	Any organization with sales forces selling tangible products or insurance	Banks, Insurance Companies, Computer and Telephone Companies
Typical Qualifications	Managers often hold Bachelor's or higher degrees in the Arts or Business Administration	Bachelor's or higher degrees required in the physical sciences, engineering, architecture or law	Incumbents often hold degrees in the arts, marketing, or related to the products sold	Academic degrees or other qualifications required in computer science, mathematics or accounting
Typical Job Titles **Level I**	Chief Operating Officer, Executive Vice President, General Manager	Director, Electrical Engineering, Vice President - Operating Systems, Chief Engineer	V.P. Marketing or Sales, General Sales Manager	Vice-President - Finance, Manager, Technical Services
Level II	Superintendent, Mine Manager	Superintendent, Product Engineering, Division or Department Head	District or Regional Manager	Group Officer (Banks), Division Director
Level III	General Foreman, Supervisor	Engineer, Architect, Chemist, Lawyer	Sales Representative	Computer Programmer Analyst, Accountant

their early 30s. The remaining entry-level groups are in their late 30s. In general, middle managers in all hierarchies are in the early 40s, and top-level managers in all hierarchies in the middle 40s. There is a trend toward ever younger top-level managers.

THE DEVELOPMENT AND IMPLEMENTATION OF THE STEP PROGRAM

The successive phases in the development and validation of the STEP program were a logical progression in testing hypotheses related to the underlying rationale of the program.

Development of the Two Measurement Systems

The first phase in the development of this job-analysis-based program was a search for instruments that could provide (1) operational definitions of the functions performed in higher-level positions and (2) valid measurements of the abilities, skills, and attributes of present and potential incumbents of these positions.

Procedures for Analyzing Higher-Level Positions

The first requirement of the job analysis procedure was that it be able to differentiate among the functions performed by job incumbents in the twelve occupational groups defined by the three levels of functioning in the four managerial hierarchies. The first intent was to use or adapt an established job analysis procedure. To this end an extensive review was undertaken of job analysis procedures recognized in the discipline of in-dustrial-organizational psychology. At the conclusion of this review, which is summarized in Chapter 2, the decision was made to develop a job analysis instrument specifically for use with the higher-level population in the STEP program. The development of this instrument, called the Managerial and Professional Job Functions Inventory (MP-JFI) (Baehr, Lonergan, & Hunt, 1978), and the definition of its job function dimensions is also given in Chapter 2.

Chapter 3 presents the results of the empirical testing of the ability of the specially developed MP-JFI to differentiate among the functions within each managerial hierarchy, as well as to identify the functions that were common to incumbents at each organizational level, regardless of hier-archy. Each incumbent's position is defined by a profile that shows the relative importance of the functions to be performed for overall success-ful performance of the job. Composite MP-JFI Importance profiles were developed for national samples of incumbents in the twelve occupational groups that constitute the national norms for job description in the STEP program.

The MP-JFI with a different response mode was administered to the same samples of employees that took the Importance version of the MP-JFI. This Ability version of the MP-JFI produced information about the current ability levels of incumbents in the job functions. The job function Importance and Ability data were used to identify the training needs of these national samples of employees as an example of how the process could be used in organizations for targeted employee groups.

Development of Procedures for Measuring the Abilities, Skills, and Attributes of Higher-Level Personnel

The two major considerations here were the types of measures (such as mental abilities, personality measures, and background data) to be used and the procedures that would maximize the objectivity and validity of their measurement in industrial settings. Parallelling the steps undertaken for the measurement of the job functions, a review was undertaken of commonly used evaluation procedures and of reports in the professional literature of the predictive validity of the different types of measures of human ability. The information accumulated as a result of this review (summarized in Chapter 4) was used in the development of a managerial and professional test battery. The battery provides objectivity scorable measures over a wide range of human characteristics. The definitions of the dimensions measured are given at the end of Chapter 4.

Chapter 5 presents the results of an empirical investigation of the ability of the test battery to differentiate among the abilities and attributes of incumbents at the three levels of functioning in each managerial hierarchy and to identify the common and unique characteristics of incumbents at each level of functioning, regardless of hierarchy. The objective was to identify the qualities that were characteristic of the incumbents in each occupational group and that were likely to be necessary for successful performance in the various positions. Composite test score profiles were developed for national samples of employees in the twelve occupational groups that constitute the test qualification standards or norms used in the interpretation of STEP program results.

The Reliability and Validity of the Measurement Systems

Chapter 6 explores the reliability and validity of the measurement systems with respect to both the individual measurement dimensions and the composite scores. The composite scores represent the estimates of potential derived from the test battery and the job skill assessments derived through the use of the Ability version of the job analysis instrument.

The object of validations of selection and promotion procedures is to determine the relationship between the measures of human ability and independently obtained measures of job performance. It is necessary, for both professional-ethical and legal compliance considerations, to be able to demonstrate the extent to which the results of the evaluation procedures (test battery scores) can predict later performance on the job. Some of the approaches taken to validation are described below.

Performance Criterion Validations

The first approach was the traditional performance-criterion validations required by the 1970 U.S. Equal Employment Opportunity Commission (EEOC) "Guidelines on Employee Selection Procedures." In performance criterion validations, the object is generally to predict performance on the job as a whole. The results of 62 such validations undertaken for specific occupations represented in the classification matrix are summarized in Chapter 6.

Component Validity Studies

In this approach to validation, the object is to predict performance on the important components (functions) of the job. Investigations were, therefore, undertaken to identify the abilities, skills, and attributes measured by the test battery that were required for the successful performance of each of the sixteen job functions covered by the Managerial and Professional Job Functions Inventory. Given this information, it is theoretically possible to construct a matrix that identifies the best combination and magnitudes of test scores to predict the ability of the individual to perform each of the job functions. A customized and validated selection test battery could then be developed for any position for which the important functions to be performed had been identified through a job analysis. At the present time this is more of a theoretical concept than an implementable reality, but it seems highly likely that future research will provide evaluation procedures that do not require job-specific validations and are not subject to the usual restrictions of sample size.

Prediction of Earnings

In a third approach to validation, systematic use was made of the entire data base of national samples of employees in an investigation of the ability of the STEP measurement systems to predict earnings (as one measure of an individual's worth to an organization) by hierarchy (occupational specialty) and level of organizational functioning. This was done for the three types of measures provided by the STEP program. One of the questions to be answered here was the relative importance in determining earnings of (1) the particular functions that were important in the position, (2) the ability of the incumbent to perform the functions, and (3) the incumbent's test battery scores, which had been shown to predict performance. If such relationships could be shown to exist for particular occupations, it would then be necessary to determine if the relationships would hold for national samples of employees in different institutional and geographical settings.

Validity of the Derived Composites

In the most recent, and perhaps the most stringent, test of the validity of the STEP program, the derived estimates of potential for successful performance and of acquired job skills have been related to significant aspects of work behavior. It has been possible to conduct studies in organizations in which to determine whether (1) the estimates of potential for the present position predict independently obtained measures of performance in the position, (2) the job skill assessments predict supervisory ratings of proficiency, and (3) the estimates of potential for performance in future positions predict supervisors' estimates of the employee's promotability.

Applications of the STEP Program

There are two major types of applications of the STEP program. The first type is organization applications through the use of the Managerial and Professional Job Functions Inventory. These applications include studies of organizational structure, job design and clarification, the identification of group training needs, and the development of training program curricula.

The other type of application concerns the staffing and development of the human resource of the organization. The STEP program can be used for selection into any of the twelve occupational groups. But in addition to providing information concerning selection into a given position, the STEP program can, at the time of hiring, provide estimates of potential for successful performance in the next higher position. This will allow for early identification of promotable employees by the organization. The STEP program should be particularly useful for the campus hiring of professionally qualified personnel, such as engineers recruited for eventual management positions in the Line hierarchy, since a grade point average may reflect academic prowess or technical expertise but will provide little information about the individual's ability to manage. Chapter 7 describes a number of actual organizational interventions that illustrate both types of application.

Chapter 8 is devoted entirely to one application, the career counseling conference based on STEP results, which can take place at any stage in an individual's career. When entry-level (Level III) employees are considered for promotion, all individuals except those in the Line hierarchy face the decision of whether to stay within their professional specialty, where they may be acknowledged experts, or to move into management positions. This is often a critical career decision because, unless the individual has the required managerial skills, he or she is likely to stay at the middle management level with a "fast track" career coming to a sudden halt and with erstwhile colleagues being promoted to higher positions. The results of the STEP program can be used both to counsel individuals who find themselves in this situation and to minimize the occurrence of such situations.

The STEP program is peculiarly suited also for counseling individuals contemplating a move into a different hierarchy since it provides estimates of potential for vertically and horizontally linked positions in the classification matrix. Typical examples of moves across hierarchies would be managers of professionals tempted to accept Line management positions because of higher pay, chemical engineers switching to the sale of chemical products, or technical specialists, such as computer analysts, moving to positions in which they must manage their former peers.

In summary, the STEP program was designed to help select and place highly qualified individuals seeking their first career positions as well as to provide relevant information concerning suitability for promotion up any given hierarchy, horizontal movement across hierarchies, and other career changes that typically occur in one's early 40s. For high-drive managers who have reached Level 1 of a sharply pyramidal organization and who can progress no further except in the case of sudden death or early retirement of their superiors, the career questions the STEP program addresses are the individual's potential for successful performance in different organization cultures or in private practice, the type of extrinsic gratifications (such as market analysis and investing) that could be successfully undertaken to provide continuing challenge, or the preparation that could be made for constructive retirement.

In the final chapter, an attempt is made to predict some challenges to human resource management specialists that must be faced in the next decade and to describe the kind of human resource procedures that will be necessary to meet these challenges successfully.

2

A Review of Job Analysis Procedures and the Development of a Procedure for Analyzing Higher-Level Positions

The technical and practical requirements of a suitable job analysis procedure for the STEP program could be quite easily formulated and are listed below.

1. The procedure should be suitable for, and clearly differentiate among, the twelve key occupational groups in the four, three-rung managerial hierarchies illustrated in the classification matrix in Figure 1.1.
2. The procedure should provide an operational job description for each position in the classification matrix.
3. If a standardized analysis instrument is used, it should conform to the same standards of professional construction, including the reliability and validity of its measures, as those required of psychological tests for the measurement of human abilities.
4. The procedure should be time- and cost-effective for large-scale use in organizations and also be legally defensible.
5. The procedure should be implementable by job incumbents, their supervisors, or other knowledgeable organizational personnel rather than by specially trained job analysts or consultants. This requirement would not only reduce costs but would also give organizational personnel the feeling that they had made a significant contribution in describing their respective positions.
6. The procedure should not be restricted to use in the STEP program, but should also serve as the basis for a wide range of human resource management procedures including job description and design, job clarification, and the identification of training needs.

A rather wide-ranging review of currently available job analysis procedures was undertaken in an attempt to find a procedure that could satisfy or be adapted for use in the STEP program.

A REVIEW OF JOB ANALYSIS PROCEDURES

Although there are many different ways of classifying approaches to job analysis, we found it useful first to divide them into the less-structured procedures and the structured procedures that used standard classification systems or standardized instruments as the major vehicle in the analysis. The latter were again divided on the basis of the job descriptors used in the instrument, primarily into instruments using worker-oriented as opposed to job-oriented descriptors. Worker-oriented descriptors describe the position in terms of the human attributes required for successful performance, whereas the job oriented descriptors describe the position in terms of the activities and functions to be performed for overall successful performance.

Less-Structured Approaches to Job Analysis

Less-structured job analysis procedures can be used to elicit information about the activities performed in a job or the human attributes required for the performance of the job. Of these approaches, the most frequently used are various types of interviews with incumbents, supervisors, or others familiar with the job; observation and analysis of the job; or actual performance of the job by the job analyst. The observation of performance is more readily applied to repetitive job cycles, as found in some industrial settings, or to such positions as those of municipal bus operator and police officer, where observation can take the form of "ride-alongs" through a tour of duty. For most higher-level staff or line executive positions, however, observation of performance on the job would be difficult to achieve if not disruptive and inappropriate.

Interviews may be either "in-depth," conducted with individuals, or interviews conducted in a group setting with incumbents, supervisors, managers, and members of the personnel department. One variant of the group interview is "brainstorming" or the normative group process. The basic principle here is the deliberate alteration of thought process, that is, to use the creative mind at one time and the judicial mind at another time rather than trying to think critically and imaginatively at the same time.

An example of the use of brainstorming as one approach to job analysis occurred in a national validation study for the selection of municipal bus operators (Baehr, 1976). The brainstorming group consisted of a cross section of organizational personnel that included Assistant Superintendents, District Supervisors, and Station Masters, many of whom had previously been bus operators. An hour's concentrated work produced (after researchers edited and eliminated duplications) some fifty characteristics regarded as essential for the successful performance of bus operators. The group assisted in classifying these characteristics as physical, cognitive, and behavioral requirements. Phrased in the language of the group, some of the physical requirements were good coordination, reaction time, hearing, and sight. Cognitive requirements were expressed as the need for "common sense," ability to follow instructions, ability to make out Day Cards, ability to write accurate accident reports, and good communication skills. Some of the required behavioral characteristics that emerged were dependability, self-confidence, keeping a cool head in a tight spot, and consideration for people. The classified list, obtained in a short period of time, was a valuable resource for the selection of tests in the trial battery and also served as the basis for a worker-oriented job analysis instrument.

These less-structured procedures provide insight into the requirements of a job and a wealth of information not readily obtainable by other means. As illustrated in the bus operator analysis, they can also provide the content for the development of scales and instruments used in the more structured procedures. Another example of this application is the Behavior Observation Scaling methodology based on the critical incidents technique pioneered by Flanagan (1954), which was an outgrowth of the Aviation Psychology Program, established in 1941, by the United States Air Force in World War II. Through a series of studies such as the identification of the specific reasons for failure to learn to fly, identification of the specific reasons for failure of bombing missions, and a large-scale systematic effort to gather specific incidents of effective and ineffective behavior in combat, the general principles of the critical incident technique were developed.

In industrial and business settings, where it has been used by a number of researchers, the technique translates into the systematic collection of critical incidents of behavior that lead, respectively, to good or poor performance outcomes. The technique is the basis of the "behavioral events" interviews conducted by McBer and Company (McClelland, 1978) and has also been extensively used by Dunnette and his associates. Of particular interest to us was a study by one of Dunnette's associates, Borman (1973), in which he constructed Behavior Observation Scales (BOS) for line supervisors. He then hypothesized the behavior attributes that would be required for successful performance of each of the identified behavior dimensions and selected tests that he considered to be measures of the hypothesized attributes. Finally, the tests were cross validated against performance ratings on the identified performance dimensions and useful validities obtained for five of the six dimensions. It is conceivable that Behavior Observation Scales could have been constructed for the twelve occupational groups in our rational classification system, the vertical and horizontal links on the BOS identified, and the test battery used to predict BOS performance ratings. But the scales are specific to occupation and time of construction and would have required redevelopment for changes in technology and the economy or for expansion to additional hierarchies and would thus not have been cost-effective. However, Borman's study does provide a clear example of the logical progression from the functions to be performed in a position, to the attributes required to perform them, to tests to measure the attributes and, finally, the validation of the tests against actual performance on the job.

Structured Worker-Oriented Approaches

A review of these approaches provided valuable information on methods used to link taxonomies of work behavior and human attributes. Notable among these was the extensive work done by McCormick and his associates in the course of the development of the Position Analysis Questionnaire (PAQ) (McCormick, Jeanneret, & Mecham, 1969).

The 182 behaviorally related job activities (job elements) used in the PAQ are the result of replicative factor analyses reported by Jeanneret and McCormick (1969) for Form A of the PAQ and later study by Marquardt and McCormick (1974a) using Form B of the PAQ for a sample of 3,700 jobs. Both studies consisted first of an overall analysis of the job elements, then of an analysis of the job elements within each of the six divisions of the PAQ. The divisions were defined as follows: Division 1: Information Input, Division 2: Mental Process, Division 3: Work Output, Division 4: Relationships with Other Persons, Division 5: Job Context, and Division 6: Other Job Characteristics. There was also a General Division that was not included in the overall analysis. The job elements of the PAQ provide a standardized system for describing a wide variety of jobs, although McCormick's samples tended to include a larger proportion of higher-level jobs.

The link between this job taxonomy and human attributes was established through replicative studies with Form A (Mecham & McCormick, 1969) and Form B (Marquardt & McCormick, 1974b) and produced similar results. In the Form B study, eight to eighteen industrial psychologists rated the relevance of seventy-six human attributes to each of the job elements of the PAQ with satisfactorily high pooled reliability ratings. Thirty-seven of the seventy-six human attributes were obtained from a list produced by Theologus, Romashko, and Fleishman (1970) as a result of efforts undertaken at the American Institutes for Research to provide a unifying set of variables for describing human task performance. The thirty-seven attributes, each with its own definition, covered human performance in the sensory, perceptual, cognitive, psychomotor, and physical areas.

There was substantial correspondence in the factorial structures obtained from the separate principle components analyses of the job element data and the attribute data. Dunnette's comments in connection with the earlier study are also appropriate here.

The underlying similarity of the two sets of factor structures is, in a way, a kind of first requirement for concluding that fundamental similarities exist between taxonomies based on estimated importance of task elements for getting jobs done and the aptitudinal and adaptive attributes judged to be important in each of those task elements. This is an important finding, for it lays the groundwork for the further argument (basic to the concept of synthetic validity) that if a given kind of work activity, task element, or job dimension is found to be common to different jobs, then the human attributes necessary for doing those jobs ought also to be the same or similar. (Dunnette, 1976, p. 508)

The PAQ has also been involved in more direct and extensive studies of synthetic (component) validity with Forms A and B. In the Form B study, the United States Training and Employment Service supplied, for a total of 141 jobs, incumbents' dimension scores and the traditional validity coefficients for the dimensions of the General Aptitude Test Battery (GATB) (Dvorak, 1956). The 141 jobs were found to correspond with 659 positions for which PAQ job dimension scores and attribute profiles could be developed based, respectively, on the 37 job data dimensions and the 23 attribute dimensions derived from the analysis of 2,300 jobs. The job and attribute data were regressed separately in a double cross-validation design against the GATB scores and against the validity coefficients. The final results indicated that GATB scores were better predicted than the validity coefficients and that the attribute data predicted the test scores just about as well as the job data. The range of correlations over the nine dimensions of the GATB for the prediction of the mean GATB dimension scores was .46 to .76 for the job data and .47 to .75 for the attribute data. In later studies (McCormick, DeNisi, & Shaw, 1979) the PAQ dimensions were related to commercially used tests. Since the PAQ job data consists of worker-oriented behavior characteristics, it is not applicable for some of the requirements of the STEP program, those of job design and organization development. For the latter applications, the job descriptors must consist of the actual activities performed in the position. To date, the major applications of the PAQ have been for job classification and for job evaluation directed toward determining base wage and salary rates.

Primoff is one of the rather limited number of practitioners who has implemented personnel procedures based on component validity studies. The actual procedure was called the *J*-coefficient (job-coefficient) (Primoff, 1955). It was developed for use by the United States Civil Service Commission for selecting tests for trades and industrial jobs in the federal service at a time when emergency manpower needs placed a heavy strain on the testing facilities of the commission. Primoff describes the

J-coefficient as an approximation of the coefficient obtained from traditional validation procedures, a view with which Wherry (1955) concurs in his review of the coefficient.

To calculate the *J*-coefficient it is necessary to have (1) a list of elements (behavior units) covering the skills, abilities, and attributes required for successful performance of the job; (2) trained analysts who follow a standardized checklist procedure when interviewing incumbents or experts to determine the degree to which each element is required for the successful performance of the job; and (3) a matrix of standardized and stabilized beta weights for the elements on each test used in the evaluation of individuals. The *J*-coefficient is the sum, for all elements, of the cross products of the beta weights for the tests and the job values obtained from the job analysis.

Since the 1950s there have been considerable refinements and additions to the job elements, including measures of potential and motivation (Primoff, 1969). Still later Primoff (1972) reported the results of a study that showed that, with proper directions and definition of the elements, the job analysis could be performed by knowledgeable incumbents and supervisors (as opposed to job analysts) and that six raters were sufficient to achieve acceptable reliability.

These are important results for the objectives of the STEP program since, from the outset, it was intended that the job analysis should be conducted by organization personnel. In addition, after the relationships between the job analysis measures and measures of human attributes had been established, it seemed likely that component validity studies would be one approach taken in investigating the validity of the procedure.

A number of other well-developed job analysis systems should at least be briefly mentioned. One of these is Functional Job Analysis (FJA), developed in the course of research undertaken for the third edition of the Dictionary of Occupational Titles (DOT) (1965). The original application was to improve job placement and counseling for workers registering for employment at local employment service offices. Since then, FJA has been adapted for use in business and industrial organizations (Fine, 1974).

The first step in applying FJA for a given position is the development of task statements, with a strictly defined structure, by job analysts. The task is then rated on ordinal scales with respect to the handling of Data, People, and Things. The descriptors of these scales at lower levels are job activities that tend to shade into behavior attributes at higher, more complex levels. The Data function has a seven-point scale that ranges from activities at the low level like "comparing" and "copying" up to "synthesizing," which is defined as "takes off in new directions on the basis of personal intuitions, feelings, and ideas" (Fine & Wiley, 1971, p. 33). The People function is a nine-point scale ranging from "taking instructions" to "negotiating" and "mentoring," and the Things function is an eight-point scale ranging from "tending" and "handling" to "setting up" and "precision working." For a complete analysis, the job is also rated on additional scales of human abilities such as "general educational development," "mathematical development," and "language development."

Among other well-known job analysis procedures is an occupational classification system developed by Holland et al. (1970), based on the theory that personality types are reflected by vocational choice. In this system classifications are made with respect to six categories of jobs defined as: Realistic, Investigative, Artistic, Social, Enterprising, and Conventional. Occupations are coded with respect to three of the classifications. For example, a sales position may be coded ESC, which indicates that incumbents most resemble people in the Enterprising occupations and, to a lesser extent, those in the Social and Conventional occupations. Holland et al. describe reasonably successful attempts to link the six categories of jobs to job dimension scores on the PAQ. In a later study, an attempt was made to link the Holland and the Owens (1968) background data classification systems (Neiner & Owens, 1985). Although these systems are useful for many purposes, they are clearly not geared toward job description in terms of work activities, job clarification, or job design.

Structured Work-Oriented Approaches

If a work-oriented approach is taken (where the job is described with respect to the activities that must be performed) a decision must be made concerning the optimal level of the specificity of the job descriptors. Specific tasks and activities can necessarily describe only single and possibly fractionated aspects of the job. Use of more generalized items is likely to describe the work behavior underlying broader job functions. Very generalized items describing work behavior are likely to shade into attributes that facilitate that behavior. A good example of this shading from work activities to human attributes is the job descriptors used by Fine as he moves up the Data, People, and Things scales. The next logical extrapolation is that jobs be described directly in terms of the human attributes required for their performance, as is the case in the calculation of the *J*-coefficient. A description of the relationship between the specificity of job descriptors used and the range of jobs that the structured, pencil-and-paper job analysis instruments cover is shown in Table 2.1, using as benchmarks some of the job analysis systems reviewed in this chapter.

The use of specific tasks as job descriptors in a job-oriented job analysis approach was typified by Morsh (1964) in his studies of positions in the United States Air Force. Morsh's work centered around the construc-

Table 2.1
The Relationship between the Content of Job Descriptors and the Range of Jobs Covered

Item Content	Range of Jobs Covered	Job Analysis Instruments
Specific	Individual Jobs	Task Inventories for U.S. Air Force Positions – Morsh (1964)
General	Same Category of Jobs	Managers – Tornow & Pinto (1976)
		Managers – Hemphill (1959)
		Supervisors – Prien (1963)
		Clerical – Chalupsky (1962)
Generic	Different Jobs	Required Attributes for Any Combination of Work Behaviors – McCormick, Jeanneret & Mecham (1969)
		Required Attributes Related to Tests – Primoff (1955)

tion of job inventories. One, for example, covered all levels of an airman career ladder from apprentice through journeyman and supervisor to superintendent; another for officer jobs from junior officer through company grade to staff officer. These inventories can be economically administered to large numbers of incumbents and the resulting data can be subjected to a computerized hierarchical grouping procedure to identify and describe job types. They admirably fulfilled Morsh's objectives of facilitating training for promotion to consecutive positions in a particular Air Force career ladder. However, even if the approach were adapted to industrial occupations, the extreme specificity of the items as exemplified by "Types Air Force Form 246 (Record of Emergency Data) whenever a change occurs" would preclude its use for comparisons across functional departments.

An example of an approach with descriptors that dealt with broader job functions, determined through factor analysis, for a particular occupation was the research done on clerical personnel by Chalupsky (1962) and the Supervisor Position Description Questionnaire developed by Prien (1963). On an even broader level, closer to the objectives of the STEP program, was a position description procedure for executives developed by Hemphill (1959) that employed 10 factorially determined dimensions. This procedure could be applied across companies and across business functions in a way that would make clear the similarities and differences among executive positions regardless of the company in which the positions existed.

Tornow and Pinto (1976) elaborated and considerably refined the original research conducted by Hemphill and developed an instrument called the Management Position Description Questionnaire (MPDQ). Their approach was a factor analysis of MPDQ responses from 433 position incumbents, covering a wide range of managerial levels and functions, which revealed 13 independent job factors. All positions were then compared and grouped into 10 homogeneous clusters in terms of the similarities and differences in their 13-factor job profiles. These clusters, which were cross validated on a hold-out sample of 56 cases, form the bases of a managerial job taxonomy. Six of the ten clusters are defined in terms of their mean profiles on the thirteen position factors. The first three defined clusters represent upper-, middle-, and beginning-management positions, and the remaining three clusters represent marketing, personnel, and legal functioning departments. It is of considerable interest that this empirical study produced job classification dimensions that closely resemble those employed in the rational classification system used in the STEP program illustrated in Figure 1.1. Both systems classify positions with respect to three levels of management and with respect to a number of occupational specialties. One major difference between the two classification systems, however, is that in the STEP system occupational groups are defined at each management level within an occupational specialty (hierarchy), whereas in the Tornow and Pinto study no indication is given of the managerial levels included in the "functional department" (occupational specialty) clusters. Another major difference is that, as its name implies, that MPDQ was developed exclusively for managerial positions, while the target population in the STEP program covers a wider range of higher-level positions, including such nonmanagement positions as engineers, architects, lawyers, computer analysts, actuarial personnel, and sales representatives.

Although the MPDQ came the closest of the instruments reviewed to satisfying the job analysis requirements of the STEP program, it was decided that a quantitative job-oriented job analysis instrument would be specifically developed for the purpose of analyzing higher-level management and professional positions.

DEVELOPMENT AND DESCRIPTION OF THE MANAGERIAL AND PROFESSIONAL JOB FUNCTIONS INVENTORY (MP-JFI)

The development of the inventory rested on two basic assumptions: (1) that there was considerable overlap in the functions performed by occupational groups at higher levels and that what differentiated such groups was the relative and differing emphasis placed on these functions in any given position in a particular organization, and (2) that it would be possible to write a series of descriptors or "generic" job items that would refer to underlying job requirements rather than to specific functions performed.

The latter assumption became particularly important when dealing with different occupations and automatically excluded the use of any item immediately identifiable as pertaining to a specific occupation. For example, "the ability to make accurate sales forecasts" would almost certainly be regarded as "relevant" or "important" for sales positions and would probably be regarded as "not relevant" by most managerial and professional personnel. Yet, there is some element of forecasting in many higher-level positions. Research and development professionals must make decisions with respect to the structure of new experiments or approaches on the basis of past results, and managers must judge the possible soundness of executive decisions on the basis of past results and present operating conditions. Thus an item phrased in the form, "the ability to predict future results on the basis of past history and experience," could be regarded as "relevant" for a number of different types of positions. The object in writing these generic items was to maintain a fine balance between having them sufficiently general with respect to the basic behavior involved so that they could be used across occupations, but not so general or diluted that they would be equally applicable to all occupations.

Development of the Preliminary Form of the Job Analysis Instrument

The trial form of the instrument consisted of 122 generic job items derived from the literature, from conventional job descriptions, and from job clarification programs developed by the Human Resources Center of The University of Chicago. The items were written in a style suitable for use by job incumbents. After considerable experimentation with different response modes such as "number of times performed" and the "time spent" on the activity, the "importance" of the activity for overall successful performance was selected to describe the jobs.

In early versions of the instrument, respondents were first asked to sort all items (each printed on a separate card) into two piles—one pile for items regarded as relevant to the job and the other for items that did not apply to the specific work involved. Next, they were asked to count the number of cards that had been placed in the "relevant" pile. A printed table included with the response materials indicated how many cards out of any number chosen as relevant should be sorted into each of five categories to produce a normal distribution of job-item importance. Finally, respondents distributed each of the relevant cards into the required proportions of importance and placed each set into an appropriately labeled envelope, with a separate envelope for the "not relevant" category.

The trial instrument was administered to about 600 male industrial employees in nine occupational classifications. These classifications ranged from first-line supervisors through middle- and upper-management personnel in the Line management hierarchy as well as personnel in sales and sales management and in research and development. Twelve underlying job dimensions were determined through factor analysis of the importance ratings assigned to the randomized items, with rotation to oblique simple structure (Baehr, 1967) and incorporated into a job description instrument called the Work Elements Inventory. This instrument was used by the Human Resources Center of The University of Chicago with satisfactory results as one approach to job analysis. The Work Elements Inventory also received very favorable comment in a review of job analysis research by Prien and Ronan (1971).

However, despite its relatively successful usage record, there were a number of practical and theoretical disadvantages that contributed to a decision to revise the instrument. On the practical side, dealing with individual cards made for a very "bulky" instrument, it required supervised administration for optimal results and large-scale mail administration was very expensive. On the theoretical side, the variously sized "nonrelevant" category complicated statistical handling of the data. If the nonrelevant items were used in the analysis there was the danger of their carrying undue weight in the calculation of measures of association. On the other hand, use of only relevant items produced varying and incomplete data matrices that were difficult to handle. Furthermore, in the late 1970s, it was thought that the inventory should be revised and expanded to incorporate possible new job dimensions created by developments in the economy, by increased governmental controls of the environment, and by changes in personnel policies and practices resulting from the Civil Rights Act of 1964.

Development of the Present Form of the Job Analysis Instrument

Two hundred trial items were assembled in a pencil-and-paper format that could be machine scored. They were administered to a vocationally heterogeneous sample of 893 employees. The sample included approximately equal numbers of public- and private-sector employees and ranged from industrial sales representatives and other nonmanagement specialist personnel to chief executive officers. The response technique was a forced, four-interval, rectangular distribution. In other words, the respondent was asked to sort the items so that there were approximately equal numbers in each of the four categories or ranges on an importance scale described as "little or none," "less than average," "more than average," and "outstanding" (See Figure 2.1). It should be noted that, although this rating procedure results in a rectangular distribution for the total number of items included in the inventory, the distributions of the individual items are essentially normal. The reasons for the choice of a forced distribution response technique are discussed in the next section of this chapter.

Using the forced distribution data, a completely new exploratory factor analysis was performed, using a principal axis factor extraction and orthogonal (Saunders, 1962) and oblique (Hendriksen and White, 1964) rotations to simple structure. The solution yielded sixteen underlying job function dimensions. Although the solutions were essentially similar, the oblique solution yielded the clearer structure. The stability of the twelve job functions dimensions in the preliminary form of the instrument is attested to by the fact that the original twelve dimensions all appeared again, in spite of a ten-year time lapse, a different response technique, and a different sample of employees. The titles of the dimensions, with short definitions, are given in Appendix 2.1 at the end of this chapter. The items that contribute to the sixteen job function dimensions are randomly presented in a booklet that is the present form of the instrument called the Managerial and Professional Job Functions Inventory (MP-JFI) (Baehr, Lonergan, & Hunt, 1978).

TECHNICAL AND OPERATIONAL CHARACTERISTICS OF THE MP-JFI

Further discussion of the rationale underlying the construction of the MP-JFI is given in Baehr (1987a) and the basic statistical data and the details of the statistical analyses are given in the *Managerial and Professional Job Functions Inventory Interpretation and Research Manual* (Baehr, in press). Some of the salient technical characteristics and operational considerations in the implementation of the MP-JFI are summarized below.

Use of the Forced Distribution Response Technique

The forced distribution is admittedly an irksome response technique. However, it has been our experience in administering the MP-JFI that respondents will accept the technique if they understand why it is being used. For smooth administration, therefore, the respondents should be given an explanation, before administration, of the benefits of using the technique. There were two major reasons for the choice of the technique:

Figure 2.1
Format for Obtaining the Four Equal-Interval Scale

Managerial and Professional Job Functions Inventory

	Little or None	Less Than Average	Below Average	Above Average	More Than Average	Outstanding	
57. Taking responsibility for the safety record of the group							
58. Developing interpersonal skills to facilitate communication of both facts and feelings							
59. Fairly determining an individual's potential for increased responsibility							
60. Developing and maintaining effective discipline							
61. Continually improving and developing one's own skills							j
62. Developing or assisting in programs to validate organization selection procedures according to federal guidelines							
63. Describing the objectives of the organization to community groups							
64. Handling complaints about the organization's products or services							
65. Forecasting long-range developmental needs of the organization							
66. Seeing that costs are kept within budget							k
67. Consulting with others to insure that new procedures are installed smoothly							
68. Participating actively in committees set up to review work progress and problems							
69. Effectively communicating research results or technical ideas to those who will implement them.							
70. Making immediately needed decisions on the basis of incomplete information							
71. Encouraging the work group to make its own decisions and to communicate them to the supervisor							
72. Making on-the-spot decisions in order to meet production deadlines							l
73. Recognizing the effect of the physical work environment on attitudes toward safety							
74. Knowing how to communicate relevant information to different groups							
75. Evaluating the work performance of others							
77. Assuming a new position in the organization as a vehicle for continuing personal development							
78. Implementing special training programs for newly hired members of minority groups							m
79. Sponsoring or supporting community, civic, and charity affairs							
80. Informing people about new organization products or services							
81. Establishing tentative criteria for evaluating results in key areas of organizational activity							
82. Knowing and understanding policies applicable to management of capital assets							
83. Recommending changes in established policies whenever needed							
84. Coordinating the work from different groups or departments							
Approximate Final Column Totals	7	7	14	14	7	7	n

first to provide a common base for the comparison of the MP-JFI profile scores; second to prevent conscious or unconscious biasing or manipulation of responses.

Common Base for Comparisons

The MP-JFI profiles compare jobs with respect to the importance of the functions performed, or employees with respect to their ability to perform the important functions of the job, depending upon whether the Importance or the Ability version of the instrument is used. The forced distribution technique provides a common base by minimizing the effects of the "constant errors of judgment" such as respondents (1) rating all items as being of "above average" importance for the job or representing "above average" ability for the employee, (2) avoiding hard decision making by rating all items as average ability (or importance), and (3) making an overall judgment with respect to the level of ability (or importance) of the items and rating them all fairly similarly, rather than making a judgment with respect to each item. The objective of the technique is to force respondents to consider each item individually and to make an accurate judgment concerning their relative ability to perform it, or when rating importance, the relative importance of the function for the position. The general tendency is for respondents to rate the majority of the items as important for the job, which results in severely skewed distributions. Such distributions will not provide an accurate or realistic base for job comparisons.

Prevention of Biased or Manipulated Responses

Another reason for the use of the forced distribution technique and the randomization of the items in the booklet is to minimize the opportunity for respondents to bias the results. In order to bias results in some desired direction, the respondents need two pieces of information that they do not have—knowledge of the items that contribute to each job function dimension, and the names of the dimensions that have been empirically identified as important for a given position.

There is a natural tendency for respondents to bias results in a favorable direction, especially when making self-assessments of ability. The concern is sometimes expressed by respondents that the use of the technique results in a distorted picture of their abilities. To ensure that the forced distribution technique did not impose artificial and unrealistic restrictions on employees describing their abilities, great care was taken in the construction of the MP-JFI to ensure that about two-thirds of the items were relevant and differentially important for each of the higher-level positions for which the inventory was intended. There are, thus, no positions for which all sixteen functions are equally important. It seems extremely unlikely that during the course of a work life an employee will have acquired equally high facility in sixteen job functions that pertain to such diverse positions as top executive, line supervisor, professional engineer, sales representative, or computer programmer. The object is to determine the relative job skill strengths and weaknesses of each individual.

As a further precaution to prevent biased results, it is recommended that when an employee is required to complete both the Importance and the Ability booklets within a short space of time, the Ability booklet be completed first and, if possible, a day or two be allowed to elapse before the Importance booklet is completed. Regardless of these precautions, it is a good test administration practice to emphasize that honest and thoughtful responses usually provide more favorable results for the respondent and certainly provide more useful ones.

Four-Interval versus Two-Interval Response Technique

An accurate and valid description of the functions to be performed in a position is essential for the successful implementation of the STEP program and the rigorous four-interval response technique has, therefore, consistently been used for job description. The four-interval technique has also been used for self and for supervisory assessments of ability. However, supervisors are often required to assess the ability of a number of employees in the work group and, under these circumstances, the use of the four-interval technique becomes tedious, time-consuming, and burdensome. In an attempt to alleviate this situation a two-interval technique, which requires that the respondent use only the two middle columns on the scale to assess half of the items as above average and half as below average ability, was tried experimentally. The product moment correlations between the scores derived from the four-interval and two-interval response techniques were calculated separately for the Importance and Ability scores. For both types of score, highly significant correlations of about .9 or greater were obtained between the scores derived from the four-interval and two-interval techniques. This high degree of association between the corresponding scores together with small standard errors of estimate suggest that the two-interval technique, while retaining most of the advantages of the four-interval technique, does not result in a significant loss in accuracy. The two-interval technique is therefore recommended for Ability ratings used for individual respondents and especially when a supervisor is required to assess the ability of a number of employees. This should save half the time required to complete the MP-JFI Ability ratings.

Reliability and Independence of the MP-JFI Dimension Scores

A requirement for the professional use of a psychological measurement instrument is that its measurements be reliable. In other words, the instrument should be internally consistent. Also, administrations of the instrument at different times to the same respondent should produce similar scores unless there has been some intervention that can reasonably be expected to affect a change in the scores.

Reliability

Job function dimension scores were calculated for a sample of 822 vocationally heterogeneous individuals who had responded to the instrument by giving each item an equal weight when calculating the sum of the Importance responses of the items identified as defining a factorial dimension or job function. Thereafter, Cronbach's alpha coefficient of reliability was calculated for each of the job function scores. These are given in Table 2.2. Apart from one "outlier" of .48, the reliability coefficients range from .62 to .93 with a mean of about .82. This is regarded as acceptable for subscores from a multiple-score test. It should also be borne in mind that, when used operationally, MP-JFI job importance profiles are based on composites of at least, and preferably more than, 10 responses made by incumbents or their supervisors with respect to the job under consideration. The reliability estimates for composite profiles would, of course, be proportionally higher than for responses made by an individual. The reliabilities of the job skill assessments for individuals, based on composites of selected Ability scores, are given in Chapter 6.

Independence

Another technical requirement for multiscore psychological measurement instruments is that the dimension scores obtained from the instrument be relatively independent. In other words, the different dimension scores should not be largely repetitive measures of the same skill or ability. The independence of the dimensions was tested by calculating the product moment dimension intercorrelations for the sample of subjects used to calculate the reliabilities. Approximately half of the dimension intercorrelation coefficients (59/120) fell within the range of $+.15$ to $-.15$, which indicates almost total independence. This is considered a gratifying result for dimensions derived from an oblique rotational solution. Approximately a quarter of the remaining items (27/120) fell within the range of $+.15$ to $+.45$ and the remaining quarter (31/120) within the range of $-.15$ to $-.45$. There are, thus, no really substantial correlations among the dimension scores, which indicates that there are no severely overlapping dimensions.

It is also reasonable to speculate about the independence of the Ability and Importance scores, especially when these are both assessed by the same respondent. Common wisdom suggests that there should be some correspondence between these scores since it is reasonable to expect that employees will be most likely to acquire skills in the functions that are important for the job and that their level of job skill may be low in functions that they are not called on to perform.

Table 2.2
Alpha Reliability Coefficients for MP-JFI Job Function Scores Calculated on 882 Personnel in Higher-Level Positions

Dimensions	Number of Items	Alpha
1. Setting Organizational Objectives	10	.81
2. Financial Planning and Review	6	.62
3. Improving Work Procedures and Practices	9	.63
4. Interdepartmental Coordination	7	.64
5. Developing and Implementing Technical Ideas	9	.87
6. Judgment and Decision Making	8	.48
7. Developing Group Cooperation and Teamwork	10	.74
8. Coping with Difficulties and Emergencies	8	.67
9. Promoting Safety Attitudes and Practices	9	.93
10. Communication	8	.63
11. Developing Employee Potential	9	.88
12. Supervisory Practices	9	.87
13. Self-development and Improvement	9	.86
14. Personnel Practices	10	.83
15. Promoting Community-Organization Relations	10	.81
16. Handling Outside Contacts	9	.86

To test the degree of association between corresponding Importance and Ability scores, product moment correlations were calculated for each of the 16 MP-JFI dimensions. This was done separately for incumbents in the four hierarchies. The average correlation for the 16 dimension scores for the hierarchies were as follows: Line hierarchy, $r = .52$ ($N = 162$); Professional hierarchy, $r = .52$ ($N = 195$); Sales hierarchy, $r = .60$ ($N = 162$); and Technical hierarchy, $r = .55$ ($N = 275$). These results indicate that, in all hierarchies, Importance and Ability scores have 36 percent or less of their variance in common. This is a moderate degree of overlap that does not preclude the use of these two measures in determining training needs.

The information given in this chapter concerns the technical soundness of the constructed instrument. Chapter 3 investigates the ability of the MP-JFI to differentiate across levels and hierarchies in the rational classification system.

NOTE

Portions of this chapter are adapted from M. E. Baehr, "Job Analysis Procedures for Higher-Level Executive and Professional Positions," in J. W. Jones,

B. D. Steffy, and D. W. Bray (Eds.), *Applying Psychology in Business: The Handbook for Managers and Human Resource Professionals* (Lexington, MA: Lexington Books, 1991), 169–183.

APPENDIX 2.1: DEFINITIONS OF THE MP-JFI DIMENSIONS

ORGANIZATIONAL AREA

1. *Setting Organization Objectives.* Formulating the overall mission and goals of the organization; setting short- and long-range objectives that are significant and measurable and that incorporate future predictions; evaluating alternative structures for future organizational operations (10 items).

2. *Financial Planning and Review.* Making economic decisions and managing capital assets; establishing a budget and independent controls to assure that the budget is met; maintaining accurate financial records using up-to-date procedures (6 items).

3. *Improving Work Procedures and Practices.* Analyzing, interpreting, and evaluating operating policies within the organizational structure; ensuring that new procedures are installed smoothly (9 items).

4. *Interdepartmental Coordination.* Understanding and coordinating the problems and work activities of different departments within the organization; using informal communication lines as well as work committees to gain and disseminate information across the organization (7 items).

LEADERSHIP AREA

5. *Developing and Implementing Technical Ideas.* Originating technical ideas and designs; translating technical ideas into feasible solutions to organizational needs; leading technical projects and writing appropriate reports; helping the organization adjust to and evaluate technical changes (9 items).

6. *Judgment and Decision Making.* Analyzing incomplete information to make decisions; being flexible in nonroutine decisions; acting on decisions concerning resource and work force allocation; accepting responsibility for the consequences of both one's own and one's subordinates' decisions (8 items).

7. *Developing Group Cooperation and Teamwork.* Encouraging and building work group relations that will lead to better exchange of ideas, improved decision making, more open communication, higher morale, and a sense of purpose; recognizing destructive problems and conflicts within the work group (10 items).

8. *Coping with Difficulties and Emergencies.* Efficiently working under pressure; effectively handling unexpected problems, day-to-day crises, and emergency situations; quickly analyzing operation breakdowns and setting priorities for action (8 items).

9. *Promoting Safety Attitudes and Practices.* Taking responsibility for the identification and elimination of job safety and health hazards; promoting and

communicating safety practices and regulations to employees; investigating possibly job-related accidents and illnesses (9 items).

10. *Communications.* Monitoring and improving both external communication channels and internal upward and downward lines; developing, testing, and seeking feedback on one's own communication skills; conducting effective meetings (8 items).

HUMAN RESOURCES AREA

11. *Developing Employee Potential.* Evaluating employees' present performance and potential in order to create opportunities for better utilization of their abilities; examining and responding to employee dissatisfaction; assisting others in overall career development (9 items).

12. *Supervisory Practices.* Clarifying subordinate's job functions and responsibilities; motivating employees while maintaining discipline and control; seeing that subordinates maintain established standards of performance and accepting personal responsibility for those who do not (9 items).

13. *Self-Development and Improvement.* Formulating self-improvement goals; using feedback from others to help assess one's own strengths and weaknesses; improving one's own skills by participating in developmental programs; and, by assuming new positions, coordinating personal career goals with organizational need (9 items).

14. *Personnel Practices.* Ensuring that the organization adheres to federal equal employment opportunity requirements in its employee selection procedures; keeping informed on current issues and procedures in employee selection; developing and implementing special recruiting and training programs for minority applicants (10 items).

COMMUNITY AREA

15. *Promoting Community-Organization Relations.* Staying informed on community social, economic, and political problems and their relevance to and impact on the organization; accepting responsibility for the ongoing relationship between the organization and the community; actively seeking information from, and disseminating information to, the community about the organization (10 items).

16. *Handling Outside Contacts.* Promoting the organization and its products to outside contacts and clients; handling and entertaining long-term clients, suppliers, and visitors so as to properly convey the organization's relationship with them; expediting customers' special requests and handling their complaints about the organization (8 items).

3

Identification of the Functions Performed by Managerial Hierarchy and Level of Organizational Functioning

The ability to clearly identify and differentiate among the important functions characteristically performed by the occupational groups in the classification matrix would attest to both the structural reality of the classification system and the job analysis procedure used to define the jobs. In order to test the first requirement for the practical use of the MP-JFI, two analyses of variance were undertaken. One was to determine whether or not there were significant differences in the functions performed at different levels of functioning for the total group of employees and, if so, at the different levels of functioning separately within each hierarchy. The second analysis sought to determine whether or not there were significant differences in the functions performed by incumbents in the four different hierarchies (occupational specialties) and, if so, whether or not there were also significant differences in functions performed separately at each level of organizational functioning in the different hierarchies.

In short, the objective of the analyses was to identify the important functions performed at different levels of organizational functioning in different hierarchies or occupational specialties and, even more narrowly, within each of the twelve occupational groups. The composite MP-JFI profiles of the employees in the twelve occupational groups would provide operational job descriptions of these positions on a national level. These job descriptions could serve as standards that would allow an organization to determine the extent to which its job structures resembled those of comparable positions in similar organizations nationwide.

The second section of this chapter deals with the job skill levels of the occupational groups and the identification of training needs.

THE NATIONAL SAMPLE DATA BASE

The sample of line, professional, sales, and technical personnel who had completed the MP-JFI dates from 1978. Table 3.1 shows the total sample of 1,605 cases, classified by level in each hierarchy and by type of business. The first three columns of Table 3.1 represent employees in largely industrial, profit-making organizations as opposed to employees in the fourth and fifth columns, which represent employees in largely governmental, not-for-profit organizations. It was hypothesized that factors such as the stress involved in meeting profit margins and the merit promotional and pay systems in industrial organizations as opposed to the then civil service promotion by tenure and payment by grade level would result in some significant differences in the functional job descriptions.

It was decided, therefore, to exclude the not-for-profit organizations from the sample. The remaining 1,358 cases (84.6% of the sample) were regarded as employees in profit-making institutions in the United States and were used in subsequent analyses. In analyzing the similarities and differences in functions performed by this vocationally heterogeneous group of employees, we are seeking general trends, or the predominant functions usually performed by the various occupational groups. There will probably always be some variation in the functions performed by similar occupational groups in different organizations possibly due to some differences in operational conditions or organization work environments.

ANALYSIS OF THE JOB FUNCTIONS

The employees in the organizational groups listed in Table 3.1 completed the MP-JFI with respect to the importance of the activities that they performed in their positions. The importance values for the factorially determined clusters of activities contribute, respectively, to the 16 MP-JFI job function or dimension scores. The average dimension scores for each occupational group were converted to normalized standard scores with a mean of 50 and a standard deviation of 10. The dimension means, standard deviations, normalized standard scores, and the numbers in each occupational group are given in the *Managerial and Professional Job Functions Inventory Interpretation and Research Manual* (Baehr, in press). The occupational group profiles, based on the normalized standard scores, are shown for each of the three levels in the Line, Professional, Sales, and Technical hierarchies, respectively, in Figures 3.1, 3.2, 3.3, and 3.4. In these figures the numbers given in the SS column are, for each of the 16 job functions listed, the average of the standard score importance values ascribed to the function by each of the three occupa-

Table 3.1
Classification of the Cases in the Sample by Type of Business, Hierarchy, and Occupational Level

Business	Industry	Banking	Hospital	Government	Voluntary	Total	Percent
Level							
Line I	58	10	7	11	1	87	5.4%
Line II	144	14	9	7	1	175	10.9%
Line III	241	1	27	0	0	269	16.8%
Prof. I	87	7	5	44	4	147	9.2%
Prof. II	99	22	3	76	1	201	12.5%
Prof. III	160	8	1	86	1	256	16.0%
Sales I	29	5	2	0	0	36	2.2%
Sales II	39	10	1	0	0	50	3.1%
Sales III	134	0	0	0	0	134	8.3%
Technical I	24	37	5	5	0	71	4.4%
Technical II	43	67	3	9	0	122	7.6%
Technical III	4	51	1	1	0	57	3.6%
Total	1062	232	64	239	8	1605	100%
%	66.2%	14.4%	4.0%	14.9%	0.5%	100%	

tional groups in a given hierarchy. For example, in Figure 3.1, 67 in the SS column is the average importance value ascribed to the Objective Setting function by executives (E) in the Line hierarchy. Similarly, 58 and 45 are the average importance values, respectively, of middle managers (M) and lines supervisors (L) for the Objective Setting function in the Line hierarchy. These numbers have been plotted on the normalized standard score scale shown at the top of the grid.

There is a direct relationship between the equal-internal standard score scale shown at the top of the grid and the conventional centile (percentile) scale shown at the bottom of the grid. Thus, a standard score of 50 (at the mean of the 0 to 100 SS scale) always converts to a centile of 50. This is interpreted to mean that a standard score of 50 (obtained either as an average for an occupational group or by an individual) exceeds that of 50% of the normative population. Similarly, it will be seen, by comparing the standard score and centile scales, that a standard score of

Figure 3.1
Average Job Function Importance Scores for Level I Executives (E), Level II Middle Managers (M), and Level III Line Supervisors (L) in the Line Hierarchy

CATEGORY	Scale	CS	SS	Normalized Standard Score Scale	Prob
ORGANIZATION				37.5 40 42.5 45 47.5 50 52.5 55 57.5 60 62.5	
1. Objective Setting		96	67	EEEEEEEEEEEEEEEEEEEEEEEEEEEEEEEEEEEEEEEEEEEEEEEEEE	.000***
		79	58	MMMMMMMMMMMMMMMMMMMMMMMMMMMMMMMMMM	
		31	45	LLLLLLLLLLLLLLLL	
2. Financial Planning		73	56	EEEEEEEEEEEEEEEEEEEEEEEEEEEEEEEEEEEEE	.000***
		73	56	MMMMMMMMMMMMMMMMMMMMMMMMMMMMMM	
		21	42	LLLLLLLL	
3. Work Practices		66	54	EEEEEEEEEEEEEEEEEEEEEEEEEEEEEEEEE	.000***
		66	54	MMMMMMMMMMMMMMMMMMMMMMMMMM	
		50	50	LLLLLLLLLLLLLLLLLLLLLLLLLL	
4. Coordination		58	52	EEEEEEEEEEEEEEEEEEEEEEEEEEE	.000***
		76	57	MMMMMMMMMMMMMMMMMMMMMMMMMMMMMMMM	
		46	49	LLLLLLLLLLLLLLLLLLLLLLLL	
5. Developing Technical Ideas		24	43	EEEEEEEEEE	.000***
		24	43	MMMMMMMM	
		34	46	LLLLLLLLLLLLLLLL	
LEADERSHIP					
6. Decision Making		73	56	EEEEEEEEEEEEEEEEEEEEEEEEEEEEEEEEEEEEE	.000***
		73	56	MMMMMMMMMMMMMMMMMMMMMMMMMMMMMM	
		42	48	LLLLLLLLLLLLLLLLLLLL	
7. Developing Teamwork		69	55	EEEEEEEEEEEEEEEEEEEEEEEEEEEEEEEEEEEE	.804
		69	55	MMMMMMMMMMMMMMMMMMMMMMMMMMMM	
		69	55	LLLLLLLLLLLLLLLLLLLLLLLLLLLLLLLLLLLL	
8. Coping with Emergencies		18	41	EEEEEEE	.000***
		34	46	MMMMMMMMMMMMM	
		82	59	LLLLLLLLLLLLLLLLLLLLLLLLLLLLLLLLLLLLLLLLLLLL	
9. Promoting Safety		34	46	EEEEEEEEEEEEEEEE	.000***
		54	51	MMMMMMMMMMMMMMMMMM	
		84	60	LLLLLLLLLLLLLLLLLLLLLLLLLLLLLLLLLLLLLLLLLLLLLL	
10. Communications		73	56	EEEEEEEEEEEEEEEEEEEEEEEEEEEEEEEEEEEEE	.000***
		62	53	MMMMMMMMMMMMMMMMMMMMMMMM	
		34	46	LLLLLLLLLLLLLLLL	
HUMAN RESOURCES					
11. Developing Employee Potential		76	57	EEEEEEEEEEEEEEEEEEEEEEEEEEEEEEEEEEEEEEEE	.000***
		69	55	MMMMMMMMMMMMMMMMMMMMMMMMMMMM	
		58	52	LLLLLLLLLLLLLLLLLLLLLLLLLLLLLL	
12. Supervisory Practices		46	49	EEEEEEEEEEEEEEEEEEEEEEE	.000***
		54	51	MMMMMMMMMMMMMMMMMM	
		66	54	LLLLLLLLLLLLLLLLLLLLLLLLLLLLLLLLLL	
13. Self-Development		27	44	EEEEEEEEEEEE	.067
		38	47	MMMMMMMMMMMMMM	
		38	47	LLLLLLLLLLLLLLLLLL	
14. Personnel Practices		58	52	EEEEEEEEEEEEEEEEEEEEEEEEEEE	.165
		58	52	MMMMMMMMMMMMMMMMMMMMMM	
		66	54	LLLLLLLLLLLLLLLLLLLLLLLLLLLLLLLLLL	
COMMUNITY					
15. Community Relations		73	56	EEEEEEEEEEEEEEEEEEEEEEEEEEEEEEEEEEEE	.000***
		62	53	MMMMMMMMMMMMMMMMMMMMMMMM	
		54	51	LLLLLLLLLLLLLLLLLLLLLLLL	
16. Outside Contacts		62	53	EEEEEEEEEEEEEEEEEEEEEEEEEEEEEE	.000***
		46	49	MMMMMMMMMMMMMMMMMM	
		42	48	LLLLLLLLLLLLLLLLLLLL	

Centile Scale: 11   16   23   31   40   50   60   69   77   84   89

*** p < .001.

Figure 3.2
Average Job Function Importance Scores for Level I Executives (E), Level II Middle Managers (M), and Level III Professionals (P) in the Professional Hierarchy

CATEGORY	Scale	CS	SS	Normalized Standard Score Scale	Prob

Column headers for Normalized Standard Score Scale: 37.5 40 42.5 45 47.5 50 52.5 55 57.5 60 62.5

ORGANIZATION

1. Objective Setting
- 90 / 63 / EEEEEEEEEEEEEEEEEEEEEEEEEEEEEEEEEEEEEEEEEEEEEEEEEEE / .000***
- 84 / 60 / MMMMMMMMMMMMMMMMMMMMMMMMMMMMMMMMMMMMMMMM
- 69 / 55 / PPPPPPPPPPPPPPPPPPPPPPPPPPPPPPPPPPPPPPPP

2. Financial Planning
- 62 / 53 / EEEEEEEEEEEEEEEEEEEEEEEEEEEEEEEEEEEEEE / .760
- 62 / 53 / MMMMMMMMMMMMMMMMMMMMMMMMMMMMM
- 62 / 53 / PPPPPPPPPPPPPPPPPPPPPPPPPPPPPPPPPP

3. Work Practices
- 58 / 52 / EEEEEEEEEEEEEEEEEEEEEEEEEEEEEEEEE / .001***
- 66 / 54 / MMMMMMMMMMMMMMMMMMMMMMMMMMMMMM
- 50 / 50 / PPPPPPPPPPPPPPPPPPPPPPPPPPPPP

4. Coordination
- 66 / 54 / EEEEEEEEEEEEEEEEEEEEEEEEEEEEEEEEEEEE / .380
- 76 / 57 / MMMMMMMMMMMMMMMMMMMMMMMMMMMMMMMMMMM
- 66 / 54 / PPPPPPPPPPPPPPPPPPPPPPPPPPPPPPPPPPPP

5. Developing Technical Ideas
- 42 / 48 / EEEEEEEEEEEEEEEEEEEEEEEE / .000***
- 42 / 48 / MMMMMMMMMMMMMMMMMMM
- 58 / 52 / PPPPPPPPPPPPPPPPPPPPPPPPPPPPPPPPPPP

LEADERSHIP

6. Decision Making
- 73 / 56 / EEEEEEEEEEEEEEEEEEEEEEEEEEEEEEEEEEEE / .000***
- 73 / 56 / MMMMMMMMMMMMMMMMMMMMMMMMMMMMMMMMMMM
- 31 / 45 / PPPPPPPPPPPPPPPP

7. Developing Teamwork
- 62 / 53 / EEEEEEEEEEEEEEEEEEEEEEEEEEEEEEEE / .000***
- 62 / 53 / MMMMMMMMMMMMMMMMMMMMMMMMMMMMM
- 27 / 44 / PPPPPPPPPPPPPP

8. Coping with Emergencies
- 18 / 41 / EEEEE / .000***
- 18 / 44 / MMMMMMMMM
- 50 / 50 / PPPPPPPPPPPPPPPPPPPPPPPPPPP

9. Promoting Safety
- 34 / 46 / EEEEEEEEEEEEEEEEE / .000***
- 34 / 46 / MMMMMMMMMMMMM
- 58 / 52 / PPPPPPPPPPPPPPPPPPPPPPPPPPPPPPPPPPP

10. Communications
- 73 / 56 / EEEEEEEEEEEEEEEEEEEEEEEEEEEEEEEEEEEE / .000***
- 73 / 56 / MMMMMMMMMMMMMMMMMMMMMMMMMMMMMMMMMMM
- 42 / 48 / PPPPPPPPPPPPPPPPPPPPPPPP

HUMAN RESOURCES

11. Developing Employee Potential
- 69 / 55 / EEEEEEEEEEEEEEEEEEEEEEEEEEEEEEEEEEEE / .000***
- 69 / 55 / MMMMMMMMMMMMMMMMMMMMMMMMMMMMMMMMMMM
- 21 / 42 / PPPPPPPPPP

12. Supervisory Practices
- 46 / 49 / EEEEEEEEEEEEEEEEEEEEEEEEE / .000***
- 54 / 51 / MMMMMMMMMMMMMMMMMMMMMMM
- 27 / 44 / PPPPPPPPPPPPPP

13. Self-Development
- 34 / 46 / EEEEEEEEEEEEEEEEE / .000***
- 38 / 47 / MMMMMMMMMMMMMMM
- 62 / 53 / PPPPPPPPPPPPPPPPPPPPPPPPPPPPPPPPPPPPPP

14. Personnel Practices
- 66 / 54 / EEEEEEEEEEEEEEEEEEEEEEEEEEEEEEEEEE / .648
- 66 / 54 / MMMMMMMMMMMMMMMMMMMMMMMMMMMMMM
- 58 / 52 / PPPPPPPPPPPPPPPPPPPPPPPPPPPPPPPPPPP

COMMUNITY

15. Community Relations
- 62 / 53 / EEEEEEEEEEEEEEEEEEEEEEEEEEEEEEEE / .000***
- 54 / 51 / MMMMMMMMMMMMMMMMMMMMMMM
- 73 / 56 / PPPPPPPPPPPPPPPPPPPPPPPPPPPPPPPPPPP

16. Outside Contacts
- 46 / 49 / EEEEEEEEEEEEEEEEEEEEEEEEE / .004**
- 46 / 49 / MMMMMMMMMMMMMMMMMMM
- 58 / 52 / PPPPPPPPPPPPPPPPPPPPPPPPPPPPPPPPPPP

Centile Scale: 11 16 23 31 40 50 60 69 77 84 89

** p < .01.   *** p < .001.

41

Figure 3.3
Average Job Function Importance Scores for Level I Executives (E), Level II Middle Managers (M), and Level III Sales Representatives (S) in the Sales Hierarchy

CATEGORY	Scale	CS	SS	Normalized Standard Score Scale	Prob

ORGANIZATION

1. Objective Setting — CS: 86, 69, 58 — SS: 61, 55, 52
EEEEEEEEEEEEEEEEEEEEEEEEEEEEEEEEEEEEEEEEEEEEEEEE
MMMMMMMMMMMMMMMMMMMMMMMMMMMMM
SSSSSSSSSSSSSSSSSSSSSSSSSSSSSSSS — .000***

2. Financial Planning — CS: 62, 50, 50 — SS: 53, 50, 50
EEEEEEEEEEEEEEEEEEEEEEEEEEEEEEEEE
MMMMMMMMMMMMMMMMMM
SSSSSSSSSSSSSSSSSSSSSSSSS — .342

3. Work Practices — CS: 66, 31, 31 — SS: 54, 45, 45
EEEEEEEEEEEEEEEEEEEEEEEEEEEEEEEEEEE
MMMMMMMMMMM
SSSSSSSSSSSSSSS — .000***

4. Coordination — CS: 58, 38, 38 — SS: 52, 47, 47
EEEEEEEEEEEEEEEEEEEEEEEEEEEEEE
MMMMMMMMMMMMMM
SSSSSSSSSSSSSSSSSSS — .000***

5. Developing Technical Ideas — CS: 24, 34, 69 — SS: 43, 46, 55
EEEEEEEEEEEE
MMMMMMMMMMMMMM
SSSSSSSSSSSSSSSSSSSSSSSSSSSSSSSSSSSSSSSS — .000***

LEADERSHIP

6. Decision Making — CS: 73, 62, 21 — SS: 56, 53, 42
EEEEEEEEEEEEEEEEEEEEEEEEEEEEEEEEEEEE
MMMMMMMMMMMMMMMMMMMMMMMMMM
SSSSSSSSSS — .000***

7. Developing Teamwork — CS: 62, 76, 27 — SS: 53, 57, 44
EEEEEEEEEEEEEEEEEEEEEEEEEEEEEEEEEEE
MMMMMMMMMMMMMMMMMMMMMMMMMMMMMMMMMMMMM
SSSSSSSSSSSSSSS — .000***

8. Coping with Emergencies — CS: 27, 27, 62 — SS: 44, 44, 53
EEEEEEEEEEEEE
MMMMMMMMMM
SSSSSSSSSSSSSSSSSSSSSSSSSSSSSSSSSSSSSS — .000***

9. Promoting Safety — CS: 21, 27, 38 — SS: 42, 44, 47
EEEEEEEEE
MMMMMMMMMM
SSSSSSSSSSSSSSSSSSSS — .000***

10. Communications — CS: 73, 62, 62 — SS: 56, 53, 53
EEEEEEEEEEEEEEEEEEEEEEEEEEEEEEEEEEEE
MMMMMMMMMMMMMMMMMMMMMMMMMM
SSSSSSSSSSSSSSSSSSSSSSSSSSSSSSSSSSS — .525

HUMAN RESOURCES

11. Developing Employee Potential — CS: 76, 82, 18 — SS: 57, 59, 41
EEEEEEEEEEEEEEEEEEEEEEEEEEEEEEEEEEEEEEEE
MMMMMMMMMMMMMMMMMMMMMMMMMMMMMMMMMMMMMMMMMM
SSSSSS — .000***

12. Supervisory Practices — CS: 62, 73, 18 — SS: 53, 56, 41
EEEEEEEEEEEEEEEEEEEEEEEEEEEEEEEEEE
MMMMMMMMMMMMMMMMMMMMMMMMMMMMMMMMMM
SSSSSS — .000***

13. Self-Development — CS: 34, 54, 79 — SS: 46, 51, 58
EEEEEEEEEEEEEEEEE
MMMMMMMMMMMMMMMMMMMMMM
SSSSSSSSSSSSSSSSSSSSSSSSSSSSSSSSSSSSSSSSSSSSSSSS — .000***

14. Personnel Practices — CS: 66, 42, 34 — SS: 54, 48, 46
EEEEEEEEEEEEEEEEEEEEEEEEEEEEEEEEEE
MMMMMMMMMMMMMMMMMM
SSSSSSSSSSSSSSSSS — .000***

COMMUNITY

15. Community Relations — CS: 54, 46, 62 — SS: 51, 49, 53
EEEEEEEEEEEEEEEEEEEEEEEEEE
MMMMMMMMMMMMMMMMMM
SSSSSSSSSSSSSSSSSSSSSSSSSSSSSSS — .000***

16. Outside Contacts — CS: 76, 76, 79 — SS: 57, 57, 58
EEEEEEEEEEEEEEEEEEEEEEEEEEEEEEEEEEEEEEEE
MMMMMMMMMMMMMMMMMMMMMMMMMMMMMMMMMMMMMM
SSSSSSSSSSSSSSSSSSSSSSSSSSSSSSSSSSSSSSSSSSSSSSSS — .000***

Normalized Standard Score Scale: 37.5 40 42.5 45 47.5 50 52.5 55 57.5 60 62.5

Centile Scale: 11 16 23 31 40 50 60 69 77 84 89

*** p < .001.

42

Figure 3.4
Average Job Function Importance Scores for Level I Executives (E), Level II Middle Managers (M), and Level III Technical Specialists (T) in the Technical Hierarchy

Normalized Standard Score Scale: 37.5 40 42.5 45 47.5 50 52.5 55 57.5 60 62.5

CATEGORY	Scale	CS	SS	Plot	Prob
ORGANIZATION					
1. Objective Setting		90	63	EEEEEEEEEEEEEEEEEEEEEEEEEEEEEEEEEEEEEEEEEEEEEEEEEEEE	.000***
		79	58	MMMMMMMMMMMMMMMMMMMMMMMMMMMMMMMMMM	
		58	52	TTTTTTTTTTTTTTTTTTTTTTTTTTTTTT	
2. Financial Planning		82	59	EEEEEEEEEEEEEEEEEEEEEEEEEEEEEEEEEEEEEEEEEEEEE	.648
		73	56	MMMMMMMMMMMMMMMMMMMMMMMMMMMMMMMM	
		82	59	TTTTTTTTTTTTTTTTTTTTTTTTTTTTTTTTTTTTTTTTTTTTT	
3. Work Practices		66	54	EEEEEEEEEEEEEEEEEEEEEEEEEEEEEE	.095
		66	54	MMMMMMMMMMMMMMMMMMMMMMMMMMMM	
		58	52	TTTTTTTTTTTTTTTTTTTTTTTTTTTT	
4. Coordination		66	54	EEEEEEEEEEEEEEEEEEEEEEEEEEEEEE	.001***
		66	54	MMMMMMMMMMMMMMMMMMMMMMMMMMMM	
		46	49	TTTTTTTTTTTTTTTTTTTTTTTTT	
5. Developing Technical Ideas		34	46	EEEEEEEEEEEEEEEEE	.648
		34	46	MMMMMMMMMMMMM	
		42	48	TTTTTTTTTTTTTTTTTTTTT	
LEADERSHIP					
6. Decision Making		73	56	EEEEEEEEEEEEEEEEEEEEEEEEEEEEEEEEEEEEEE	.000***
		62	53	MMMMMMMMMMMMMMMMMMMMMMMMMMMMM	
		42	43	TTTTTTTTTTTTT	
7. Developing Teamwork		62	53	EEEEEEEEEEEEEEEEEEEEEEEEEEEEEEEE	.858
		62	53	MMMMMMMMMMMMMMMMMMMMMMMMMMMM	
		62	53	TTTTTTTTTTTTTTTTTTTTTTTTTTTTTTTTTTT	
8. Coping with Emergencies		18	41	EEEEE	.001***
		27	44	MMMMMMMMM	
		42	48	TTTTTTTTTTTTTTTTTTTTT	
9. Promoting Safety		21	42	EEEEEEEEE	.394
		21	42	MMMMMM	
		27	44	TTTTTTTTTTTT	
10. Communications		73	56	EEEEEEEEEEEEEEEEEEEEEEEEEEEEEEEEEEEEEE	.290
		62	53	MMMMMMMMMMMMMMMMMMMMMMMMMMMMM	
		62	53	TTTTTTTTTTTTTTTTTTTTTTTTTTTTTTTTTTT	
HUMAN RESOURCES					
11. Developing Employee Potential		69	55	EEEEEEEEEEEEEEEEEEEEEEEEEEEEEEEEEEE	.003**
		76	57	MMMMMMMMMMMMMMMMMMMMMMMMMMMMMMMMM	
		58	52	TTTTTTTTTTTTTTTTTTTTTTTTTTTT	
12. Supervisory Practices		54	51	EEEEEEEEEEEEEEEEEEEEEEEEEE	.962
		62	53	MMMMMMMMMMMMMMMMMMMMMMMMMMMMM	
		54	51	TTTTTTTTTTTTTTTTTTTTTTTTTT	
13. Self-Development		27	44	EEEEEEEEEEEEE	.000***
		38	47	MMMMMMMMMMMMMMM	
		69	55	TTTTTTTTTTTTTTTTTTTTTTTTTTTTTTTTTTTTT	
14. Personnel Practices		58	52	EEEEEEEEEEEEEEEEEEEEEEEEEEEE	.018*
		58	52	MMMMMMMMMMMMMMMMMMMMMMMMMMM	
		42	48	TTTTTTTTTTTTTTTTTTTTT	
COMMUNITY					
15. Community Relations		66	54	EEEEEEEEEEEEEEEEEEEEEEEEEEEEEE	.000***
		54	51	MMMMMMMMMMMMMMMMMMMMMMMM	
		79	58	TTTTTTTTTTTTTTTTTTTTTTTTTTTTTTTTTTTTTTTTTTTT	
16. Outside Contacts		46	49	EEEEEEEEEEEEEEEEEEEEEEEE	.010**
		58	52	MMMMMMMMMMMMMMMMMMMMMMMMM	
		66	54	TTTTTTTTTTTTTTTTTTTTTTTTTTTTTTTTTT	

Centile Scale: 11 16 23 31 40 50 60 69 77 84 89

* p < .05.   ** p < .01.   *** p < .001.

55 (given at the top of the grid) corresponds to a centile of 69 (given at the bottom of the grid) and thus exceeds 69% of the normative population.

In this instance, the normative population consists of the total number of employees in the twelve occupational groups in the classification matrix that will be referred to as the Higher-Level Population (HLP). In Figures 3.1 through 3.4, the centile values that correspond to the standard score importance value are given in the column labeled CS. Thus, in Figure 3.1, the importance value of 67 ascribed by executives to the Objective Setting function exceeds that of 96% (the number given in the CS column) of the Higher-Level Population. Similarly, the importance values for the Objective Setting function for middle managers and line supervisors in the Line hierarchy exceed 79% and 31% of the HLP, respectively.

An examination of the four figures shows that, in each of the four hierarchies, there appear to be systematic and often substantial differences among the importance values ascribed to a particular job function by the occupational groups at the different levels of the hierarchy. In the case of the Objective Setting function, these substantial, systematic differences occur in all four hierarchies, with executives always being the highest scoring group. By contrast, for the Promoting Safety function in the Line hierarchy (Figure 3.1), and to a lesser extent in the Professional hierarchy (Figure 3.2), there are systematic differences but the Level III occupational groups, rather than their respective executives, are the highest scoring groups. Again, in contrast to the Objective Setting factor, which shows the same pattern of scores in all four hierarchies, Promoting Safety shows meaningful systematic differences only in the Line and Professional hierarchies and is of less than average importance for all occupational groups in the Sales (Figure 3.3) and Technical (Figure 3.4) hierarchies. The job functions are differentially important for the different occupational groups. It is the particular pattern of the importance values across the sixteen job functions that provides the operational job description for each occupational group.

The following section describes statistical analyses undertaken to determine whether the observed differences in the standard score values are merely due to chance or whether they represent significant differences in the functions performed and thus the demands of the occupational groups' respective jobs. Some of the results of these analyses are given as probability values in the extreme right-hand column labeled Prob on each figure and will be discussed in the following section.

Significant Differences in the Importance of Functions Performed at Different Levels of Organizational Functioning

The statistical significance of the differences among the importance values for the three occupational-level groups (regardless of hierarchy) were determined for each of the 16 MP-JFI factors through one-way analyses of variance. The results indicated that 14 of 16 dimensions had differences across the three levels that were significant beyond the .001 level of confidence (d.f., 2, 1,337). Of the two remaining dimensions, Handling Outside Contacts had a difference that was significant at the .05 level of confidence, and Personnel Practices showed a nonsignificant difference. The above results clearly indicate that the MP-JFI can differentiate among the importance scores for functions performed at the three different levels of functioning in the total sample. In order to determine whether or not the MP-JFI could differentiate equally well across levels in the separate hierarchies, the one-way analyses were rerun separately for each hierarchy. The resulting F and probability values (p) are given in the column labeled Prob in Figures 3.1 through 3.4. An examination of the probability column in Figure 3.1 shows that 13 of the 16 MP-JFI dimensions (marked with three stars) have significant differences across levels in the Line hierarchy with probability values beyond the .001 level of confidence (d.f., 2, 490). In other words, the probability of the differences among the three levels in the Line hierarchy on 13 of the 16 MP-JFI dimensions being due to chance is less than 1 in 1,000. Comparable figures for the Professional and Sales hierarchies are, respectively, 13 out of 16 (d.f., 2, 390) and 14 out of 16 (d.f., 2, 218), with all but one difference significant beyond the .001 level of confidence. The Technical Specialist hierarchy is the latest and thus the least well defined hierarchy to be added to the classification matrix. In this hierarchy, 9 out of 16 (d.f., 2, 233) of the MP-JFI dimensions have significant differences, of which 6 are beyond the .001 level of confidence.

Overall, these results indicate that the MP-JFI can differentiate among the important functions performed at the different levels of functioning for the total group of higher-level employees and separately within each hierarchy.

Significant Differences in the Importance of Functions Performed in Different Hierarchies

An analysis of variance was also run to compare MP-JFI Importance scores across hierarchies. When the analysis was run for the total sample, regardless of level of functioning, all 16 of the differences among the hierarchies on the MP-JFI Importance scores were significant beyond the

.001 level of confidence (d.f., 3, 1,336). In order to determine whether or not the significant differences occurred at all levels of functioning, the analyses were run separately at each of the three levels. The resulting F and probability values (p) are given in the *Managerial and Professional Job Functions Inventory Interpretation and Research Manual* (Baehr, in press).

At Level III where four different jobs are being compared (first-line supervisor, professional, sales representative, and technical specialist), all 16 of the MP-JFI dimensions show significant differences beyond the .001 level of confidence (d.f., 3, 613). At Level II, the middle management level for all four hierarchies, 14 out of 16 are significant at least at the .05 level of confidence (d.f., 3, 444). Of the 14, only 7 are significant at least at the .001 level, which was the standard use for the comparisons made at Level III. Finally at Level I, the general management and executive level for each hierarchy, only 7 out of 16 are significant at least at the .05 level of confidence (d.f., 3, 273). Of the 7, only 2 are significant at the more stringent .001 level of confidence.

Overall, these results show an interesting decrease in the number of MP-JFI dimensions that differentiate across hierarchies at successively higher levels of functioning. Using the more stringent .001 level of confidence, 16 out of 16 MP-JFI job functions differentiate at Level III, where four distinctly different jobs are being compared. This number drops to 7 out of 16 job functions at Level II, probably because of the emergence of the common managerial functions. At Level I, only 2 of the 16 job functions differentiate among the four hierarchies, which indicates that, when the managerial or vice presidential level is reached, largely similar functions are performed, regardless of the hierarchy that the manager ascended. This indicates that, regardless of the functional department in which the career is started, if the employees progress to top management levels, largely similar functions are important for overall successful performance and that the different professional, technical, or other specialist skills that employees may possess have little bearing on successful performance as a manager.

Common Functions Performed by Level and Hierarchy

The demonstration of significant differences among the functions performed as perceived by incumbents in the different occupational groups in the classification matrix supports the reality or meaningfulness of the classification system and also the ability of the job analysis instrument to identify these differences. However, for studies of organizational structure, job design, and the development of training course curricula, it is important also to know what functions are common to occupational groups in different hierarchies and at different levels of organizational functioning.

The important functions common to the hierarchies at each level were identified using the quite stringent requirement that at least one of the four occupational groups at a given level have an importance value of 54 or higher (on a standard score scale of 0 to 100) for the MP-JFI function, and that the other groups at the same level had normalized standard score values of at least 53 or more for the function. This procedure will identify the functions that are both important and common to the hierarchies at each level of functioning. Thereafter, to ensure that an important function was not overlooked in any hierarchy, all remaining functions at each level in each hierarchy with a normalized standard score importance value of 53 or larger were listed. The only exception to these rules occurs for an importance score of 52 for Developing Technical Ideas, at Level III in the Professional hierarchy. This score was included because it had appeared with higher importance values in previous analyses of the data, and because it was significantly higher for professionals than for executives in the hierarchy. The common and unique factors for executives in the four hierarchies are shown in Table 3.2, those for middle managers in Table 3.3, and the functions for the Level III (entry-level) occupational groups in Table 3.4.

Common Functions at Each Level

In view of the results of the analysis of variance, which show that only 2 of the 16 job functions are significantly different across hierarchies for top-level executives, it is not surprising to find a considerable degree of overlap in the functions performed by the executive groups in Table 3.2. Six of the most important functions are common to executives in all four hierarchies. These are Objective Setting, Decision Making, Financial Planning, Communications, Developing Employee Potential, and Developing Teamwork. In addition, Work Procedures and Practices and Community/ Organization Relations are common to three hierarchies. Two job functions are common to two hierarchies and Supervisory Practices is unique to the Sales hierarchy.

In general, top-level executives perform at least three different types of functions: the major emphasis is on the steering and operational functions such as Objective Setting and Decision Making, followed by functions that deal specifically with the development of the work force, such as Developing Employee Potential and Developing Teamwork and, at a somewhat lower level of importance, functions that involve the community outside of the work place, such as Community/Organization Relations and Dealing with Outside Contacts.

The common and unique functions performed by middle managers are shown in Table 3.3. There is some overlap with the top-executive steering

Table 3.2
Common and Unique Functions Performed at the Executive Level in Each Hierarchy

LINE		PROFESSIONAL		SALES		TECHNICAL	
Objective Setting	67	*Objective Setting	63	Objective Setting	61	Objective Setting	63
Decision Making	56	Decision Making	56	Decision Making	56	Decision Making	56
Communications	56	Communications	56	*Communications	56	*Communications	56
Dev. Employee Potential	57	Dev. Employee Potential	55	Dev. Employee Potential	57	Dev. Employee Potential	55
Financial Planning	56	*Financial Planning	53	Financial Planning	53	*Financial Planning	59
*Dev. Teamwork	55	Dev. Teamwork	53	Dev. Teamwork	53	*Dev. Teamwork	53
Work Practices	54			Work Practices	54	Work Practices	54
Comm./Org. Relations	56	Comm./Org. Relations	53			Comm./Org. Relations	54
		*Interdept. Coordination	54			Interdept. Coordination	54
		Personnel Practices	54	Personnel Practices	54		
Outside Contacts	53			*Outside Contacts	57		
				Supervisory Practices	53		

*Common to all levels of the hierarchy

and operational functions, although for middle managers these functions are at a somewhat lower level of importance. This overlap is to be expected since some of the middle managers may well have acquired the skills necessary to facilitate their promotion to higher-level positions. A number of the functions common to middle managers stress the nurturing of employees and smoothness of operations in the immediate work group as represented by Developing Employee Potential, Developing Teamwork, Work Procedures and Practices, and Supervisory Practices (common to two hierarchies) and in the Professional hierarchy also Personnel Practices. In addition, coordination across functional departments is considered important in three of the four hierarchies.

In accordance with the results of the analysis of variance, Table 3.4 shows that there is relatively little overlap in the functions performed by the Level III (entry-level) occupational groups in the four hierarchies. Only two functions are common to as many as three hierarchies. One of these is Self Development and Improvement, which could be expected of this younger group of technical specialist personnel at the start of their careers, and the other is Community-Organization Relations. The interaction with the community probably takes somewhat different forms in the different hierarchies. The most direct interaction would be that of sales representatives. In the Technical hierarchy, accountants employed by accounting consulting agencies often have direct customer service and account responsibility. The more academically inclined personnel in the Professional hierarchy probably represent their organizations through such activities as presentations at professional conventions and consulting with government committees. The remaining functions performed by Level III personnel are either common to only two hierarchies or are unique to each hierarchy.

Common Functions in Each Hierarchy

Some important functions are common to all three levels in a hierarchy, and may be thought of as characteristic functions for that occupational specialty. In the Line hierarchy, Developing Teamwork appears at all three levels. In the Professional Hierarchy, the strongest emphasis at all levels in the hierarchy is on Objective Setting followed by Interdepartmental Coordination and Financial Planning. Predictably, the function that is important at all levels in the Sales hierarchy is Handling of Outside Contacts followed by Communications. Finally, in the Technical hierarchy, there is a strong emphasis at all three levels on Financial Planning. This is logical in view of the fact that a large percentage of the employees in this hierarchy are employed in financial institutions. The other functions common to three levels in this hierarchy are Communications and Developing Teamwork.

Table 3.3
Common and Unique Functions Performed at the Middle Management Level in Each Hierarchy

LINE		PROFESSIONAL		SALES		TECHNICAL	
Objective Setting	58	*Objective Setting	60	Objective Setting	55	Objective Setting	58
Decision Making	56	Decision Making	56	Decision Making	53	Decision Making	53
Communications	53	Communications	56	*Communications	53	*Communications	53
Dev. Employee Potential	55	Dev. Employee Potential	55	Dev. Employee Potential	59	Dev. Employee Potential	57
*Dev. Teamwork	55	Dev. Teamwork	53	Dev. Teamwork	57	*Dev. Teamwork	53
Financial Planning	56	*Financial Planning	53			*Financial Planning	56
Work Practices	54	Work Practices	54			Work Practices	54
Interdept. Coordination	57	*Interdept. Coordination	57	Supervisory Practices	56	Interdept. Coordination	54
						Supervisory Practices	53
Comm./Org. Relations	53	Personnel Practices	54	*Outside Contacts	57		

*Common to all levels of the hierarchy

Table 3.4
Common and Unique Functions Performed by Entry-Level Occupational Groups in Each Hierarchy

Occupational Groups

LINE SUPERVISORS		PROFESSIONALS		SALES REPS.		TECHNICAL SPECIALISTS	
		Self-Development	53	Self-Development	58	Self-Development	55
		Comm./Org. Relations	56	Comm./Org. Relations	53	Comm./Org. Relations	58
		*Financial Planning	53			*Financial Planning	59
				*Communications	53	*Communications	53
				*Outside Contacts	58	Outside Contacts	54
		Dev. Tech. Ideas	(52)	Dev. Tech. Ideas	55		
*Dev. Teamwork	55					*Dev. Teamwork	53
Coping with Emergencies	59			Coping with Emergencies	53		
		*Objective Setting	55				
		*Interdept. Coordination	54				
Promoting Safety	60						
Supervisory Practices	54						
Personnel Practices	54						

*Common to all levels of the hierarchy

51

EMPIRICAL DEVELOPMENT OF A JOB TAXONOMY

The second approach taken in investigating the reality of the classification matrix was similar to that used by Tornow and Pinto (1976) in the empirical development of a job taxonomy. This was briefly reviewed in Chapter 2. The first step taken by Tornow and Pinto was the development of a job description instrument called the Management Position Description Questionnaire (MPDQ). Both the MP-JFI and the MPDQ have factorially determined job function dimensions but the sample of 433 position incumbents used in the development of the MPDQ dimensions differed from that used for the MP-JFI in that it did not include nonmanagement professional and specialist personnel. The MPDQ sample consisted entirely of managers selected to represent three broad levels of functioning in a number of different occupational specialties in different companies.

The analysis produced 13 MPDQ factors or job function dimensions. The factor scores were generated for each of the 433 managers and were presented as a 13-dimension profile of standard scores. The next objective of the study was to determine how similar each of the management positions (represented by a 13-dimension profile) was to each of the others. This was accomplished through a clustering procedure (Ward & Hook, 1963) that, after some checking procedures, indicated that there were ten clusters of fairly similar profiles, six of which were interpretable clusters. Three of the six interpretable clusters were thought to represent upper-, middle-, and lower-management positions, respectively, and the remaining three clusters were defined as representing functional departments.

Tornow and Pinto suggested that their job clusters could serve as a means for classifying jobs. Such a classification scheme would be generally similar to the classification matrix used in the STEP program except that it would not cover any nonmanagement professional or technical specialist positions. The STEP classification matrix covers a wider range of higher-level positions. In addition, in the STEP classification matrix, positions within each occupational specialty are subdivided into three levels of functioning, whereas the MPDQ occupational specialty clusters give no indication of level of functioning or the differences in the complexity of the jobs included in the cluster. In spite of these differences, the broad similarities between the two classification systems prompted a replication of the MPDQ analysis using MP-JFI profiles to describe the positions.

Cluster Analysis of MP-JFI Job Profiles

A sample was selected so that each of the 12 occupational groups in the three-level, four-hierarchy matrix were represented by 30 cases for a total sample of 360 cases. One case was later dropped because of an incorrectly completed Inventory. The majority of the cases (263 or 73%) consisted of individuals who had participated in the career counseling conferences in the management development seminars conducted by The University of Chicago in Vail, Colorado, during the years 1978 to 1986. They thus represent a national sample of higher-level personnel drawn from business and industrial organizations throughout the United States. An individual's assignment to one of the twelve occupational groups was the result of a mutual decision reached after preliminary discussion between the career counselor and the individual. The remaining cases, generally at lower levels in the hierarchies since lower-level personnel seldom attend the Management Development Seminars at Vail, were drawn from organizations that had participated in validation studies for specific occupational groups conducted by the Human Resources Center of The University of Chicago and later by London House.

For each of the 359 complete MP-JFI Inventories, the raw scores for the 16 MP-JFI dimensions were converted to normalized standard scores, using as the normative base a national sample of 900 cases with representation of all 12 occupational groups. The normalized standard scores were subjected to a clustering procedure based on the squared Euclidian distance using the average linkage method (Alenderfer & Blashfield, 1984). Successive solutions for 4 through 12 clusters were obtained. The 12-cluster solution was most easily interpreted. Ten of the 12 were well-defined clusters ranging in size from 12 to 61 job profiles. The eleventh cluster appeared to be a broad representation of higher-level managers and the twelfth represented two cases who had incorrectly completed their Inventories. In view of some of the small cluster sample sizes (shown in the N column in Table 3.6) it was decided not to compute solutions with larger numbers of clusters and to interpret the 12-cluster solution. The averages for the 16 MP-JFI factor scores are given for each cluster in Table 3.5. The clusters in the table are given in the order in which they are interpreted rather than in the order in which they appeared in the analysis.

Interpretation of the MP-JFI Cluster Profiles

Two reference criteria were used in the interpretation of the composite MP-JFI profiles for the clusters. The first criterion was established by comparing each of the composite MP-JFI profiles, successively, with the 12 normative occupational group profiles shown in Figures 3.1 through 3.4. This was accomplished through a computerized profile analysis program (Orban, 1984). Correlations of .5 or greater are shown in Table 3.6. It was occasionally necessary to report correlations of lower magnitude when these were the highest obtained for the cluster. The lower-magni-

Table 3.5
Mean Normalized Standard Score Cluster Profiles on the MP-JFI Functions

MP-JFI Dimensions	A	B	C	D	E	F	G	H	I	J	K
1. Objective Setting	60	54	38	54	47	49	44	60	48	57	58
2. Financial Planning	51	51	42	52	54	49	46	50	54	67	49
3. Work Practices	48	58	43	56	39	52	52	58	46	60	61
4. Coordination	55	63	47	47	44	47	50	57	42	54	55
5. Technical Ideas	45	42	48	56	57	56	46	59	48	50	40
6. Decision Making	54	57	50	44	47	50	58	58	52	56	58
7. Developing Teamwork	52	57	72	40	43	55	53	51	56	49	60
8. Coping with Emergencies	41	47	64	47	56	48	61	48	52	48	49
9. Promoting Safety	45	47	60	55	50	47	64	47	50	45	51
10. Communications	60	64	49	47	47	50	43	54	51	51	53
11. Employee Potential	53	55	53	43	42	51	48	52	64	52	63
12. Supervisory Practices	48	53	67	43	42	50	52	49	59	52	58
13. Self-Development	51	50	47	49	53	66	48	42	52	50	35
14. Personnel Practices	49	54	52	58	50	48	57	49	53	45	59
15. Community Relations	58	50	45	65	51	47	52	46	47	50	53
16. Outside Contacts	55	54	48	56	66	51	46	47	54	47	51

(Clusters)

tude correlations are shown in parentheses in Table 3.6, and the highest correlations for the cluster are underlined. The second criterion was the common and unique factors identified for the occupational groups given in Tables 3.2 through 3.4.

Cluster A: Executives

Table 3.6 shows that the composite MP-JFI profile for Cluster A has its highest correlations (ranging from .74 to .86) with the Level I occupational groups in each of the four hierarchies. The most important job functions indicated on the Cluster A composite profile shown in Table 3.5 are 1. Objective Setting (60), 10. Communications (60), 15. Community Relations (58), 4. Coordination (55), 16. Outside Contacts (55), 6. Decision Making (54), and 11. Employee Potential (53). Five out of these seven factors are listed in Table 3.2 as common to the executive groups in the four hierarchies and the remaining two factors, Coordination and Outside Contacts, are common to two of the executive groups. These results strongly suggest that the Cluster A composite profile describes the common functions performed by top-level executives, regardless of hierarchy.

Cluster B: Middle Managers

Table 3.6 shows that the composite MP-JFI profile for Cluster B has its highest correlations (ranging from .63 to .70) with the MP-JFI profiles of the Level II occupational groups in the Line, Professional, and Technical hierarchies and the Level I group in the Sales hierarchy. The highest job function scores on the profile are 10. Communications (64), 4. Coordination (63), 3. Work Practices (58), 7. Developing Teamwork (57), 6. Decision Making (57), and 11. Employee Potential (55). These six job functions are all listed as common to three or four of the hierarchies for middle managers in Table 3.3 and the cluster is interpreted as representing the common aspects of middle management positions in the classification matrix.

Cluster C: Line Supervisors

The Cluster C composite MP-JFI profile has only one high correlation with a normative occupational group profile, a .78 with the Level III supervisors in the Line hierarchy. The highest job function scores on the cluster profile are 7. Developing Teamwork (72), 12. Supervisory Practices (67), 8. Coping with Emergencies (64), 11. Employee Potential (53), and 14. Personnel Practices (52). All of these functions, with the exception of 11. Employee Potential, are listed as the most important functions performed at Level III in the Line hierarchy in Table 3.4 and thus clearly represent the functions performed by line supervisors.

Cluster D: Nonmanagement Professionals

The only high correlation (.79) of the composite Cluster D MP-JFI profile occurs with the Level III group in the Professional hierarchy. The highest job function scores on this profile are 15. Community Relations (65), 14. Personnel Practices (58), 5. Technical Ideas (56), 3. Work Practices (56), and 16. Outside Contacts (56). Of these functions, only Community Relations and Developing Technical Ideas occur as important functions at Level III in the Professional hierarchy in Table 3.4. Although this fit was not as close as those discussed for previous clusters, it is the closest that was observed for this cluster. The cluster is thus interpreted as representing the functions performed by nonmanagement professionals in the Professional hierarchy.

Cluster E: Sales Representatives

The only high correlation for the MP-JFI composite profile of this cluster was .78 with Level III of the Sales hierarchy. The highest job functions scores represented by the cluster's composite profile are 16. Outside Con-

Table 3.6
Correlations between the Composite MP-JFI Profiles of the 12 Identified Clusters and the 12 Occupational Group Normative Profiles

CLUSTER	DEFINITION	N	CORRELATIONS WITH OCCUPATIONAL GROUP NORMATIVE PROFILES			
			Line	Professional	Sales	Technical
LEVEL CLUSTERS						
A	Executives	61	L I .86 L II .62	P I .79 P II .68	S I .74	T I .78 T II .68 T III .51
B	Middle Managers	33	L I .55 L II .70	P I .62 P II .69	S I .69	T I .54 T II .63
OCCUPATIONAL GROUP CLUSTERS						
C	Line Supervisors	13	L III .78			
D	Nonmanagement Professionals	12		P III .79		
E	Sales Representatives	31			S III .78	
F	Technical Personnel	27			S III (.34)	T III (.36)
HIERARCHY CLUSTERS						
G	Line Executives and Managers	24	L III .83			T III .51
H	Professional Executives and Managers	52		P I .53 P II .55		
I	Sales Executives and Managers	55			S I (.21) S II .78	
J	Technical Executives and Managers	34	L I .53			T I .65 T II .60
K	Higher Level Managers	15	L I .59 L II .77	P I .60 P II .67	S I .64	T I .51 T II .60
	Inaccurate Data	2				
	Eliminated	1				
		360				

Note   a. Correlations less than .50 given in parentheses.
b. The highest correlations for each cluster are underlined.

tacts (66), 5. Technical Ideas (57), 8. Coping with Emergencies (56), 2. Financial Planning (54), and 13. Self-Development (53). All of these, with the exception of Financial Planning, occur for the Level III occupational group in the Sales hierarchy in Table 3.4 and the cluster is interpreted as representing the functions performed by sales representatives.

Cluster F: Technical Specialist Personnel

This is the most poorly defined cluster with no correlations with the normative group profiles that exceed .5. The cluster's highest correlation is .36 with the Level III occupational group in the Technical hierarchy and .34 with the Level III group in the Sales hierarchy. The cluster's composite MP-JFI profile shows only three really important functions, with the next highest importance value being only 52. The three important functions are 13. Self-Development (66), 5. Technical Ideas (56), and 7. Developing Teamwork (55). Rather surprisingly, in view of the low correlations with the normative group occupational profiles, two of these functions appear as important at Level III of the Technical hierarchy in Table 3.4 and the third, Technical Ideas, fits quite logically with technical/specialist functions. The best fit for this cluster composite profile is considered to be with that of technical specialists in the Technical hierarchy.

Cluster G: Line Executives and Middle Managers

The highest correlation for this cluster's composite MP-JFI profile (.83) occurs with Level III in the Line hierarchy. Although Cluster C also has its only high correlation with Level III in the Line hierarchy, there are some significant differences among the important job functions represented by the C and G cluster profiles. For example, the Cluster G profile has an importance value of 58 on the higher-level managerial function of 6. Decision Making as compared to an importance value of only 50 for this function on the Cluster C profile, which represents first-line supervisors. Again, the Cluster C profile has an importance value of 67 for the 12. Supervisory Practices function, which characterizes line supervisors, as opposed to an importance value of only 52 for this function on the Cluster G profile. Although Cluster G is not well defined, its most likely interpretation is that it represents middle- and upper-level management functions in the Line hierarchy.

Cluster H: Executives and Middle Managers of Professional Personnel

The composite MP-JFI profile for Cluster H has its highest correlations with the executive (.53) and middle management (.55) normative group profiles in the Professional hierarchy. The most important factors on the Cluster H composite profile are 1. Objective Setting (60), 5. Technical Ideas (59), 6. Decision Making (58), 3. Work Practices (58), and 4. Coordination (57). Three of these factors are common to Levels I and II of the Professional hierarchy, and the remaining factors, Work Practices and Technical Ideas, occur at Levels II and III of the hierarchy, respectively. The Cluster H composite profile thus represents the functions common to executives and middle managers in the Professional hierarchy.

Cluster I: Executives and Managers of Sales Personnel

The composite MP-JFI profile for Cluster I has its highest correlation (.78) with the Level II Sales occupational group profile and its next highest correlation with the Sales I profile. The most important functions on the composite cluster profile are 11. Employee Potential (64), 10. Communications (51), 12. Supervisory Practices (59), 7. Developing Teamwork (56), and 2. Financial Planning (54). Of these functions, three are common to the Level I and II groups in the Sales hierarchy, and the remaining function, Financial Planning, appears at Level I in the Sales hierarchy. There appears, therefore, to be a fairly good fit between the cluster profile and the common function performed at Level I and II of the Sales hierarchy. The cluster is, therefore, interpreted as representing the functions performed by sales executives and middle managers.

Cluster J: Executives and Managers of Technical Personnel

The composite MP-JFI profile for Cluster J has its highest correlation (.65) with the Technical I profile and its next highest correlation (.60) with the Technical II profile. The most important functions on the composite Cluster J profile are 2. Financial Planning (67), 3. Work Practices (60), 1. Objective Setting (57), 6. Decision Making (56), 4. Coordination (54), 11. Employee Potential (52), and 12. Supervisory Practices (52). The Financial Planning function typifies this hierarchy and appears with high-importance values at all three levels. In addition, six of the seven factors listed above are common to Levels I and II of the hierarchy and the seventh (Supervisory Practices) is important at Level II. The Cluster J composite profile clearly represents the functions common to executives and middle managers in the Technical hierarchy.

Cluster K: Higher Level Management Personnel

The composite MP-JFI profile for Cluster K shows high correlations with the Level I and II occupational groups in all hierarchies except for the Sales hierarchy, where it shows a high correlation only with the Level I occupational group. This cluster is tentatively interpreted as representing the functions performed by all higher-level management personnel as opposed to the largely nonmanagement personnel at Level III.

Given the benefit of the doubt about the least well defined F and G clusters, the obtained clusters can be represented in Figure 3.5. In sum-

Figure 3.5
Diagrammatic Representation of the Overlap between the Derived Clusters and the STEP Occupational Classification System

Levels			Hierarchies		
	LINE	PROFESSIONAL	SALES	TECHNICAL
I	LI	PI	SI	TI
II	LII	PII	SII	TII
III	LIII	PIII	SIII	TIII

mary, there are sufficient functions common to all executives at Level I in the hierarchies and common to all middle managers at Level II to produce two clusters of profiles that represent the functions performed at these two levels of functioning in the classification matrix. Since there are very few functions performed in common at Level III of the classification matrix, clusters at this level appear that represent the functions performed by each of the occupational groups in the four different hierarchies. Finally, there is sufficient overlap in the functions performed by the Level I and II occupational groups in each particular hierarchy to produce clusters that represent the functions of the management as opposed to the nonmanagement personnel in that hierarchy.

Two approaches were taken in testing the reality and usefulness of the classification matrix. In the first approach, the classification matrix was established on logical grounds and positions assigned to the resulting occupational groups without reference to their MP-JFI profiles. Thereafter, the results of successive analyses of variance indicated that the MP-JFI could differentiate among the functions performed in the twelve occupational groups.

In the second approach, no assumptions were made concerning a possible classification scheme and profiles that described all of the occupational groups were subjected to a cluster analysis procedure. The interpretations of the obtained clusters again supported the concepts underlying the classification matrix used in the STEP program. It appears, therefore, that the STEP classification scheme can be used for describing the vast majority of higher-level professional specialist and management positions in business and industrial organizations. It can also provide a structure for a variety of human resource procedures.

ANALYSIS OF EMPLOYEES' ABILITIES

The MP-JFI can, with a different response mode, be used to assess employees' ability levels, or competency, in the sixteen job functions. Self-assessments of ability can be obtained by asking the employee to take all of his or her work experience into consideration and rate his or her ability to perform the activities described by the 140 items in the Inventory. Precisely the same procedure and scale intervals used to assess Importance were employed to assess the relative ability to perform each item, to calculate the job function Ability scores, and to convert the raw Ability scores to normalized standard scores. It is thus possible to make direct comparisons between the corresponding Importance and Ability scores for a given job function obtained by an individual or an occupational group.

The job function Ability means, standard deviations, normalized standard scores, and the numbers in each occupational group in the classification matrix are given in the *Managerial and Professional Job Functions Inventory Interpretation and Research Manual* (Baehr, in press). In order to explore the relationship between the importance of a function for a position and employees' assessed ability to perform the function, the Ability scores were subjected to the same series of analyses as those reported for the Importance scores.

Significant Differences in the Job Function Ability Scores at Different Levels of Organizational Functioning and in Different Hierarchies

Analyses of the statistical significance of the difference among the Ability scores for the three occupational levels, regardless of hierarchy, revealed that 14 out of 16 MP-JFI dimensions had significant differences beyond the .001 level of confidence (d.f., 2, 1,337) and the remaining functions, Objective Setting and Communications, had differences that were significant at the .01 level of confidence and nonsignificant, respectively. These results are very similar to but not identical to those obtained for the Importance scores.

When the analyses were repeated separately for the four hierarchies, the results show some surprising differences from those obtained for the Importance scores. The number of significant differences for the hierarchies are as follows. Line: 15 out of 16 (d.f., 2, 292), Professional: 2 out of 16 (d.f., 2, 227), Sales: 13 out of 16 (d.f., 2, 304), and Technical: 8 out of 16 (d.f., 2, 245). The lack of significant differences in the Professional hierarchy leads us to speculate that in this hierarchy engineering, architectural, or other professional skills are maintained even when the rela-

tive importance of functions performed changes with ascent up the hierarchy. This is true to a lesser extent in the Technical hierarchy.

Analyses were also run to determine the significant differences in the
Ability levels of functions in the different hierarchies. When all levels are
combined in the analysis, 12 out of 16 MP-JFI dimensions show significant differences (d.f., 3, 1,044). Done separately by level, the results are
analogous to those obtained for the Importance scores. At Level III, 14
out of 16 MP-JFI dimension scores have significant differences (d.f., 3,
387); the significant differences reduce to 11 out of 16 at Level II (d.f., 3,
395); and reduce still further to 7 out of 16 at Level I (d.f., 3, 248).

The similarity in the results obtained for the Importance and Ability
scores suggests, as could be expected, that if they are to remain employed, employees will acquire relatively higher levels of skill in the functions that are important for the position. A direct comparison of corresponding Importance and Ability scores leads to the identification of the
training needs of individuals or of groups. This is one of the important
applications of job analysis that is described in greater detail in Chapter
7. For illustrative purposes, this procedure was followed for the national
samples of employees used in the analyses of variance.

Identification of Training Needs

At each level in each hierarchy the occupational group's normalized
standard score for Importance was compared with that for Ability and
differences of five or more standard score points between corresponding
scores identified. By rule of thumb, based on the standard errors of measurement given in Chapter 6, a difference of five standard score points
(one-half standard deviation) was regarded as likely to be significant when
the composite profiles are based on large numbers of cases. The identified significant differences are shown in Table 3.7.

Since the results given in Table 3.7 are based on national samples of
employees, the significant discrepancies between corresponding Ability
and Importance scores may be regarded as an indication of national training
needs. It is clear from Table 3.7 that the predominant training need is in
Communications, which occurs in every hierarchy at Levels I and II. It
also appears in the Technical hierarchy at Level III. The other common
training need is for Supervisory Practices at Level II in the Professional
and Technical hierarchies. This seems reasonable since it is at Level II in
these hierarchies that employees move from nonmanagement professional and technical positions to the management of professional and
technical personnel.

Another interesting observation that can be made about the results is
that the discrepancies appear only for functions that are of above average (Importance score>50) and generally of considerably higher impor-

Table 3.7
Significant Differences between Corresponding Ability (A) and Importance (I) Scores by Hierarchy and Level

Level	Line		Professional		Sales		Technical	
	A	I	A	I	A	I	A	I
I			Objective Setting	58	63				
	Communications 46	56	Communications	48	56	Communications 51	56	Communications 46	56
II	Communications 46	53	Communications	46	56	Communications 48	53	Communications 46	53
			Supervisory Practices	56	51			Supervisory Practices 53	48
III			Self-Development	44	53				
			Financial Planning	47	53				
	Coping with Emergencies 53	59							
	Promoting Safety 51	60					Communications 48	53

tance for the different occupational groups. This is evident from the fact that all of the functions listed in Table 3.7 also appear in Tables 3.1 through 3.4, which show the important and common functions at each level of the hierarchies. The only exception is Supervisory Practices at Level II in the Professional hierarchy, which has an importance value of 51. The procedure described here can be used within an organization to identify training needs and also to develop training curricula.

The Development of Training Curricula

The identification of training needs leads naturally to speculations on the training curricula that will help to address those needs. When the MP-JFI has been used to identify the job functions dimensions for which training is required, then a natural approach to the development of training curricula is through an analysis of the item responses that contributed to the job function Ability score.

The results described in the previous section indicate that Communications is a pervasive training need for higher-level personnel. This is underscored by the fact that communications is included in the curriculum of virtually all management development programs. Procedures for the development of training curricula for the Communications function are described in Baehr (1984a) and are summarized below. Procedures for addressing training in Supervisory Practices, which is an important consideration for middle managers, are discussed in Chapter 7, together with other applications of the STEP program.

In the majority of management development programs, communication training focuses on presentation skills in one-on-one or small group situation. Language skills, including breadth of vocabulary and fluency of verbal expression, certainly play a part in effective communication. For this reason, tests specifically designed to measure facility in written and spoken language are included in the managerial and professional test battery. However, the items that contribute to the MP-JFI Communications factor, given below, suggest that effective communication in an organizational setting requires other skills in addition to facility in the English language.

MP-JFI Item No.

10.   Establishing effective processes for internal and external communication.

26.   Keeping communication channels open both upward and downward in the organization.

42.   Identifying possible barriers to communication within the organization.

58.   Developing interpersonal skills to facilitate communication of both facts and feelings.

74.   Knowing how to communicate relevant information to different groups.

90.   Conducting effective meetings.

105.   Regularly testing the openness of communication between self and others.

119.   Actively seeking feedback on communication sent to others.

An examination of the items suggests that there are at least three aspects of communication in organizational settings that should be considered for inclusion in communication training programs. The first aspect, typified by item 58, is the behavioral requirement of the *appropriate use of affect and nonverbal communication cues* when imparting information. For example, employees are much more likely to feel rewarded and motivated if the fact that they have exceeded all set quotas for the period is communicated with enthusiasm and in a congratulatory tone rather than as a dry fact. A remedial exercise in this area that comes to mind is participation in specially developed role-playing exercises in which the communicator and listener switch roles and personally experience the impact of different styles of communicating the same basic facts. Another approach would be to make independent video recordings of the same presentation by the different members of the training program with subsequent playback to the group. It is often an enlightening experience to hear and see oneself in action! In addition, group members would learn through discussion aimed at the identification of the most effective presentations and the reasons the presentations were effective.

A second aspect concerns *communication to groups* and includes establishing criteria for determining what should be communicated to different groups (item 74), formal presentations, and the means for conducting effective meetings (item 90). There is a body of reading available on conducting effective meetings, including the well-known questioning and listening techniques and presentation exercises such as those used in assessment centers. Video recordings of members conducting simulated meetings could also be effectively used here. Decisions concerning what should be communicated to different groups, or how far communications should go down the line, will be largely determined by organization policy. Training is this area would probably be conducted in-house rather than in a stranger lab, or national training group session, and may well consist mainly of clarifying the organization's policies with respect to the communication of different types of information.

A much less frequently covered aspect of communication concerns the *formal and informal channels of communication within the organizational setting.* Representative items deal with establishing the communication channels (item 10), directed effort toward keeping them open (item 26), identifying barriers to communication (item 42), and seeking feedback on communications sent to others (item 119). The preponderance of items suggests that a session on formal organization structures and their effects on communication modes could be very appropriately included in a communication program. Other sessions on formal and informal channels of communication in the organization would also be helpful. For example, ways of overcoming the effects of the well-known phenomenon of some lower-level managers deliberately withholding relevant information from their employees to enhance their own sense of power could be discussed. One way of determining whether or not this situation exists would be, on occasion, to seek feedback from the employees themselves concerning the information that should have been relayed to them.

Comparison of the Measured Abilities of Fortune 500 and Inc. 500 CEOs

The introduction to this chapter stated that the identification of the important functions performed, and the corresponding levels of job skill in the different occupational groups, represented general trends among higher-level employees in profit-making institutions. It further stated that there would be some variation in the functions performed (and thus the required job skills of similar occupational groups) in different organizations, possibly due to differences in operational conditions or organization work environments. A study conducted by Moretti, Morken, & Borkowski (1989) specifically investigated the properties that distinguished high-level executives in large established organizations, as represented by organizations on the Fortune 500 roster, and executives on the Inc. 500 roster, which signified that the organizations were among the fastest growing entrepreneurial companies.

The study was implemented by asking a random selection of chief executive offers (CEOs), in organizations on the two then-current rosters, to participate in the study by completing a managerial and professional test battery and the Ability version of the MP-JFI. Participation was rewarded by a telephoned feedback of results to each CEO. The final sample consisted of thirty-five CEOs from each roster. Differences on the managerial and professional test battery will be described in Chapter 5, which deals with the characteristic abilities, skills, and attributes of incumbents in the different occupational groups. The job skill differences between the two groups of CEOs are summarized below.

Table 3.8 shows the average Ability scores of the Fortune 500 and Inc. 500 CEOs for the sixteen job functions covered by the MP-JFI. The functions are presented in the order of the Importance value of the national norm for Level I executives in the Line hierarchy. This number is given in the first column of Table 3.8. The final column in the table labeled Prob. shows the probability of the observed differences between the two groups of CEOs being due to chance.

An examination of Table 3.8 reveals a number of interesting facts: (1) The Ability levels of the Fortune 500 CEOs more closely resemble the Line Executive Importance norms, since they decrease fairly systematically as the levels of importance of the factors decrease. (2) If the Line Executive Importance norm is used as a standard, and a five point difference is regarded as significant, Fortune 500 CEOs have only one identified training need, that for the Communications function (indicated by an asterisk). The need for training in Communications is even more acute for the Inc. 500 CEOs. They would also have three other job functions for which training would be required if they were to consider a move to a Fortune 500 company. (3) An examination of corresponding Ability scores for the two groups of executives together with the probability of significant differences in the Prob. column in Table 3.8 indicates that the Fortune 500 CEOs have significantly higher levels of Ability on six and the Inc. CEOs on three of the job functions, respectively.

In general, Fortune 500 CEOs have higher levels of acquired job skills in the functions related to the handling of employees in established and conservative organizations, such as Developing Employee Potential, Developing Teamwork, Communications, and in representing the organization in the community. By contrast, the CEOs in the rapidly expanding entrepreneurial organizations show facility in Coping with Difficulties and Emergencies, which will inevitably surface in a rapidly changing environment, in Developing Technical Ideas, which leads to the development of new products, and in marketing these products through Outside Contacts and promotions. These findings are important for organizations in selecting executives who are likely to be successful in implementing their particular goals and objectives and for individuals in selecting the work environment that will enable them to best utilize their natural skills and talents. Although these differences are important, the fact that these high-level executives in American Institutions have similar levels of Ability on seven of the sixteen job functions should not be overlooked. In particular, what these executives have in common are high levels of Ability in

Table 3.8
A Comparison of the Job Skills of Fortune 500 and Inc. 500 Chief Executive Officers

Job Function	Importance Line Exec. Norm	Ability Fortune 500	Ability Inc. 500	Prob.
Objective Setting	67	63	63	
Dev. Employee Potential	57	54	50	.004
Decision Making	56	57	54	
Communications	56	50*	40*	.0001
Financial Planning	56	53	52	
Comm./Org. Relations	56	62	55	.0001
Dev. Teamwork	55	51	46*	.027
Work Practices	54	51	53	
Outside Contacts	53	54	58	.005
Inter. Coordination	52	49	47*	
Personnel Practices	52	54	51	
Supervisory Practices	49	46	43*	.006
Promoting Safety	46	48	44	.032
Self-Development	44	46	48	
Dev. Tech. Ideas	43	42	52	.0001
Coping With Difficulties	41	46	52	.003

* Identified training needs in comparison with the Line executive norm.

some of the core high-level functions such as setting the overall objectives for the organization, making the decisions that will implement the objectives, and the financial planning that will inevitably be associated with these activities.

The results of the statistical analyses described in this chapter have established the viability and usefulness of the classification system for higher-level positions and have enabled us to identify the common and unique functions performed by the national occupational groups in the classification matrix. A parallel form of the job analysis instrument has allowed us to identify the levels of acquired job skill or competency of the national occupational groups on the important functions for their respective positions. We have also been able to compare the job skills of two groups of CEOs at comparable levels of responsibility in organizations with clearly different organizational structures and work environments.

The job functions are differentially important for different occupational groups and also, to some extent, in different work environments. Clearly, employees will require different combinations of skills for successful performance in the different positions. Common logic suggests that the speed of acquisition and the final level of skill acquired for the various job functions will vary for individuals, depending on their qualifications or the particular aptitudes and behavior attributes that they can bring to bear in their performance of the job. The thrust of the following research was to determine the particular abilities, skills, and attributes necessary for the successful performance of each of the MP-JFI job functions.

To this end, some current procedures for evaluating employees and the different types of psychological measurements used in employee evaluations were reviewed. The results of the review are summarized in Chapter 4 and prompted the development of a psychological test battery specifically for use with higher-level management and professional specialist personnel.

NOTE

I am indebted to Ronald Prenta for his computer analysis of the MP-JFI job profiles discussed in this chapter.

4

A Review of the Procedures and Measures Used in Employee Evaluations and the Development of the Managerial and Professional Test Battery

The two major considerations in the development of a process for the evaluation of potential new hires and current employees were the types of measures (such as cognitive abilities, personality attributes, and background data) to be used and the procedure that would maximize the objectivity and validity of the measurements in industrial settings. At the outset, the objectives and expected users of the STEP program determined some of the requirements with respect to both content and method of measurement. Some of these requirements are listed below.

1. Where there are significant differences in the functions performed by different occupational groups there should be corresponding differences in the measured abilities, skills, and attributes (ASAs) of the employees who perform them.

2. The process should provide, for individuals or for occupational groups, valid measures over a wide spectrum of human ability and behavior.

3. The process should be time- and cost-effective for large-scale use in organizations and should also be legally defensible.

4. The process should be usable by qualified human resource personnel in organizations, human resource consultants, clinicians, and vocational counselors with minimum specific training in the administration of the program.

5. The process should not serve a single human resource function, such as initial hiring, but should be applicable throughout the individual's career in the organization including personal development, gauging promotability, career pathing, and succession planning.

In a first attempt to identify an evaluation procedure that met these objectives, a brief review was undertaken of currently used employee evaluation procedures.

A REVIEW OF EMPLOYEE EVALUATION PROCEDURES

Over the years, three commonly used methods for the evaluation of personnel for human resource decision making, each with its variants and used in various combinations, have remained in the mainstream of psychological practice. Defined in broad terms, these are the personal interview, assessment centers, and standardized psychological tests.

The Personal Interview

The earliest and most ubiquitous evaluation procedure is the personal interview. The interview may appear in various forms and for various purposes during the selection process. The most common objectives of selection interviews are (1) initial screening; (2) evaluation of the candidate, with or without knowledge of results of other steps in the selection process; and (3) an opportunity for the potential supervisor to talk with the candidate. Regardless of the type of evaluation procedure used, one or more of these interviews is likely to be used at some stage in the selection process.

To keep the reviews within the scope of this chapter, discussion will be confined to the evaluation interview, which is intended to assess the candidate's suitability for the position. The process of the evaluation interview may vary from a strictly structured or loosely patterned procedure to the use of what are known as the standard interviewing techniques and to in-depth clinical interviews, with or without the use of projective tests.

Of the evaluation interviews, the clinical interview is probably the most affected by the expertise of the interviewer, and by his or her intimate knowledge of the requirements for successful performance in key positions in the organization. The writer has only once had the opportunity of comparing results obtained from projective tests, and the overall performance assessment (OPA) from a clinical interview, with results obtained from standardized tests in a performance criterion validation (Industrial Relations Center, The University of Chicago, 1967). The sample was 54 insurance sales representatives, and the performance criterion measure was a composite of appraisals from two or more managers, derived through the use of the paired comparison technique. The product moment correlation of the OPA with the criterion was $+.34$ $(p<.05)$, as compared with a correlation of $+.63$ $(p<.001)$ between the criterion and an estimate of potential based on an interpretation of the results from the standardized test battery. An uninterpreted regression of standardized test scores against the criterion produced a multiple correlation of .69 ($p<.001$) with 6 predictors. Meehl (1954), in an extensive investigation of clinical and statistical validity, found the latter to be superior. These findings hold for the present study, as indicated by validity coefficients of .69 for statistical prediction versus .34 for clinical prediction.

In the light of these results, it seemed likely that use of the standard interview techniques would better suit the purposes of the STEP program. Ever since the classic McGill University studies (Webster, 1964), investigators have studied the effects of different variables on the decision-making process and subsequent interview outcomes.

A much-investigated variable is the effect of supplying interviewers with information about the candidate, such as biographical information, prior to the interview. This effect was investigated by Tucker and Rowe (1977) in a carefully controlled interview situation where the same applicant was interviewed by 28 employment interviewers, half of whom had been provided with an application form prior to the interview. Their results indicated no significant difference ($t(26) = .027$, $p>.05$) between the mean decision times of the two groups and also no significant difference between the mean degrees of rated confidence in the decision expressed by the two groups. However, interviewers with access to the application form generated more nonapplication information (based on the results of a postinterview questionnaire) than those without knowledge of the application blank, and Tucker and Rowe concluded that the application blank is an important tool in the employment interview.

These seemingly logical results obtained by Tucker and Rowe have not been universally upheld. Dipboye, Fontenelle, and Garner (1984), in a study of the effects of previewing the application on interview processes and outcomes found, like Tucker and Rowe, that previewing the application form increased the amount of correct nonapplication information gathered. This increased information did not, however, appear to enhance the interview outcome, since nonpreview interviewers made more reliable evaluations of the applicants' performance and fit to job. Dipboye et al. conceded, however, that a number of variables, such as assessing videotaped rather than face-to-face interviews, the type of application information provided, and interviewer style and expertise, may have contaminated their findings.

Heneman III, Schwab, Huett, and Ford (1975) investigated interviewer validity as a function of interview structure, biographical data, and interviewee order. They found generally low inter-rater reliabilities and validities for predicting ratings on a job performance scale, based on a job analysis, for all interview conditions. Results of an analysis of variance indicated that the main factor in influencing judges' validity was the order of applicant presentation. In other words, judges' ratings are influenced by prior candidates through "contrast effects." Unhappily, these findings add still another variable to the large number that have to be controlled in interview validation research.

It was hoped that structured or patterned interviews would reduce some of the variables affecting interview outcomes and be a more suitable vehicle for employee evaluation. Janz (1982) compared patterned behavior description interviews to unstructured (standard) interviews. The results indicated that although rater reliability was higher for interviewers using standard techniques (.71 versus .46), the validity of the patterned behavior interviews was significantly and substantially higher than for the standard interviews as indicated by coefficients of .54 ($p<.001$) versus .07 (ns). These clear results were somewhat marred by the nonrandom assignment of students to interview conditions and the more extensive training afforded the patterned behavior interviewers. Bentz (1983) found that the validity of patterned interviews could be increased by structuring them in a way that produced thought-provoking, problem-solving responses rather than yes-no responses.

A wider review of the literature did not produce much greater clarity about the validity of the evaluative employee interview than that presented here. If research results do indeed indicate a trend, it is toward supplying the interviewer with *relevant* information before the interview. Supplying the interviewer with biographical information with undetermined relationships to job performance may well detract from interview validity. Furthermore, some form of structuring seems desirable, providing it produces thought-provoking responses. Structuring could be expected to increase validity and control for extreme differences in interviewer style and expertise. It also seems desirable to have job-behavior-oriented interview content, if for no other reason than that the interview will then be in accordance with the spirit of the "Uniform Guidelines on Employee Selection Procedures" (1978). Finally, if interview assessments are one of the major criteria in an employment decision, they should be subjected to the same validation procedures as a standardized psychological test.

The Assessment Center

The assessment center, as it is currently known, is based on procedures developed during World War II in Germany, by the War Office Selection Board (WOSB) in Britain, and by the American Office of Strategic Services (OSS) to evaluate the qualification of candidates to serve overseas in irregular or special assignments. The first attempt to demonstrate the validity of these procedures resulted in the seminal publication *Assessment of Men*, produced by the OSS Assessment Staff (1948).

The first operational use of assessment centers in industry was in 1958 by the Michigan Bell Telephone Company. Assessment centers were later also established in such organizations as Standard Oil of Ohio, IBM, Sears, and General Electric. Their use in industry produced validation studies for such purposes as the measurement of potential for business management (Bray & Grant, 1966) and the selection of salesmen (Bray & Campbell, 1968). Consistent use of assessment centers by organizations also made possible longitudinal studies, such as that conducted at AT&T (Bray, Campbell & Grant, 1974).

Assessment centers enjoyed a rapidly increasing popularity, which probably peaked in the late 1970s. Contributors to the increased popularity were the appealing face validity of assessment centers and the establishment of consulting companies that would either conduct standard assessment exercises or assist companies in developing their own exercises (Development Dimensions, Inc., 1975). In addition, after the establishment of legal requirements concerning adverse impact, the generally held belief that assessment centers did not discriminate against women and minorities was a great attraction.

Actually, the results of studies investigating the possibility of race and sex bias in assessment center ratings have been mixed. Hamner, Kim, Baird, and Bigoness (1974) and Huck and Bray (1976), for example, did report some evidence of race and sex bias, while Schmidt and Johnson (1973) found no sex bias either in peer ratings or promotion rates. In an interesting study, Schmitt and Hill (1977) found some evidence that the presence of race and sex bias was, to some extent, a function of the racial composition of the assessee and assessor groups. They stressed, however, that the results were of marginal statistical and practical significance. Protagonists of assessment centers have claimed that any bias that may exist in center assessments has not resulted in the wide-scale adverse impact against minorities repeatedly demonstrated for standardized psychological tests. These are not, however, parallel situations. Assessment centers typically deal with higher-level positions, while psychological tests are most often used for entry- and lower-level positions. Our own experience in administering a psychological test battery to higher-level personnel is that there is little or no evidence of adverse impact against either sex or race groups (Baehr & Moretti, 1985).

The increased popularity and prominence of assessment centers in the 1970s led inevitably to a close scrutiny of the methods of assessment employed and the validity of overall assessment ratings (OAR). In the typical operation of an assessment center, a content-oriented job analysis is undertaken to identify the dimensions (constructs) that will measure potential for a generalized behavior concept (e.g., business management) or performance in a particular position (e.g., sales representative). Since assessment centers generally deal with higher-level positions, the dimensions to be measured are generally fairly complex such as, for example, analytical skills, interpersonal skills, initiative, and persuasiveness. These dimensions are then assessed by a number of different methods, either purchased or developed. The methods used for assessment are usually selected from behavior simulations, leaderless and assigned leadership group discussions, dyadic discussions, and quantified assessments from peer- or self-ratings or from projective or standardized tests (MacKinnon, 1975).

The use of a number of methods for assessing a variety of traits lends itself to the analysis of assessment ratings by the multitrait-multimethod technique (Campbell & Fiske, 1959). To demonstrate validity through application of this technique, it is necessary to show that the intercorrelations for the same trait assessed by different methods are demonstrably higher than the intercorrelations of different traits assessed by the same method. A number of investigations have shown that this hoped-for result is not always achieved. Sackett and Dreher (1982), in fact, showed a reverse situation to exist through their multitrait-multimethod (and factorial) analyses of the rating made in three different assessment centers. The most dramatic results were for one center where the average correlation for the same trait assessed by different methods was .07 (with correlations for some traits being zero), whereas the average correlation among different traits assessed by the same method was .64 (with correlations for some methods being .7 or higher). They concluded, "For the organizations discussed here, the results provide virtually no support for the view that the assessment center technique generates dimensional scores that can be interpreted as representing complex constructs such as leadership, decision making, or organizational acumen." They also concluded, "These findings, if replicated in other operational assessment centers, should caution against relying on traditional content validation in the assessment center context" (p. 409).

The rather disconcerting findings reported above lead naturally to the question of just what the assessment center is measuring or attempting to predict. The claims and counterclaims for the validity of the overall assessment rating in predicting a variety of criteria such as progress in management level, salary, performance, and ratings of potential were succinctly summarized by Turnage and Muchinsky (1984). Their own study results seem to indicate that what is best predicted by assessment center ratings is "who will get promoted."

The major problem with assessment center validation studies seems to reside, as it does in most validation research, in the identification of reliable and valid criterion measures. Assessment center validation research is particularly prone to distortion and contamination by a number of factors. A frequent source of contamination is a poorly conducted job analysis to identify the constructs to be rated. This leads naturally to poorly defined rating dimensions and poorly trained assessors. A number of the job analysis procedures reviewed in Chapter 2 could be used. When the assessments are predominantly for higher-level positions, use of a work-oriented standardized job analysis procedure such as the MP-JFI would ensure that the process was demonstrably job related. Furthermore, each MP-JFI rating dimension is clearly defined by the items (job activities) that contribute to it.

Another frequently encountered difficulty in the administration of assessment centers is the aggregation of data over time, locations, and raters. Even in a single assessment setting, the method to be used in combining ratings from the different assessors is open to question. The most generally used procedure involves negotiating sessions (which are sometimes long and costly) to arrive at a consensus. One obvious danger here is that some individuals, by virtue of such factors as standing, seniority, perceived greater qualifications, or merely natural assertiveness, may dominate the negotiations and thus undermine the consensus approach.

In an assessment procedure for the selection of Applicants for Postulancy in the Episcopal Church, a consensus approach was taken in combining the separate ratings made by an ordained priest, the applicant's pastor, an academician from the seminary, a lay person, and an elected chairman. A comparison of the resulting "Recommended" and "Not Recommended" groups of applicants on the scores of a series of psychological tests showed virtually no significant differences. By contrast, the mechanically obtained sum of the separate assessments yielded a number of significant and interpretable differences in test scores and thus appeared to be the potentially more valid measure (Baehr, 1986). In a comparison of consensus and mechanically derived assessment center dimension ratings for a group of 110 police candidates, Pynes, Bernardin, Benton, and McEvoy (1988) found the two types of ratings to be highly correlated. Furthermore, the fact that the consensus derived and mechanically derived ratings both correlated with the overall assessment rating at .71 suggested that the commonly used team-meeting process may be superfluous. It was estimated that the elimination of the process could save the organization over $6,000 a year.

One of the most difficult sources of contamination to combat is promotions made by managers with prior knowledge of assessment results. Turnage and Muchinsky (1984) suggested that a more subtle form of contamination is the assessor's ability to evaluate candidates according to the organization's decision maker's point of view of the "right type" of people. Regardless of the structure of the assessment center or the methods used, if an organization is to invest the time and money required, logic and prudence seem to require a clear definition of what is to be measured and an examination of the measures to be used through both content and performance criterion validation studies.

Standardized Psychological Tests

Evaluations made through the use of standardized psychological tests have had an even longer and more turbulent history than have assessment centers. The widespread and often inappropriate use of employment tests decreased dramatically after the passage of the Civil Rights Act of 1964, with its Title VII, prohibiting discrimination in employment on the basis of race, sex, or national origin. The 1970 "Guidelines on Employee Selection Procedures" (U.S. Equal Employment Opportunity Commission, 1970), which defined specific and often complex requirements for selection test validation, caused many employers to discontinue test use entirely. However, the same "Guidelines" expanded the definition of a test to *any* procedure on which selection and promotion decisions were based.

As it gradually became evident that it was generally more difficult to demonstrate the validity of alternative procedures, there was a return to the use of standardized tests. This trend has continued, and a survey of test usage conducted by the American Society for Personnel Administration (1985) showed that 24% of the 299 companies surveyed were testing more than they had a year ago, 39% were testing more than five years ago, and 44% were considering expanding their testing.

As in other selection procedures, the central issue around which controversy has revolved is the demonstration of validity. The 1970 "Guidelines" recognized only the classical performance criterion validation procedure (in either its concurrent or predictive modes), in which it had to be demonstrated that the tests predicted independently obtained measures of performance in a position. The association between the tests and performance criterion measures is usually expressed as a product moment or multiple correlation, and the "Guidelines," in my opinion, misguidedly accepted a minimum sample size of 30 for these traditionally large-sample statistical techniques. One of the more controversial requirements of the 1970 "Guidelines" was separate validations for ethnic (or other) groups when there were significant differences among such groups on either the predictor or criterion measures. This has become known as "differential validity."

The conflicting validation results obtained in job-specific studies were a major factor in introducing the concept of "validity generalization" popularized by John E. Hunter and Frank L. Schmidt and their associates (Schmidt, Hunter, and Urry, 1976; Schmidt & Hunter, 1977; Schmidt, Hunter, Pearlman, & Shane, 1979). They also extended validity generalization principles applied to job-specific studies to race-specific differential validity studies, to indicate that there were no true racial differences in test validity (Schmidt, Berner, & Hunter, 1973). Researchers who have questioned these conclusions (Bartlett, Bobko, & Pine, 1977; Boehm, 1977;

Katzell & Dyer, 1977) have been roundly critiqued by Hunter and Schmidt (1978), with subsequent rebuttals by those critiqued in the same journal.

Stated in its simplest terms, proponents of this type of validity generalization maintain that variations in subgroup validation results are due largely to inadequate sample size and other artifacts such as criterion unreliability and restriction of range in both the predictor and criterion measures. Perhaps the greatest contribution made by Hunter and Schmidt was to highlight the fallacy of relying on the results of studies based on small samples and inadequately investigated criterion measures. Fortunately, some of the conditions which gave rise to such studies have been ameliorated by the "Uniform Guidelines on Employee Selection Procedures" (1978). The 1978 "Guidelines" (1) accept content and construct validation procedures in addition to performance criterion studies; (2) have changed the requirements of differential validity studies to the demonstration of "test fairness"; and, particularly important from the point of view of practical application, (3) have encouraged the use of consortium or multiunit validation studies. In consortium studies, departments or organizations with essentially similar jobs may be combined in a single validation study. Such studies not only generate large sample sizes but offer the opportunity of replicative investigations of the predictor and criterion measures, and the relationships between them, by race and location of the participating subgroups.

Investigations of predictor and criterion measures for samples of different racial groups should not be concerned with only the magnitude of the correlations between the variables, which is indicated by the slope of the regression lines, but also with their intercepts. If the magnitude of the correlation between test scores and performance is the same for, say, groups of minority and white subjects and the regression lines have the same intercept, then the regression lines are collinear and the relationship between test scores and performance will be the same for the subjects in both groups. If, on the other hand, the magnitude of the correlation is the same but the intercepts are significantly different, then the regression lines will be parallel and the relationship between test and performance scores will be different within each group. In other words, if a hiring cutoff point is set at a given level of performance, it will correspond to different test scores for the two groups. This reflects the fact that the underlying distributions of test scores for the two groups have significantly different means, and it frequently happens that the minority subjects comprise the lower scoring group. In order to avoid claims of adverse impact when there are significant differences in racial group test score means, some test publishers and practitioners have statistically equalized the means of the two groups or "adjusted" the test scores of the lower scoring group. Another practice, which has the same effect, is to rank order the subjects according to test score separately in the two groups and to hire by rank order. These would seem to be dubious professional practices unless it can be demonstrated that there is no difference in the actual job performance of the two groups.

In addition to multiunit validation studies, the 1978 "Guidelines" have endorsed the concept of "transportability" of validation results. This permits the use of properly conducted performance criterion validation results by an organization that has not participated in a validation when "the incumbents in the user's job and the incumbents in the job or group of jobs on which the validity study was conducted perform substantially the same work behaviors, as shown by appropriate job analyses both of the job or group of jobs on which the validity study was performed and on the job for which the selection procedure is to be used" (1978 "Guidelines," excerpted from the *Federal Register*, 1978, p. 38299). This clearly obviates the necessity of repeated validations for essentially similar jobs.

Many, among others Guion (1976), have emphasized the necessity of general principles and theories in establishing a science. But there are many approaches to generalization in the personnel field. One is the Hunter and Schmidt generalization procedures for job-specific validities obtained from small samples. Another is the consortium validation and transportability procedures in the 1978 "Guidelines." A third, less well known procedure, is what was earlier called synthetic validity and later more appropriately named component validity by McCormick (see Mecham & McCormick, 1969). In contrast to traditional validations that attempt to use test measures to predict performance on the job as a whole, the object of component validity research is to predict performance on the separate, identified components of the job. This research is predicated on the assumption that the requirements of any given job component will be comparable in the case of any job in which that same component occurs. It follows that if a matrix could be established that related the separate job components to the required measurable attributes or test scores, then it would be possible to deduce the required attributes for any job with known components. This approach not only avoids the necessity of job specific validations but even the restrictions due to sample size.

As a result of this review, it was decided that the requirements of the evaluation procedure in the STEP program would best be met by the use of objectively scorable psychological tests that could be administered to individuals or groups. It was further decided that a variety of approaches would be taken to determine the validity of the resulting test battery.

THE DEVELOPMENT OF THE MANAGERIAL AND PROFESSIONAL TEST BATTERY

Once it was decided to use objectively scorable pencil-and-paper tests, the question arose as to the particular aspects of human ability and behavior that the tests should measure. The decision was ultimately reached that, at least for the trial form of the managerial and professional test battery, the tests should cover as wide a span of human behavior as possible. To this end, it was decided to have at least one anchor test in each of the following five major areas of human behavior that are traditionally subject to psychological testing: (1) background and experience, (2) cognitive or mental abilities, (3) special aptitudes, (4) temperament and personality, and (5) emotional health. A brief review of the history of test development in each of these areas and a description of the tests selected from those available on the market or specially constructed for the area follows. The definitions of the scoring dimensions of all the tests is given at the end of the chapter in Appendix 4.1.

Background and Experience

Most hiring decisions involve some use of background information about the individual. Indeed, personal background data, in a variety of forms, has been used for over three decades for the prediction of many aspects of human behavior, including work performance. The person who is perhaps best known for research in connection with background data is William A. Owens. He attributes its widespread and continuing use to the belief that what an individual has achieved or failed to achieve in the past will be the best predictor of the pattern of the individual's future performance. He has supported this measurement axiom with extensive validity evidence listed in a comprehensive review of the development and application of biographical data (Owens, 1976).

The most usual forms in which biodata has been used is in personal interviews, application blanks, and personal history questionnaires. The history of its usage in the industrial context has been largely one of increasing standardization of item format and objectivity of the procedures to produce data that lends itself to conventional psychometric evaluations. The most usual formats of items used in biographical questionnaires are: a dichotomous yes-no response, multiple choice, or, for attitudinal items, a scaled response. After the standardization of item format, the next logical development was to test the predictive efficiency of the individual items or groups of items.

One approach to determining predictive efficiency was to validate each item separately with respect to some criterion, such as work performance, and to use the high-validity items to produce either a weighted or unweighed sum as an overall score on the questionnaire. This approach has been criticized on at least two grounds, one of which is that it represents a "dust bowl" empiricism that precludes psychological interpretation (Dunnette, 1962). Another criticism is that the approach produces high primary (initial) validity that sinks significantly in cross validation (Scollay, 1957; Hughes, Dunn & Baxter, 1956; Wernimont, 1962). In a later study, Brown (1978) cites possible causes for the decrease in cross validity such as restriction in range when determining the validity of a test in use and, particularly, the use of small sample sizes in the development of the original keys. In his study, Brown investigates the long-term validity of a personal history item scoring key developed on a 1933 sample of 10,111 life insurance agents by checking the validity of the original key on a 1939 sample of 857 agents and a 1969–1971 sample of 14,738 agents. His results indicated that there was little loss in validity over both the 6-year and 38-year validation periods despite drastic labor market and economic changes and changes in the job itself. He attributes this outcome to scoring key confidentiality, test maintenance, and adequate developmental sample size. These results, however, are both organization- and job-specific.

In a still more recent study (Rothstein, Schmidt, Erwin, Owens, & Sparks, 1990) items were keyed for job relevance on large samples obtained from multiple organizations and retained only when they showed cross validity across organizations. At a later stage, cross validation was performed on approximately 11,000 first-line supervisors in 79 organizations. The authors claim that results obtained from meta-analyses constitute the first large-sample evidence of validities that generalized across organizations, age levels, sex, levels of education, supervisory experience, and company tenure in the noncognitive domain.

Even if keyed background data can be shown to generalize across a variety of operational conditions for a given occupation, it would not suit the purposes of the STEP program, primarily because a specifically validated instrument would be required for each occupation dealt with and also because, as Dunnette noted earlier, such empirical keying would at least hamper if not preclude a dynamic interpretation of test results.

An alternative and currently widespread approach to grouping biodata items by psychometric clustering or by factorial procedures, which produce interpretable dimensions, was used in the construction of biographical inventories used in the STEP program. The standard procedure for the construction of all multiscore tests in the STEP program, regardless of item content or the behavioral area covered by the test, was to administer the research version of the test to representative samples of the target population and to calculate the intercorrelations of the item responses. The underlying dimensions represented in the system of intercorrelations were determined empirically through multiple-factor analysis with subsequent rotation of the dimension axes to simple structure. The obtained dimensions are defined by, and consist of, identified groups of items and become the basis for scoring and reporting the test results.

Background data research that culminated in the development of the instrument used in the managerial and professional test battery was initiated in the late 1950s. The initial instrument was developed to screen male applicants for higher-level positions. This instrument showed substantial validity for selection for a wide variety of occupations (Baehr & Williams, 1968; Baehr, Furcon, & Froemel, 1968; Baehr, 1976). As adequate sample sizes became available, a comparable but separate instrument was developed for women in higher-level positions, which was used successfully in selection validation studies (Baehr, 1981).

In the early separately developed instruments for men and women, there was some overlap in the background dimensions but also a number of dimensions that were unique to either sex. An experimental scoring of groups of men and women on both instruments suggested that factors that were unique to one sex (as determined by the separate analyses) might also be meaningful for the other sex. These results prompted the construction of an instrument to which both men and women could respond.

The items from the two instruments were combined in a single booklet and edited to remove all sexist references. In addition, 57 completely new items were included for research purposes. The resulting inventory had 150 items and was administered to 500 men and women in a variety of higher-level occupations. A multiple-factor analysis of the responses produced 21 factors of which 16 were well defined by items and clearly interpretable. The items in these factors were reproduced in a booklet and the resulting instrument, the Experience and Background Inventory (EBI) (Baehr & Froemel, 1980), was the anchor test for the background area in the managerial and professional test battery.

The use of background data for prediction in organizational settings has become a sensitive and legal issue in connection with the successive federal "Guidelines" that prohibit discrimination against minority and other protected groups. Contrary to expectations, however, there has been empirical evidence that background data has less discriminatory impact against minority groups than conventional cognitive tests (Sparks, 1965; Baehr, Furcon, & Froemel, 1968).

In order to investigate the possibility of sex differences in responses to the EBI, the average dimension scores of groups of approximately 200 each of men and women were subjected to t-tests of the significance of the differences between the means. Of the 16 scoring dimensions, 11 had significant sex group differences. Of these, the male subgroup scored higher on 7 dimensions and the females on 4. Males, as a group, scored higher on dimensions that deal with aspiration level, drive, finances, and general and traditional family responsibility. Females, as a group, scored higher on factors dealing with school achievement, type of college majors, group leadership skills, and cooperative family responsibility. There were no significant group differences on factors dealing with school activities, professional work and vocational satisfaction, adjustment to the parental family environment, job and personal stability, and degree of participation in active relaxation pursuits. Overall, these results indicate that sex group membership will not necessarily be a determinant for a consistently high-score EBI profile.

The passage of years has seen an ever increasing number of women entering the work force on a full-time basis; the enforcement of legislation to ensure equal opportunity for women and minorities in employment; and changing attitudes toward the family structure, including an increasing trend for husband and wife to share equally in the raising of the children and providing for the family. These developments have led to a closer congruence between the work motivations of men and women. In the course of career counseling interviews, the writer has noticed that many career women show a typically "male" profile on the EBI and it is not too unusual to find men who show what has been traditionally regarded as the "female" profile. Although there will probably always be sex group differences on the dimension scores, it is thought that the use of the EBI will fairly represent the background and motivational needs of individuals of both sexes.

Mental Abilities

The first research on cognitive measures (as opposed to measures of sensory and motor skills) in describing differences in human behavior is generally attributed to Alfred Binet in his study of the learning problems of French schoolchildren (Binet, 1903). The first Binet test was published in 1905. The translated and greatly revised American version, developed by Lewis Terman of Stanford University, was published in 1916, with later revisions in 1937 and 1960. All of the Binet tests involve tasks or items of increasing difficulty, and although there are differences in the way they are calculated, all of the Binet tests produce a single score that is generally regarded as an average of a number of different abilities (Dunnette, 1976). Spearman (1927) first formulated the theory of a single, unitary general factor of intelligence.

Thurstone (1938, 1944) pioneered multiple-factor analysis and identified a number of specific primary mental abilities that have survived pretty much unchanged to the present day. Thurstone (1947) also defined the correlational relationship between tests that would produce a general factor, as defined by Spearman, in either a first-order analysis (correlations between test scores) or a second-order analysis (correlations between correlated primary abilities).

Definitions of specific mental abilities proliferated in the many years of research undertaken by Guilford (1959, 1967), some of which, such as the concept of divergent thinking, have survived and been unique contributions to theories of intelligence.

The early meta-analysis and validity generalization studies conducted by John E. Hunter and Frank L. Schmidt were applied predominantly to cognitive measures and have been associated with a return to an emphasis of a single general factor of intelligence as the most effective predictor of performance (Hunter, 1986; Schmidt, 1988). This view has been strongly contested by other investigators (Goldstein & Patterson, 1986; Seymour, 1986; Prediger, 1989).

More than two decades of research conducted by the Human Resources Center of The University of Chicago on more than 70 measures of ability and personality with a data base of more than 5,000 higher-level personnel does not support the overriding importance of g as a predictor for these personnel. Rather, in addition to high levels of g, specific intellectual skills are differentially important for success in different higher-level occupations. Chapter 5 will show that written and spoken language skills are of preeminent importance for success at top levels of management and that the visual perceptual skills are the strongest predictors for nonmanagement engineers and technical specialists.

Four tests of specific mental abilities were included as anchor tests in the managerial and professional test battery (hereafter referred to as the test battery). There are two verbal and two nonverbal tests, all of which are derived from Thurstone's landmark studies of the primary mental abilities and the visual perceptual skills. The two verbal tests are Word Fluency (Human Resources Center, 1961) and the Bruce Vocabulary Inventory (Bruce, 1959). The Word Fluency test consists of a sheet ruled for 5 columns and 16 rows. Each column is head with a category title (such as "Automobiles," "Colors," "Tools") and the rows are headed with letters selected from the alphabet. The respondent is asked to fill each box with an example from the appropriate category, starting with the appropriate letter. There are 80 boxes to be filled. The score is the total number of boxes in which the subject has written acceptable responses within the 10-minute time limit. The test measures the speed of relevant verbal associations and high scores are associated with facility in extemporaneous speaking. Having a large vocabulary does not necessarily ensure fluency of verbal expression. The Word Fluency test only has 16% of its variance in common with the Bruce Vocabulary Inventory ($r = .41$, $N = 2,317$, $p < .001$).

The Bruce Vocabulary Inventory measures the breadth of English vocabulary through an untimed synonyms test consisting of 100 increasingly difficult items. The respondent is instructed to select the one word in a row of five words that means the same or most nearly the same as the first word in the row. In order to control for correct answers being due to chance, the respondents are instructed to complete all items and to guess if they are unsure. The measures of vocabulary and verbal fluency were included in the battery since the communication skills are universally held to be important requirements for successful management.

The two nonverbal tests are Nonverbal Reasoning (Corsini, 1957) and Closure Flexibility (Thurstone and Jeffrey, 1984). Nonverbal Reasoning is an untimed, multiple choice, paper-and-pencil test. The 44 items each consist of sets of 5 pictures. The respondents are instructed to look at the first picture then to identify which picture from the remaining four "goes with" the first picture. The score is the total number of correct answers. There is no time limit. The test's intent is to obtain a measure of deductive and analytical reasoning ability (through the solution of pictorial problems) that is unaffected by language facility. The highest correlation among the mental abilities is between Nonverbal Reasoning and Closure Flexibility ($r = .50$, $N = 2,916$, $p < .001$).

Closure Flexibility is a classical embedded figures test. Each of the test's 49 items consists of a figure, presented on the left of the page, followed by a row of 4 more complex drawings to the right. Some of these 4 more complex drawings contain the given figure in its original size and orientation. The respondent is instructed to indicate, for each drawing, whether it does or does not contain the figure. The score is the number of correct responses minus the number of wrong responses given within a 10-minute time limit. The construct measured by the test is the ability to hold a configuration in mind despite distraction (Thurstone, 1944). In addition to its relationship to deductive and analytical reasoning, it has moderately strong correlations with dimensions from an objective test of reaction time, measured under normal and stress conditions, which will be described later.

Special Aptitudes

Only two special aptitudes (sales aptitude and potential for creative and innovative behavior) were assessed by the test battery. Sales aptitude was measured by a test generally available on the market, called the Sales Aptitude Check List (Personnel Research and Development Corporation, 1960/1985) and creative potential was measured by the Cree Questionnaire (Thurstone & Mellinger, 1957/1985).

Over three decades ago, both L. L. Thurstone (1950) and J. P. Guilford (1959) commented on the importance of, and demand for, creative and inventive talent not only in the arts but in science, industry, and the professions as well. Interest in creativity grew along with the awareness that there is no direct relationship between creativity and intelligence in that a certain level of intelligence is necessary for creative and innovative behavior, but high levels of intelligence do not ensure creativity. Our research has supported this hypothesis. The range of correlations between the measure of creative potential and the four specific mental abilities in the test battery is from .09 to .16 (Baehr & Orban, 1989).

Both Thurstone and Guilford described creativity in terms of personality and behavior, which is the theory underlying the construction of the Cree Questionnaire. Thurstone and Mellinger began their research by identifying the behavior characteristics that differentiated a group of engineers, judged to be creative on the basis of patents and inventions, from another group of engineers who were similar in most respects but were not creative. The 145 differentiating items were incorporated into the Cree Questionnaire. For each item, the respondents are asked to circle a "Y" if the behavior described is typical of them, an "N" if it is not typical of them, and a "?" if they are undecided. The overall creative potential score is the number of times the respondent's responses are the same as those of the identified creative group, and thus represents the degree to which the respondent's behavior is similar to that of other creative individuals. In a separate study, J. E. Furcon (1965) determined the factorial structure of the items and defined the 13 underlying dimensions of the creative personality. The test has recently been revised for use in the STEP program. The first step in the revision was to eliminate all of the items that contributed to the 3 dimensions that showed the lowest correlations with the overall creative potential score. The second step was to calculate point biserial correlations between each of the remaining items and the overall creative potential score. The correlations ranged from $-.20$ to $+.44$ and all items with a correlation of less than $r = +.14$ were eliminated. These revisions resulted in a shorter (58-item) test with greater cohesiveness and without appreciable loss in the reliability of the dimension scores. Indeed, about half of the remaining ten dimension scores had increased alpha reliability coefficients.

The Sales Attitude Check List is composed of 31 forced choice items. Each item consists of a tetrad in which two statements describe what would ordinarily be perceived as favorable sales behavior and two that describe unfavorable sales behavior. The respondents are asked to select one statement that is most like their behavior and one that is least like their behavior. Only one of the two pairs of statements (favorable and unfavorable) in a tetrad have been shown to be associated with sales performance. The respondent's score is the number of times that the item shown to be related to sales performance in each pair is selected. The test is designed to tap some fairly basic behavioral attributes of successful salespeople in a fairly wide range of sales occupations. The test has shown validity in selection validation studies conducted over a number of years by the Human Resource Center, previously known as the Industrial Relations Center (1967, 1970).

Temperament and Personality

In this area, every effort has been made to avoid lengthy questionnaires with overt structures and response techniques vulnerable to conscious or unconscious distortion of responses. The anchor test in this area is the Temperament Comparator (TC) (Baehr, 1957/1985) and is the product of the continuation of studies by Thurstone (1951) that reduced the 13 sets of scores obtained from the Guilford-Martin inventories (Guilford, 1940; Guilford & Martin, 1943a, 1943b) to nine linearly independent factors. A later study by Baehr (1952) further reduced the factors to five that are measured in the TC through responses to 18 traits. The factors and their contributing traits are defined in Appendix 4.1.

Responses to the TC are made through the use of the paired comparison technique. Each of the 18 traits is compared with every other trait, and respondents have to indicate which of the pair is more characteristic of their behavior. Various combinations of five trait scores contribute to the five factors. The paired comparison technique minimizes distortions resulting from constant errors of judgment, such as a possible tendency for respondents to rate themselves in a consistently favorable direction. The technique also provides a measure of the consistency with which respondents are judging their behavior and is, thus, a built-in measure of the quality of the respondent's responses. The first intended use of the consistency score was to ensure that the behavior dimension scores of respondents with very low consistency, or near-random responses, were not given serious consideration in the interpretation of test results. However, in the course of routine analyses of test battery scores it was observed that there were systematic differences in the consistency scores for different occupational groups. For example, Chapter 5 will show that executives typically have significantly higher consistency scores than do any of the other occupational groups in the classification matrix.

Since there was no immediate logical explanation of why one occupational group should be more consistent in rating their behavior than any other, it was hypothesized that the consistency score represented an independent quality or attribute over and above its psychometric properties, which provide a check of the quality of the responses.

Studies of self-awareness (Duval & Wicklund, 1972) have demonstrated that self-awareness, or a firm self-image, promotes greater consistency in the way in which individuals perceive themselves. As one approach to testing this hypothesis a parallel form of the Temperament Comparator, called the Observational Assessments of Temperament (Baehr, 1979a), was developed to measure the three most predictive of its five behavior dimensions. The two forms used precisely the same traits. The essential difference between the forms was that in the TC the ratings were semi-disguised, since the respondent sees only the trait pairs and is unaware of the behavioral dimensions to which the traits contribute, whereas in the parallel form the traits were listed under the behavioral dimension to which they contribute, and the respondents were required to rate their behavior with respect to each trait separately on a five-point scale. Under these circumstances, the personal bias in assessments is uncontrolled and the respondent can either consciously or unconsciously manipulate the scores on the behavioral dimensions to which the traits contribute.

The two forms of the test were administered with a two-week time interval to 414 predominantly male higher-level managerial and professional specialist personnel. The subjects were also rated by their supervisors on the undisguised rating scale form. In the analysis of the data (Kipper & Baehr, 1988), the total sample of subjects was divided into 3 groups according to the consistency score obtained from the TC. The cutpoints in standard scores were one-half standard deviation $(SD = 10)$ above and below the mean $(M = 50)$ of a normative sample of 5,000 cases. The disguised self-assessments obtained from the TC for the 3 consistency groups (high, medium, and low) were correlated (1) with the undisguised self-assessments, and (2) with the supervisor's assessments on the undisguised form of the TC.

There was a systematic decrease in the product moment correlations between the two kinds of self-assessment (disguised and undisguised) for the high, medium, and low consistency groups for all three variables. The corresponding correlations for the two extreme consistency groups (high and low) for the three variables were as follows. Extroversion: high group $r = .45$ $(p<.001, N = 133)$ versus low group $r = .31$ $(p<.05, N = 91)$; Emotionality: high group $r = .59$ $(p<.001, N = 133)$ versus low group $r = .13$ (ns, $N = 91$); and Self-reliance: high group $r = .33$ $(p<.001, N = 133)$ versus low group $r = .28$ $(p<.05, N = 91)$.

The same pattern of decreasing magnitude of correlations between the two types of assessment was found for the correlations between the disguised self-assessments and the undisguised supervisory assessment for the Extroversion and Emotionality dimensions but there were near-zero correlations between the assessment of Self-reliance for any of the consistency groups.

A number of possible explanations were advanced for the essentially zero correlations between the self- and supervisory assessments of Self-reliance. One was the purely mechanical one that the relationship between the Self-reliance dimension and the consistency score was different from that for the other two variables. This was shown not to be the case, however, when homogeneously low-magnitude correlations were obtained for each of the three dimensions with the consistency score under all conditions of assessment.

Another plausible explanation for the lack of congruence between self- and supervisory assessments of Self-reliance was that, unlike the Extroversion and Emotionality dimensions, where assessments at either end of the continuum may be seen as being advantageous under different circumstances, only the high end of the Self-reliance dimension is seen as desirable. Self-reliance then becomes a more sensitive assessment dimension and thus more vulnerable to distortions due to personal bias. In other words, the unreliability of the self-assessments of Self-reliance may be the main reason for the lack of congruence. On the other hand, some supervisors may be intimidated by vigorous and self-reliant employees and may interpret low Self-reliance and dependence as a recognition of their authority. This introduces an emotional factor into the assessment of Self-reliance with implications for the superior-subordinate power structure that could result in biased supervisory assessments in contrast or, in addition, to unreliable self-assessments. Yet another explanation may be that the behavioral expressions of Emotionality or Extroversion are more easily recognized by supervisors than those for Self-reliance. Given the problem concerning supervisors' ratings of Self-reliance, a question may be raised about their ability to rate more complex constructs in assessment settings such as analytical skills, initiative, or decision making.

The congruent results obtained for the self- and supervisory assessments support the hypothesis that high consistency is an indication of a person's degree of self-awareness, a firm self-image, and possibly a willingness to present one's perceived self to others. It was, therefore, treated as a predictor variable in the test battery in addition to the five factors measured by the TC. It is of interest to note that although the four validity scales in the Minnesota Multiphasic Personality Inventory (MMPI) (Hathaway & McKinley, 1943) were also originally intended as checks on the validity of the clinical profile scales, high and low scores on these validity scales were associated with other differentiating factors such as background and behavior. Thus, "the particular configuration of the validity scales provides an important source of information regarding test-taking attitudes, response sets, and biases" (Newmark, 1985, p. 22).

Although every effort has been made to keep self-reports of behavior as free as possible from personal bias and other invalidating distortions, it was deemed desirable to include in the test battery some objective tests of behavior that did not require the respondents to answer questions about themselves. This is achieved for some variables through the use of The Press Test (Baehr & Corsini, 1957/1985). The Press Test is based on results of a long history of investigations in color-naming, learning, perception, and personality and temperament started by Stroop (1935). The test measures reaction time under normal and stress conditions. It consists of three parts, each of which has a strictly enforced time limit of 90 seconds.

Part I of The Press Test consists of four columns of *words* that are the names of colors. Only four color names are used. There are four corresponding columns of circles. The individual is asked to put the *first letter of each word* in the circle that corresponds with that word. Since the same four words are used repeatedly, verbal comprehension is not involved. The score is a measure of the individual's reaction time to simple verbal stimuli.

In Part II there are four columns of *colored circles*. Again, there are only four colors, the same ones for which words were used in Part I. The individual is asked to put the *first letter of each color name* in the corresponding circle. The score measures the respondent's reaction time to color stimuli. If the respondent has no color deficiency (if he or she has, the test results will be invalid), the two reaction time scores should be similar.

In Part III, there are four columns of words (the same four color names), which are generally but not always printed in inks of a color different from the color named. For example, the word yellow may be printed in green ink. Only rarely is the color word printed in the correct color ink. The individual puts the *first letter of the color of the ink* in which the word is printed in the corresponding circle. In so doing, the person has to ignore the printed word (i.e., to ignore the distracting stimulus). One's score on Part III is thus a measure of ability or willingness to work under stress. When the score is compared with the score for Part II (reaction time to color stimuli without distraction), a measure of the effect of distraction on the individual is obtained.

It was mentioned earlier that the Closure Flexibility test has moderately strong correlations with both measures of reaction time from The Press Test and its strongest correlation ($r = .31$, $N = 2,650$, $p < .001$) with reaction time under pressure. It is probably the ability to overcome visual distractions in order to concentrate on the task at hand that these scores from the two tests have in common. Chapter 5 will show that the ability to react quickly and to maintain productivity under pressure are characteristics of successful managers.

Personal-Emotional Adjustment

A knowledge of the emotional health status of an applicant or employee is important for both humanitarian and human resource management reasons. The test used in this area, the Emo (Emotional Health) Questionnaire (Baehr & Baehr, 1958/1986) was developed in clinical settings as a means for providing periodic checks on the emotional health status of patients during a course of treatment. In this form it consisted of 120 items that described symptoms of stress and pressure, such as "feeling nervous in the presence of a superior," that contributed to 10 traditional psychodiagnostic dimensions. In 1959, it was extensively revised and adapted for use in industrial and other settings. In the course of this revision, 20 neutral or positively toned items, such as "I felt full of pep and energy," were added to dilute the clinical impact of the instrument. For each of the 140 items in the Questionnaire booklet, the respondent is required first to indicate whether or not the item was experienced and, if so, to indicate the intensity of the experience on a 4-point scale. The intensity scale ranges from "Pleased" (positive effect) through "Not Affected" to "Troubled a Little" and "Troubled Very Much" (negative effect). The item responses contribute to the scores of 10 traditional psychodiagnostic dimensions and to four factorially determined second-order adjustment factors that are composites of the dimension scores.

Construct validation research has shown that the 10 traditional diagnostic dimensions, and the factorially determined key adjustment factors to which they contribute, have high and statistically significant correlations with the relevant dimensions of other clinical instruments. For example, the correlations of the Emo scores with the neuroticism variable of the Maudsley Personality Inventory (Eysenck, 1972) range from $r = .49$ to $r = .70$ for a marketing group composed of 76 sales representatives and their immediate managers. The Emo variables also showed significant correlations with the relevant diagnostic dimensions and the lie and other quality of response scales of the MMPI mentioned earlier. The Emo and MMPI have similar item content, but the Emo differs from the MMPI in having an empirically determined factorial base and in utilizing both the number and intensity of the respondent's responses to the diagnostic items. Investigation of the Emo Questionnaire's validity as a screening procedure has shown that its dimension scores and, in particular, its key adjustment factors successfully differentiate between the gainfully employed and persons hospitalized for an emotional disorder.

The diagnosis of emotional health status in occupational settings is important not only for the development of the individual and the work force but also for the success of the business enterprise. The Emo Questionnaire can be used in the selection process to identify applicants whose high levels of anxiety, failure to take responsibility, or other maladjustive tendencies are likely to make them disruptive influences and unreliable and unpredictable under stress. Emotional adjustment is also important for higher-level personnel since poor emotional adjustment in individuals who direct the work of others often has unfavorable effects on the entire work group, manifested by worker dissatisfaction, low productivity, and poor morale.

The Emo Questionnaire has been used with other psychological tests in selection test validation studies in industrial settings for over two decades. These studies were undertaken in accordance with the Equal Employment Opportunity Commission (1970) "Guidelines on Employee Selection Procedures," with the most usual statistical procedure being regression of test battery scores against various independent criteria of performance. The Emo seemed to be most predictive of performance in pressureful occupations, such as members of sales forces, where there was competition between incumbents and pressure to make sales quotas; supermarket managers, who operate within very close profit margins; and other high-level executive personnel. In the public sector, the Emo variables were effective predictors for such stressful occupations as police patrolmen, and their supervisors and managers, in large metropolitan police departments and also in a large national study for the selection of metropolitan bus operators. The Emo validation studies are described in greater detail in its *Interpretation and Research Manual* (G. O. Baehr, 1959/1987).

A small but interesting nonindustrial study in the private sector concerns the selection of child-care workers (Frost & Joy, 1987). With an ever increasing number of women moving into the work environment and ever larger numbers of children being cared for from early ages in child-care centers, the occupation of child-care worker merits the same attention given to individuals in the nursing, counseling, and other helping professions where the individual is responsible for other, and in particular dependent, persons.

The Emo was administered with the Personnel Selection Inventory (PSI-5) (London House, 1977) to 49 employees from a suburban nursing home for handicapped children. The PSI-5 measures attitudes toward theft (Dishonesty scale), violence (Violence scale), drugs (Drug-abuse scale), and emotional instability (Emotional Instability scale). The intercorrelations of the PSI-5 and Emo measures provided strong further evidence of the construct validity of both instruments. A forward-step regression of all scales against a three-year average of performance ratings produced a high significant F ratio and a multiple correlation of .65, which reduced to .48 after correction for shrinkage. The measures entering the regression model were the PSI-5 Drug-abuse scale and the Emo Withdrawal, Hostility, and Projection scales. The best prediction of length of service was obtained from three Emo scales. If confirmed on larger samples, these results suggest that, even used on its own, the Emo can be useful in selecting child-care workers who are less likely to manifest maladjustive and hostile behavior and who are more likely to be long-term employees.

During the industrial use of the Emo, a quality of response, or lie scale, was developed. This is a normative standard based on the total number of diagnostic items that the individual responded to. The most favorable scores would be in the middle range of the scale, which would indicate that the individual had about as many stressful experiences as the average for the normative group. A significantly large number of responses would be a flag for possible emotional problems and a significantly low number of responses could be due to conscious or unconscious reluctance to reveal information about the self or an inability to acknowledge or recognize stress. As in the case of the MMPI, the Emo quality of response scale, which is essentially the perceived level of stress experienced by the individual, has been found to have predictive value for job performance in addition to the function for which it was originally developed. Indeed, this overall level of response score may become one of the most important measures obtained from the Emo.

Recently, three additional quality-of-response scales have been developed. One of these, the percentage of "Not Affected" responses given to the diagnostic items, qualifies the level of response score. Even if an individual gave the normative number of responses to the diagnostic items, this could hardly be regarded as adjustive behavior if the majority of these responses were "Not Affected" or denied the affect usually associated with stressful experiences. Such responses may well flag possible schizoid behavior characteristics. The two remaining quality-of-response scales are based on the buffer or neutral items. In view of the results obtained with an overall measure based on the diagnostic items, it was considered that interesting information might be obtained from a normative scale based on the number of responses to the positively toned buffer items. This score would be qualified by the percentage of "Pleased" responses made to the buffer items, since it could hardly be regarded as adjustive behavior if the individual experienced stress in connection with what are ordinarily regarded as pleasant everyday life experiences. Even if these latter two measures are not diagnostic in their own right, they should have value when interpreting the measures of stress. It may be an indication that the individual is "coping" well if, even if stress levels are high, the individual is sufficiently buoyant to enjoy pleasant everyday life experiences as indicated by "Pleased" responses to the buffer items.

The tests described above have, over the course of years, been updated, revised, expanded, or shortened as research results indicated. They have, however, been retained as anchor tests in the managerial and profession test battery because the constructs that they measure have been shown to be consistent predictors of performance for a wide variety of occupations in diverse organizational settings. The anchor tests provide continuity in long-term research but tests of newly developed constructs, or of constructs that relate to issues of emerging importance in the business world, are included in the STEP test battery on an ongoing basis. This is done in an attempt to continually improve the predictive efficiency of the test battery and to ensure that the STEP results remain responsive to the changes in the economic environment and organizational culture.

Two measures (constructs) that have been of considerable interest to industrial-organizational psychologists, human resource specialists, and industrial managers have, for the past two years, been included in the STEP battery administered to participants in the management development seminars conducted by The University of Chicago. The two constructs were Management Responsibility and Business Ethics. The items developed to measure the two constructs were combined and randomized in a single booklet called the *Management Styles Questionnaire* (London House, 1989).

Management Responsibility (Locus of Control)

The Management Responsibility measure is based on the locus-of-control construct, formulated by Rotter (1966), that is concerned with an individual's perception of control over life events and subsequent outcomes. Individuals with an internal locus of control, "Internals," believe that they are principally responsible for determining their own fate, whereas "Externals" believe that outside forces such as luck, circumstances, or powerful others determine their fate. Newly developed constructs sometimes enjoy immediate interest and popularity that all too often fades away when the constructs are subjected to vigorous research. By contrast, Lefcourt (1981) and Rotter (1990) have pointed out that the locus-of-control construct has maintained an important role in behavioral research for over two decades.

A good deal of the research on the locus-of-control construct has been applied to behavior in organizations and its effect on the performance of executive functions (Spector, 1982). In general, "Internals" were the better overall performing executives as demonstrated by (1) preference for a participative rather than a directive management style (Runyon, 1973), (2) better solutions and greater reliability in decision making (Bonoma & Johnston, 1979; Kets de Vries, 1977), (3) greater entrepreneurship (Hornaday, 1971; Brockhaus, 1975), (4) better performance under stress (Watson & Baumal, 1967), and (5) generally more adaptive emotional health behaviors (Strickland, 1978; Kobasa, 1979).

The original forced-choice Rotter Scale was used in most of the studies cited above. Compared with general locus-of-control measures, the Management Responsibility scale is a situation-specific measure of individuals' attitudes about various management situations. The respondent rates a given statement, such as "I do not have enough control over the direction my career is taking," on a six-point scale with intervals described as "Strongly Agree," "Moderately Agree," "Slightly Agree," "Slightly Disagree," "Moderately Disagree," and "Strongly Disagree."

Administration of the Management Styles Questionnaire (MSQ) together with the STEP batteries made it possible to study the psychological correlates, over a wide range of human behavior, of both the Management Responsibility and Business Ethics scales. These results will be given later.

Business Ethics

There has been considerable research that indicates that employee theft can be predicted by pencil-and-paper integrity tests (McDaniel & Jones, 1988). The impetus for such tests in industrial settings has most often been the purely financial one of reducing organization losses due to employee theft or other counterproductive activity. Such research has also been concerned with causes of the unproductive behavior, and Jones (1983) has shown that overly stressed employees are more likely to engage in unethical behavior (e.g., illicit drug use at work, theft of company property, overly aggressive relationships with customers).

There has also been research on the ethical practices of higher-level and, in particular, executive personnel (Srivastva and Associates, 1988). It is these personnel whose decisions have far-reaching outcomes for large numbers of employees, their own highly placed peers, the organization, the environment, and even the country. In recent years we have become painfully aware of the unethical behavior of business executives resulting in insider trading scandals and junk-bond-driven turnovers that have left countless investors with devastating losses (Zetlin, 1990) and for which the reparations will eventually affect taxpayers across the country. In a report of the results of a survey of the readers of *Working Woman* on business ethics, Sandroff (1990) reports that 56% of the respondents believed that American business ethics had deteriorated in the past ten years. The report states further that

The majority of respondents said they personally have witnessed such foul play as lying to employees; expense-account abuses at the highest levels; and in-office jockeying involving favoritism, nepotism and taking credit for other people's work. Almost half have seen discrimination based on sex and color; more than a third, sexual harassment; and just under a third, lying to make a sale. And they charge that this apparent erosion of the fair-play ethic is not only disheartening but also harmful to productivity, job stability and profits in American business. (p. 113)

The items in the Business Ethics scale were geared toward managers and executives and measure an individual's attitudes toward upholding ethical business practices and standards. Several factors comprise the Business Ethics scale, including (1) general tolerance for dishonest behavior, (2) beliefs regarding how often others accurately complete monetary records, (3) attitudes toward using unethical means to "get ahead," (4) attitudes toward bending or breaking company rules or laws, and (5) attitudes toward the importance of profits versus ethics when dealing with customers or clients. Sample items include "Winning is more important than how you play the game," "Most managers tolerate a little dishonesty from their employees," and "Managers who are caught cheating on their business accounts should still be given promotions which are earned and deserved." Higher scores indicate stronger endorsement of upholding ethical business practices and standards. The items had the same six-point rating scale response format as the Management Responsibility items and were randomized with the Management Responsibility items in the Management Styles Questionnaire.

Psychological Correlates of Management Responsibility and Business Ethics

The MSQ was administered along with the STEP battery to 67 conferees at the 1989 Management Development Seminar conducted by The University of Chicago in Vail, Colorado. The sample consisted of middle managers and executives at the vice presidential level in the occupational specialties (hierarchies) covered in the STEP program. Product-moment intercorrelations were calculated between each measure in the test battery, the Management Responsibility and Business Ethics scales, and three demographic measures for the sample, which were age, years of education, and present salary.

An examination of the intercorrelates produced some unexpected information. The highest correlation ($r = .70$, $N = 67$, $p < .001$) was between the Management Responsibility and Business Ethics scales. This high level of association can be partially accounted for by "test dependence" since the items for both scales were included in one booklet. A closer examination of the items in the two scales provided another possible reason for the high correlation. It was observed that many Business Ethics items were written in a way in which the unethical act was attributed to environmental circumstances or other factors outside of the control of the individual. Cast in this mold, the Business Ethics item becomes a special case of locus of control. However, in spite of the fact that the two variables have 49% of their variance in common, only the Management Responsibility scale has a significant correlation with present salary ($r = .25$, $N = 58$, $p = .027$). In so far as present salary can be regarded as a measure of the worth of the individual to the organization, and thus serve as a performance criterion, only Management Responsibility could be considered for use as a predictor in the STEP battery. Data are now being collected to further investigate the relationship between the two scales and their value as possible predictors in the STEP battery.

Since the two variables are highly correlated, they show a similar pattern of relationships with the other measures in the STEP battery. In general, there were some moderate but potentially interesting correlations with objective measures of personal background data and the cognitive abilities and aptitudes. The most striking results, however, were the correlations with the dimensions of the Emo. The Business Ethics and Management Responsibility scales had significant correlations with, respectively, 6 and 7 of the 10 traditional diagnostic dimensions measured. The correlations are even higher with the composite adjustment factors derived from the diagnostic dimensions and the overall measure of stress response. These are shown in Table 4.1. These results corroborate the association between emotional health and unethical and counterproductive behavior mentioned by a number of researchers, which was cited earlier. The results also provide another compelling reason for the inclusion of emotional health measures in test batteries for predicting performance in the work environment.

GENERAL PRINCIPLES IN THE CONSTRUCTION OF THE MULTISCORE TESTS IN THE STEP TEST BATTERY

The construction of all multiscore tests followed the same sequence regardless of the item content of the area covered by the test. The research version of the test was administered to representative samples of the target population, and the intercorrelations of the responses to the items calculated. The underlying dimensions represented in the system of intercorrelations were determined empirically through a statistical procedure known as multiple-factor analysis. These dimensions are defined by, and consist of, identified groups of items and become the basis for scoring and reporting the test results.

In order to profile and report test results, the test raw scores were converted to normalized standard scores with a mean of 50 and a standard deviation of 10. For every subscore in every test, the conversion was done by setting the mean score for the combined sample of the twelve occupational groups in the managerial hierarchies at 50 on the normalized standard score scale. From this it follows that any one candidate's test scores will have the same meaning and can be directly compared across all areas of the test battery. It also follows that the scores for different candidates on the same variables are also directly comparable.

All test scores were thus normed for the specific population for which they are intended. For purposes of test interpretation, this population is referred to as the higher-level population (HLP). The tests in the managerial and professional test battery thus differ from most standardized psychological tests that generally use the general population as the normative base. The mean of 50 for the managerial and professional tests is

Table 4.1
Product Moment Correlations of the Business Ethics and Management Responsibility Scales with the Composite Adjustment Factors from the Emo Questionnaire

	Business Ethics			Management Responsibility		
	r	N	p	r	N	p
Adjustment Factor						
Internal Adjustment	.30	67	.006**	.21	67	.045*
External Adjustment	.39	67	.001***	.38	67	.011***
Somatic Adjustment	.21	67	.046*	.28	67	.010**
Level of Stress	.43	67	.000***	.36	67	.001***

* p < .05   ** p < .01   *** p < .001

thus a more stringent standard than the mean on most standardized psychological tests.

The specific tests used in the managerial and professional test battery are referenced in the SRA/London House (1989) *Test Catalog for Business*. Specific information about each test's construction, correlations with other tests, reliability, and validity for different purposes can be found in their respective *Interpretation and Research Manuals* also referenced in the SRA/London House *Catalog*. A summary of the reliability coefficients of the predictive dimensions in the STEP batteries is given in Table 4.2.

This chapter includes a review of current employee evaluation procedures with a view to selecting an evaluation measurement system for use in the STEP program. The reason for the decision to use standardized psychological tests as the measurement system, the rationale for the selection of the particular tests used, and the data base for their standardization are also described.

At the beginning of this chapter it was stated that one of the first requirements of the system used to evaluate the potential of employees was that, when there are significant differences in the functions performed by different occupational groups, there should be corresponding differences in the measured abilities, skills, and attributes of the employees who perform them. This requirement was tested by replicating the statistical analyses conducted for the job function scores for the measures obtained from the managerial and professional test battery. Chapter 5 reports the results of analyses of variance conducted to determine the extent to which the measures in the managerial and professional test battery differentiate across levels of organizational functioning and across hierarchies. An attempt is then made to identify the salient characteris-

Table 4.2
Summary of the Reliability Coefficients of the Predictive Dimensions Used in the STEP Battery

BACKGROUND	N	Type	Coefficient
Experience and Background Inventory			
1 School Achievement	500	Alpha	.77
5 Drive	500	Alpha	.65
6 Leadership and Group Participation	500	Alpha	.63
7 Professional Work and Vocational Satisfaction	500	Alpha	.72
8 Financial Responsibility	500	Alpha	.73
10 General Family Responsibility	500	Alpha	.69
16 Active Relaxation Pursuits	500	Alpha	.62
MENTAL ABILITIES			
Non Verbal Reasoning			
56 Items	371	K-R (21)	.77
44 Items	371	K-R (21)	.79
Word Fluency			
80 Items	48	Test-Retest	.78
80 Items	528	K-R (21)	.84
Bruce Vocabulary Inventory			
100 Items	1750	Split-Half	.92
100 Items	360	Test-Retest	.84
Closure Flexibility			
194 Items	–	Split-Half	.78
194 Items	–	Split-Half	.94

APTITUDES	N	Type	Coefficient
Cree Questionnaire			
Overall Creative Potential	496	Alpha	.78
Sales Attitude Checklist			
Sales Aptitude			–
BEHAVIOR			
Press Test			
Part I (200 items)	58	Test-Retest	.72
Part II (200 items)	58	Test-Retest	.82
Part III (200 items)	58	Test-Retest	.80
Temperament Comparator			
1 Extroversion	83	Test-Retest	.90
	759	K-R (21)	.88
2 Emotional Responsiveness	83	Test-Retest	.90
	759	K-R (21)	.89
3 Self-Reliance	83	Test-Retest	.86
	759	K-R (21)	.88
6 Personal Insight	83	Test-Retest	.80
EMOTIONAL HEALTH			
Emo Questionnaire			
KI Internal Adjustment	1193	K-R (20)	.82
KE External Adjustment	1193	K-R (20)	.83
KS Somatic Adjustment	1193	K-R (20)	.75
KG General Adjustment	1193	K-R (20)	.70

tics of the incumbents in the occupational groups in the classification matrix.

NOTE

Portions of this chapter are adapted from M. E. Baehr, "A Review of Employee Evaluation Procedures and a Description of 'High Potential' Executives and Professionals," *The Journal of Business and Psychology* 1 (1987): 172–202, and M. E. Baehr, "Identifying High-Potential Executive and Professional Personnel through Psychological Assessment," in J. W. Jones, B. D. Steffy, and D. W. Bray (Eds.), *Applying Psychology in Business: The Handbook for Managers and Human Resource Professionals* (Lexington, MA: Lexington Books, 1991), 345–356.

APPENDIX 4.1: DEFINITIONS OF ALL VARIABLES IN THE MANAGERIAL AND PROFESSIONAL TEST BATTERY

EXPERIENCE AND BACKGROUND INVENTORY

Background

1. *School Adjustment.* Adjustment and achievement in school and other academic environments.
2. *Choice of College Major.* Choice of college major influenced by intrinsic interest in vocations that benefit people and society.
3. *School Activities.* General satisfaction with social interactions at high school.

Success Orientation

4. *Aspiration Level.* Vocational choice influenced by rapid career advancement, high earnings, and high social status.
5. *Drive.* Drive for upward movement through changes of organization or within the organization.
6. *Leadership.* Active participation and demonstration of leadership skills in social, work, or professional organizations.
7. *Vocational Satisfaction.* Satisfaction with a vocation that is consistent with professional or technical training and past experience.

Responsibility

8. *Financial Responsibility.* Good financial management—the ability to earn, save, and invest.
9. *Husband-Wife Working Partnership.* Household and financial decisions shared by marriage partners.
10. *General Family Responsibility.* Family-oriented lifestyle with successful assumption of financial and family responsibility.

11. *Traditional Family Responsibility.* Traditional running of household where one partner makes greater income and makes most of the important decisions.

12. *Cooperative Family Responsibility.* Lifestyle where individual marries young, has children early, and shares household and income responsibilities.

Adjustment

13. *Parental Family Adjustment.* Pleasant and constructive attitudes in a stable early family environment.

14. *Professional-Successful Parents.* Early environment characterized by professionally educated and fairly affluent parents.

15. *Job and Personal Stability.* Established stability indicated by long-term employment and relative permanency in personal residence.

Personal

16. *Active Relaxation Pursuits.* History of enjoyment of physical activity and active sports.

MENTAL ABILITIES

1. *Nonverbal Reasoning.* Good capacity for deductive and analytical reasoning measured nonverbally.

2. *Word Fluency.* Facility and fluency in extemporaneous speaking.

3. *Vocabulary.* Breadth of English vocabulary.

4. *Closure Flexibility.* Good ability to hold a visual configuration (or concept) in mind despite visual distractions.

CREE QUESTIONNAIRE

0. *Overall Creative Potential.* Potential for intuitive thinking and creative and innovative behavior.

Social Orientation

1. *Dominance.* Socially dominant, likes to be a leader, to speak before groups, and to entertain others.

2. *Independence.* Freedom from a need for social conformity, a feeling of being "different," and confidence in oneself.

Work Orientation

3. *Autonomous Work Environment.* Preference for nonroutine and unstructured work settings.

4. *Work Under Pressure.* Ability to produce ideas best and most readily while working under pressure.

Internal Functioning

5. *Energy Level.* Behavior characterized by an abundance of energy, restlessness, general haste, and impatience.

6. *Speed of Reaction.* Decisive, quick-thinking, and easygoing behavior.

7. *Ideational Spontaneity.* Tendency to produce ideas easily, unexpectedly, and almost compulsively under all circumstances.

Interests and Skills

8. *Theoretical Interests.* High interest and participation in scientific and theoretical undertakings.

9. *Artistic Interests.* High interest and skill in artistic endeavors.

10. *Mechanical Interests.* High interest and skill in working with tools, making mechanical repairs, and in physical activities.

SALES ATTITUDE CHECKLIST

1. The similarity of the individual's sales attitudes and habits to those of successful sales representatives.

THE PRESS TEST

I. *Reaction Time to Verbal Stimuli.* The number of responses to standard verbal stimuli made in 90 seconds.

II. *Reaction Time to Color Stimuli.* The number of responses to standard color stimuli made in 90 seconds.

III. *Ability to Work Under Pressure.* Ability to maintain or even increase productivity (number of responses made to color stimuli) despite distractions.

TEMPERAMENT COMPARATOR (TC)

TC Factors

I. *Extroversion.* Demonstrative, expressive, and sometimes impulsive behavior.

II. *Emotional Responsiveness.* Emotionally responsive and enthusiastic behavior.

III. *Self-reliance.* Individually goal-oriented and self-confident behavior.

IV. *Energy.* Lively and energetic behavior that is changeable and sometimes erratic.

V. *Socially Oriented.* Seeks company. Is self-confident, and socially at ease.

TC Traits

1. *Calm.* Quiet, tranquil, and not easily disturbed.

2. *Cautious.* Exercises careful thought prior to any action.

3. *Decisive.* Makes decisions and solves problems promptly.

4. *Demonstrative.* Openly displays feelings and emotions.

5. *Emotionally Stable.* Moderate and controlled emotions.

6. *Energetic.* Works in an alert and vigorous manner.

7. *Enthusiastic.* Expression of excitement and interest in an activity.

8. *Even-Tempered.* Maintains composure in spite of provocation.

9. *Lively.* Brisk, alert, and expressive behavior.

10. *Persevering.* Persists in an undertaking despite opposition or discouragement.

11. *Prompt Starter.* Begins projects purposefully and in a timely manner.

12. *Quick Worker.* Completes projects within or before the expected time.

13. *Seeks Company.* Seeks and enjoys the company of others.

14. *Self-confident.* Believes actions will be appropriate and successful.

15. *Serious.* Grave disposition and sober trend of thought.

16. *Socially at Ease.* Feels content and secure in social settings.

17. *Steady Worker.* Works in a constant, unfaltering way.

18. *Talkative.* Ready to engage in and enjoy conversation.

Consistency

1. *Personal Insight.* Demonstrated consistency in self-ratings of behavior.

EMO QUESTIONNAIRE

Composite Factors

1. *LR(D)—Level of Stress Response.* Number of responses to the diagnostic items, or the level of admitted stressful experiences.

2. *KI—Internal Adjustment.* Freedom from generalized, unfocused tension and over preoccupation with self.

3. *KE—External Adjustment.* Self-acceptance and objective interpretation of the motives and behavior of others.

4. *KS—Somatic Adjustment.* Feeling of well-being and absence of physical complaints.

5. *KG—General Adjustment.* General buoyancy and healthy feelings of pleasure concerning everyday experiences.

Traditional Diagnostic Dimensions: Absence of tendencies toward

1. *Rationalization.* Shifting responsibility for one's own failures to other persons or the situation.

2. *Inferiority Feelings.* Anxiety manifested by lack of confidence, feelings of inferiority and self-derogation.

3. *Hostility.* Reacting to frustration by trying to belittle, harm, or bring misfortune to others.

4. *Depression.* Involuntary reactions to frustration in the form of resignation or nihilism.

5. *Fear and Anxiety.* Anxiety manifested by general tension and unjustified fears.

6. *Organic Reaction.* Frustration and anxiety channeled into physical symptoms and complaints.

7. *Projection.* Experiencing one's own unconscious hostility as being the intentional motives of others.

8. *Unreality.* Avoidance of problems by unintentionally drifting into unreality and bizarre experiences.

9. *Sex.* Maladjustment manifested by sexual or marital disturbances.

10. *Withdrawal.* Desire to reduce frustration by deliberate withdrawal from contacts and activities.

5

Analysis of the Abilities, Skills, and Attributes of Incumbents by Managerial Hierarchy and Level of Organizational Functioning

In Chapter 3, successive analyses of variance were applied to the job function scores obtained from the Managerial and Professional Job Functions Inventory (MP-JFI) in order to identify the functions performed by incumbents in the different hierarchies and at different levels of organizational functioning, and even more narrowly, in the twelve occupational groups in the classification matrix. This chapter reports the results of the same statistical procedures applied to the measures obtained from the tests in the managerial and professional test battery in order to identify the abilities, skills, and attributes of the incumbents in the different occupational groups. An attempt is also made to interpret the statistical results by developing the representative behavior profiles for the occupational groups. In order to position our results with respect to the mainstream of research in this area, some comparisons are made with results obtained by other investigators.

An early study of managerial talent by Ghiselli (1971) included some procedures that were similar to those employed here. Ghiselli selected 13 measures consisting of 3 abilities, 5 personality traits, and 5 motivational needs that were obtained through the administration of a Self-Description Inventory. He postulated two requirements that had to be satisfied for a measure to be regarded as indicative of managerial talent. One requirement was that the measure should show significant differentiations across three levels of organizational functioning, in this case, line workers, line supervisors, and middle managers. This corresponds, in our study, to analysis of variance of the test battery scores across the three levels of organizational functioning described in the classification matrix. Ghiselli's second requirement was that the measure should be related to supervisory assessments of job performance, which corresponds to the validation of the test battery measures described in Chapter 6. Because of the comparability of the procedures used in the two studies, Ghiselli's results, together with those of other investigators, will be cited from time to time. Ghiselli's sample consisted largely of 306 middle managers drawn from 90 different businesses and industrial organizations, unclassified with respect to functional department. He states in connection with the sample that "Unfortunately, at the present time, the ideal of drawing many managers from each of many firms can only be a social scientist's dream" (Ghiselli, 1971, p. 26). We have been fortunate in being able to advance toward that dream in the sample collected for this study.

THE NATIONAL SAMPLE DATA BASE

The sources described in the Acknowledgements section provided a total data base of more than 10,000 cases tested on some version of the managerial and professional test battery. Of the 10,000 cases, 4,689 were classified into occupational groups included in the four, three-rung managerial hierarchies. The 4,689 cases classified by level, hierarchy, and type of business are shown in Table 5.1. The first three columns in Table 5.1 (Industrial, Banking, and Hospital) were regarded as profit-making organizations and the fourth and fifth columns (Government and Voluntary) as nonprofit. In order to keep the analyses comparable with those conducted for the job functions, only incumbents in profit-making organizations were used in the analyses of variance described here.

IDENTIFICATION OF THE ABILITIES, SKILLS, AND ATTRIBUTES THAT DIFFERENTIATE BY HIERARCHY AND LEVEL

The incumbent employees in the occupational groups listed in Table 5.1 completed the managerial and professional test battery. As in the case of the job importance ratings for the MP-JFI, the factorially determined dimension subscores and total score for each test were converted to normalized standard scores on a scale with a mean of 50 and a standard deviation of 10.

The average scores on each of the total of 68 test dimensions were calculated for each occupational group. The occupational groups' test score means, standard deviations, and normalized standard scores for this comprehensive test battery are not presented here but individual scores will be cited when they are necessary for the interpretation of test results. The number of cases vary by test for two major reasons. First, different combinations of tests were used in the trial batteries in validations undertaken for different occupational groups. The second and ma-

Table 5.1
Classification of the Cases in the Sample by Type of Business, Hierarchy, and Occupational Level

	Business Industry	Banking	Hospital	Government	Voluntary	Total	Percent
Level							
Line I	91	9	9	17	10	136	2.9%
Line II	548	15	19	14	3	599	12.8%
Line III	614	1	49	0	0	664	14.2%
Prof. I	152	10	11	59	11	243	5.2%
Prof. II	122	29	4	80	1	236	5.0%
Prof. III	802	9	1	94	1	907	19.3%
Sales I	30	9	4	0	0	43	0.9%
Sales II	234	16	35	0	0	285	6.1%
Sales III	1056	1	67	0	0	1124	24.0%
Technical I	24	38	8	5	0	75	1.6%
Technical II	44	83	6	10	0	143	3.0%
Technical III	153	65	8	7	1	234	5.0%
Total	3870	285	221	286	27	4689	100%
%	82.5%	6.1%	4.7%	6.1%	0.6%	100%	

jor reason for the disparity in the number of cases per test, however, is the continuous upgrading and revision of the test battery. For example, as explained in Chapter 4, the Experience and Background Inventory first appeared as a unisex instrument in 1980 after more than two decades of research and thus has the smallest number of cases. The variations in the number of cases for tests and occupations are automatically taken into account in determining the statistical significance among differences in the analyses of variance.

Significant Differences in the Abilities, Skills, and Attributes of Incumbents at Different Levels of Organizational Functioning

The statistical significance of the differences among the scores for the three occupational levels (regardless of hierarchy) were determined for each of the scores in the managerial and professional test battery through one-way analyses of variance. The results were summarized by calculating the number (and percentage) of differences that were significant at or beyond the .05 level of confidence for the 24 most predictive dimensions of the test battery listed in Table 4.2 in Chapter 4, with the exception of the Sales Attitude Check List, which was only used in the Sales hierarchy.

The percentages of significant differences were calculated for different areas of the test battery as well as for the total of 23 predictors. The results indicated that in the experience and background area of the test battery, 5 out of 7 (71%) of the predictors showed significant differences across the three levels. The results for the remaining areas of the test battery and the total number of predictors were: Mental Abilities, 3 out of 4 (75%); Behavior and Emotional Health, 10 out of 12 (83%); and for the total number of predictors, 18 out of 23 (78%) of the differences across the three levels were significant. These results indicate substantial and also very similar (approximately 77%) significant differentiations for scores in all areas of the test battery.

In order to determine whether or not the same degree of differentiation would be obtained in the separate hierarchies, the one-way analyses of variance were rerun separately for each hierarchy. The percentage of differences that were significant at or beyond the .05 level of confidence for the 23 most predictive dimensions of the test battery are given in Table 5.2.

At first sight, the percentages in Table 5.2 suggest differential ability of the scores from different areas of the test battery to differentiate across organizational levels, and also a lower degree of differentiation, overall, for the Technical hierarchy. However, the uniform results obtained for the total sample and an examination of the sample sizes strongly suggest that the variability is an artifact of sample size. By heirarchy, the lowest percentage favorable response for the total number of predictors (52%) occurs for the newest and least well defined of the hierarchies, the Technical hierarchy. Table 5.1 shows that the total sample size for the Technical hierarchy is less than 500 cases as compared with over a thousand cases in each of the other hierarchies. As a result of a revision of the Experience and Background Inventory in 1980, the sample sizes in this area of the test battery were considerably reduced, especially in the Sales and Technical hierarchies, where they fell to 90 and 94, respectively. By contrast, sample sizes for the four mental ability tests in the Technical hierarchy range from 295 to 364.

It is expected that when the ongoing data collection procedures produce larger samples in the experience and background area and in the Technical hierarchy, overall, the percentage of significant differences across levels in all hierarchies is likely to be at the 70% level or higher. In general, the results in Table 5.2 indicate that different abilities, skills, and

Table 5.2
Percentage of Significant Differences Across Levels I, II, and III in the Line, Professional, Sales, and Technical Hierarchies on the 23 Predictive Test Battery Scores

Test Measures	Hierarchy			
	Line	Prof.	Sales	Tech.
Experience & Background N = 7	86%	58%	43%	29%
Mental Abilities N = 4	100%	75%	75%	75%
Behavior & Emotional Health N = 12	92%	75%	75%	50%
Total Predictors N = 23	96%	74%	70%	52%

attributes (as measured by the test battery) are characteristic of incumbents at each of the three levels in the four hierarchies.

Significant Differences in the Abilities, Skills, and Attributes of Incumbents in Different Hierarchies

Following the pattern set in the analysis of the MP-JFI, an analysis of variance was also run to compare the scores from the managerial and professional test battery across hierarchies. When the analysis was run for the total sample, regardless of level of functioning, 6 out of 7 (86%) of the differences in the background area were significant across the four hierarchies at or beyond the .05 level of confidence. The results for the remaining areas of the test battery and for the total number of predictors were: Mental Abilities, 4 out of 4 (100%); Behavior and Emotional Health, 11 out of 12 (92%); and for the total number of predictors, 21 out of 23 (91%) of the differences were statistically significant. These results indicate that, in general, there are significant differences on about 90% of the skills and attributes exhibited by incumbents across the four different hierarchies.

In order to determine whether or not the significant differences occurred uniformly at all levels of functioning, the analyses were run separately at each of the three levels. These results are summarized for different areas of the test battery and for the total number of 23 predictive dimensions in Table 5.3. When the analyses are run by level, the samples are large and thus less affected by the variations encountered when the

Table 5.3
Percentage of Significant Differences Across the Line, Professional, Sales, and Technical Hierarchies at Levels I, II, and III on the 23 Predictive Test Battery Scores

	Level of Functioning		
Test Measures	I	II	III
Experience & Background N = 7	14%	57%	100%
Mental Abilities N = 4	25%	75%	100%
Behavior & Emotional Health N = 12	17%	83%	100%
Total Predictors N = 23	17%	74%	100%

analyses were run by hierarchy. As a result, the percentages of significant differences in Table 5.3 show a similar pattern for all areas of the test battery. There were significant differences on all of the dimensions for each area of the test battery at Level III, which indicated that there were considerable differences in the abilities, skills, and attributes exhibited by incumbents in the four different occupations at Level III (first-line supervisors, nonmanagement professionals, sales representatives, and technical specialists). There was a general decrease in the percentages of significant differences at Level II, where the managerial functions come into play in all the hierarchies. The smallest percentages of significant differences (only 17% for the total number of predictors) occurs at Level I. This led to the interesting conclusion that there was considerable overlap in the abilities, skills, and attributes of top-level executives, regardless of the hierarchy that they ascended.

This pattern of a decreasing number of significant differences at ascending levels of organizational functioning is identical to that obtained in the analysis of the MP-JFI and is presumptive evidence of one of the hypotheses underlying the STEP program, which is that, when there are significant changes in the functions performed by job incumbents, there will be corresponding changes in the abilities, skills, and attributes of the job incumbents who perform them. This is one approach to demonstrating component validity that is discussed more fully in the Validity section in Chapter 6.

DEFINITION OF THE DIMENSIONS THAT DIFFERENTIATE ACROSS LEVELS OF FUNCTIONING

To date, the results of the analyses have been expressed in numerical and statistical terms. In the next section an attempt is made to express the statistical results in terms of behavior. In particular, an attempt is made to identify and describe the human abilities, skills, and attributes that differentiate among and characterize incumbents at different levels in the various hierarchies. This is done for each of the major areas of the test battery.

Experience and Background

The average score for the occupational groups at each level of functioning are shown for the Line and Professional hierarchies in Figure 5.1 and for the Sales and Technical hierarchies in Figure 5.2. In each figure, the name of the predictive dimension is given first followed by two columns of numbers. The number in the second column labeled SS, is the average of the normalized standard scores for the dimension of the individuals in the designated occupational group. For example, the average score for the group of executives in the Line hierarchy on School Achievement is 48 and this number is plotted on the normalized standard score scale shown at the top of the grid in Figure 5.1. There is a fixed relationship between the normalized standard score scale and the centile scale shown at the bottom of the grid. The centile that corresponds to a normalized standard score of 48 is 42, and this number is shown in the first column labeled CS. The final column on the table, labeled Prob., shows, for each dimension, the probability of the differences among the scores at the three levels being due to chance. Statistically significant differences are indicated by asterisks and are coded as indicated at the bottom of the figure.

An examination of Figures 5.1 and 5.2 shows significant and consistent increases in the scores for Drive/Career Progress, General Family Responsibility, and Financial Responsibility in all hierarchies, with executive (labeled E on the grid) being the highest scoring group. The single exception is Financial Responsibility in the Technical hierarchy, where all groups score above the mean.

Individuals who score high on Financial Responsibility have demonstrated their ability to manage their personal economy, to earn, save, invest, and provide for future contingencies. Those who score high on General Family Responsibility have generally married and established their families early and taken full responsibility for the family's future. They are the major decision makers and take the lead in deciding on major purchases, such as real estate and cars, and in financial investments. The

Figure 5.1
Occupational Group Means for Experience and Background Dimensions in the Line and Professional Hierarchies

Category Scale	CS Scale	SS Scale	Normalized Standard Score Scale 37.5 40 42.5 45 47.5 50 52.5 55 57.5 60 62.5	Prob.
LINE HIERARCHY				
1. School Achievement	42 46 38	48 49 47	EEEEEEEEEEEEEEEE MMMMMMMMMMMMMMM LLLLLLLLLLLLLLLL	.032*
5. Drive/Career Progress	82 66 38	59 54 47	EEEEEEEEEEEEEEEEEEEEEEEEEEEEEEEEEEE MMMMMMMMMMMMMMMMMMMM LLLLLLLLLLLLLLLL	.000***
6. Leadership & Gr. Participation	50 38 34	50 47 46	EEEEEEEEEEEEEEEEEEE MMMMMMMMMMMM LLLLLLLLLLLLLLL	.009**
7. Prof. Work & Voc. Satisfaction	50 46 21	50 49 42	EEEEEEEEEEEEEEEEEE MMMMMMMMMMMMMMM LLLLLLL	.000***
8. Financial Responsibility	73 58 27	56 52 44	EEEEEEEEEEEEEEEEEEEEEEEEEEEE MMMMMMMMMMMMMMMMMMMMM LLLLLLLLLLL	.000***
10. General Family Responsibility	84 66 27	60 54 44	EEEEEEEEEEEEEEEEEEEEEEEEEEEEEEEEEE MMMMMMMMMMMMMMMMMMMMMM LLLLLLLLLLL	.000***
16. Active Relax. Pursuits	62 62 58	53 53 52	EEEEEEEEEEEEEEEEEEEEEEEE MMMMMMMMMMMMMMMMMMMM LLLLLLLLLLLLLLLLLLLLLLL	.194
PROFESSIONAL HIERARCHY				
1. School Achievement	46 54 46	49 51 49	EEEEEEEEEEEEEEEE MMMMMMMMMMMMMMMMMM PPPPPPPPPPPPPPPPP	.225
5. Drive	76 66 38	57 54 47	EEEEEEEEEEEEEEEEEEEEEEEEEEEEEEE MMMMMMMMMMMMMMMMMMMMMM PPPPPPPPPPPPPP	.000***
6. Leadership & Gr. Participation	50 50 42	50 50 48	EEEEEEEEEEEEEEEEEE MMMMMMMMMMMMMMMMM PPPPPPPPPPPPPPPPP	.089
7. Prof. Work & Voc. Satisfaction	58 62 46	52 53 49	EEEEEEEEEEEEEEEEEEEEE MMMMMMMMMMMMMMMMMMMM PPPPPPPPPPPPPPPPPP	.000***
8. Financial Responsibility	66 66 38	54 54 47	EEEEEEEEEEEEEEEEEEEEEEEEE MMMMMMMMMMMMMMMMMMMMMMM PPPPPPPPPPPPPP	.000***
10. General Family Responsibility	84 69 34	60 55 46	EEEEEEEEEEEEEEEEEEEEEEEEEEEEEEEEEE MMMMMMMMMMMMMMMMMMMMMMMM PPPPPPPPPPPPP	.000***
16. Active Relax. Pursuits	58 66 58	52 54 52	EEEEEEEEEEEEEEEEEEEEEEE MMMMMMMMMMMMMMMMMMMMMM PPPPPPPPPPPPPPPPPPPPPPPP	.178

11 16 23 31 40 50 60 69 77 84 89

Centile Scale

* p < .05.   ** p < .01.   *** p < .001.

112

Figure 5.2
Occupational Group Means for Experience and Background Dimensions in the Sales and Technical Hierarchies

Category Scale		CS Scale	SS Scale	Normalized Standard Score Scale	Prob.
1. School Achievement	*SALES HIERARCHY*	46 38 46	49 47 49	EEEEEEEEEEEEEEEEE / MMMMMMMMMMM / SSSSSSSSSSSSSSSSS	.556
5. Drive/Career Progress		73 62 46	56 53 49	EEEEEEEEEEEEEEEEEEEEEEEEEEEE / MMMMMMMMMMMMMMMMMMMM / SSSSSSSSSSSSSSSSS	.003**
6. Leadership & Gr. Participation		46 62 62	49 53 53	EEEEEEEEEEEEEEEEE / MMMMMMMMMMMMMMMMMMMM / SSSSSSSSSSSSSSSSSSSSSSSS	.325
7. Prof Work & Voc. Satisfaction		46 38 34	49 47 46	EEEEEEEEEEEEEEEEE / MMMMMMMMMMMM / SSSSSSSSSSSS	.105
8. Financial Responsibility		66 50 38	54 50 47	EEEEEEEEEEEEEEEEEEEEEEEEE / MMMMMMMMMMMMMMMM / SSSSSSSSSSSSSS	.000***
10. General Family Responsibility		73 54 34	56 51 46	EEEEEEEEEEEEEEEEEEEEEEEEEEE / MMMMMMMMMMMMMMMMM / SSSSSSSSSSSS	.000***
16. Active Relax. Pursuits		73 73 76	56 56 57	EEEEEEEEEEEEEEEEEEEEEEEEEEE / MMMMMMMMMMMMMMMMMMMMMMMMMM / SSSSSSSSSSSSSSSSSSSSSSSSSSSSSS	.616
1. School Achievement	*TECHNICAL HIERARCHY*	46 46 62	49 49 53	EEEEEEEEEEEEEEEEE / MMMMMMMMMMMMMMMM / TTTTTTTTTTTTTTTTTTTTTTTTTTTTT	.123
5. Drive		73 69 46	56 55 49	EEEEEEEEEEEEEEEEEEEEEEEEEEEE / MMMMMMMMMMMMMMMMMMMMMMM / TTTTTTTTTTTTTTTTTTTTTT	.001***
6. Leadership & Gr. Participation		50 42 46	50 48 49	EEEEEEEEEEEEEEEEEE / MMMMMMMMMMMMMM / TTTTTTTTTTTTTTTTTTTTTT	.670
7. Prof. Work & Voc. Satisfaction		58 54 54	52 51 51	EEEEEEEEEEEEEEEEEEEEEE / MMMMMMMMMMMMMMMMMMMM / TTTTTTTTTTTTTTTTTTTTTTTTT	.566
8. Financial Responsibility		62 66 54	53 54 51	EEEEEEEEEEEEEEEEEEEEEEEE / MMMMMMMMMMMMMMMMMMMMMMM / TTTTTTTTTTTTTTTTTTTTTTTTTT	.198
10. General Family Responsibility		69 62 38	55 53 47	EEEEEEEEEEEEEEEEEEEEEEEEEE / MMMMMMMMMMMMMMMMMMMMMM / TTTTTTTTTTTTTTTTT	.001***
16. Active Relax. Pursuits		62 54 62	53 51 53	EEEEEEEEEEEEEEEEEEEEEEEE / MMMMMMMMMMMMMMMMMMMM / TTTTTTTTTTTTTTTTTTTTTTTTTTTTT	.286

Normalized Standard Score Scale: 37.5 40 42.5 45 47.5 50 52.5 55 57.5 60 62.5

Centile Scale: 11 16 23 31 40 50 60 69 77 84 89

** p < .01.   *** p < .001.

assumption is that individuals with high scores on these dimensions will be comfortable and successful is assuming financial and other types of responsibility and in directing others in the work environment.

High scores on the Drive/Career Progress factor indicate a drive for upward movement in the organization as indicated, among other things, by increasing numbers of people supervised, merit promotions, and pay raises at the same or greater rate than their age peers. The items that define the Drive factor come closest to what McClelland (1961) has defined as the need for achievement (n Ach), although there are also some elements of the need for power (n Pwr). The differentiations on the Drive factor across the three levels represented by the supervisory, middle management, and executive groups in the Line hierarchy are greatest and significant, followed closely by the differentiations among the groups in the Professional hierarchy. Although most marked in the Line and Professional hierarchies, the Drive score for executives in the other two hierarchies is at least 56, which indicates a common desire for consistent career progress and repeated achievements. These results are in accord with those of Ghiselli (1971) who found that the need for occupational achievement and for self-actualization were an integral part of managerial success.

Figures 5.1 and 5.2 show, respectively, that although they are generally well qualified and motivated, the groups of professional and technical specialist personnel both score below 50 on Drive. This is partially due to the fact that the rungs in the Professional hierarchy in organizations are often not as well defined as those in the Line hierarchy. The major reason for the low score, however, is that professionals often take lateral moves to broaden their experience and to improve their professional and technical skills, which may lead to greater intrinsic job satisfaction.

This interpretation is supported by the fact that it is only in the Professional and Technical hierarchies that the managers and executives score above the mean on the Professional Work and Vocational Satisfaction factor. Indeed, in the Technical hierarchy, the groups at all three levels score above the mean. High scorers on the Professional Work and Vocational Satisfaction factor have generally done well in college, often hold graduate degrees, have strong satisfaction with a vocation that is highly related to their past education and experience, and interact well with other professionals in the field.

A high score on the School Achievement dimension indicates outstanding precollege and later academic success, a general liking for school subjects, and freedom from hampering study habits. These characteristics often lead to rankings in the top 10% in high school, listings on honor rolls, and general satisfaction with academic performance. Although the majority of the subjects in our sample hold at least a bachelor's degree and many hold graduate degrees, early academic success does not seem

to be a characteristic of later management success, since the only significant difference occurs in the Line hierarchy, where all three groups still
score below the mean. In fact, the only two occupational groups that
score above the mean are the Level III technical specialist personnel (T)
in the Technical hierarchy and the middle managers (M) in the Professional hierarchy. These results again question the wisdom of hiring on
the basis of past academic achievement, especially if this is the main or
sole criterion.

The Leadership and Group Participation dimension consists of items
that indicate a desire for interpersonal activity and membership in various social organizations and honorary societies. A high score indicates
active participation, the holding of elective offices, and demonstration of
leadership skills in the organizations. It came as something of a surprise
that none of the four executive groups scored above the mean on this
dimension, although there are significant differences among the group
means in the Line hierarchy. The high scoring groups are the sales representatives and sales middle manager (who often still do a considerable
amount of direct selling) in the Sales hierarchy. A tentative explanation
for the high scores of these two groups is that a high level of social
interaction, and being well established as a useful and reliable member
of a group, can be used to promote visibility as a sales person and eventually promote sales.

The final factor in the experience and background area has been defined as Active Relaxation Pursuits. High scores on this dimension indicate a past history of participation in extracurricular activities at high
school, a present feeling of healthy well-being, and enjoyment and participation in physical activity, and individual and group sports. An examination of Figures 5.1 and 5.2 shows that, although the average age of this
higher-level population is 40 years, and the middle managers and executives can be expected to be in the higher-age ranges, all occupational
groups score above the mean and there are no significant differentiations
across levels in any of the hierarchies on this factor. These results indicate the continuation of an active lifestyle for all groups in this higher-
level population. It is noteworthy, however, that this lifestyle is most
characteristic of the Sales hierarchy since all of the occupational groups
in this hierarchy score more than a half standard deviation above the
mean.

Mental Abilities

The occupational group means for all the hierarchies are given in Figure 5.3 for the four mental ability tests included in the battery. It will be
seen from the Prob. column in Figure 5.3 that there are significant differences across levels on all four tests in the Line hierarchy and on three of

the four tests in the remaining hierarchies. The executives are not, however, always the highest scoring group.

There are, in fact, distinctly different patterns of mental ability scores for executives and managers as compared with nonmanagement professional and technical specialist personnel. There are significantly increasing scores on the two tests of language facility that measure, respectively, fluency of verbal expression and breadth of English vocabulary in all hierarchies, with executives and middle managers always outscoring their respective Level III groups. The next highest score for executives is for nonverbal reasoning, which measures facility in deductive and analytical reasoning.

A very different pattern of mental ability scores is evident for the group of entry-level professionals. This group has its highest scores on the two nonverbal tests that measure, respectively, deductive and analytical reasoning and ability in the visual perceptual skill of identifying and maintaining a complex diagramatic representation or concept that is embedded in a larger, distracting visual field. The latter skill, as measured by the Closure Flexibility test, has been shown to be related to facility in map reading, graphics, and mechanical ability. The group of technical specialist personnel has a score of 54 on all four tests. A characteristic that the professional and technical specialist groups have in common is that they have significantly higher scores on the Closure Flexibility test than their corresponding groups of executives.

An average score on the four tests is also calculated for each individual. This is the closest approximation to a measure of general intelligence or I.Q. in the test battery. The average mental ability scores for nine of the twelve occupational groups range from 54.0 to 56.5 on a scale of 0 to 100 and would clearly not differentiate among these groups of higher-level personnel. The three relatively low-scoring groups were sales middle managers (50.8), sales representatives (49.5), and line supervisors (46.8).

The reason for the restricted range of the average mental ability scores is that the averaging has disguised the different patterns of mental abilities exhibited by the different occupational groups. There will still, however, be a rising level of general mental ability at increasing levels of organizational functioning. This has often been demonstrated (Hunter, 1986) and is due partially to the fact that the attainment of the general or professional educational credentials, which are often prerequisites for employment in higher-level positions, is related to the individual's level of intellectual functioning. Although no one would seriously question the need for a high level of general mental functioning as a requirement for success in higher-level positions, our results indicate that the specific patterns of intellectual skills are likely to be the better predictors of performance. The results of the test of this hypothesis will be presented in Chapter 6, which deals with the validity of the test battery. We will also

Figure 5.3
Occupational Group Means for the Four Tests of Mental Ability in the Line, Professional, Sales, and Technical Hierarchies

Category Scale		CS Scale	SS Scale	Normalized Standard Score Scale	Prob.
				37.5 40 42.5 45 47.5 50 52.5 55 57.5 60 62.5	
1. Non-Verbal Reasoning	*LINE HIERARCHY*	66 66 46	54 54 49	EEEEEEEEEEEEEEEEEEEEEEEEE MMMMMMMMMMMMMMMMMMMMMM LLLLLLLLLLLLLLLLLLLLL	.000***
2. Word Fluency		82 69 38	59 55 47	EEEEEEEEEEEEEEEEEEEEEEEEEEEEEEEEEEEE MMMMMMMMMMMMMMMMMMMMMMMMMM LLLLLLLLLLLLLLL	.000***
3. Vocabulary		73 66 31	56 54 45	EEEEEEEEEEEEEEEEEEEEEEEEEEEEE MMMMMMMMMMMMMMMMMMMMMM LLLLLLLLLLLLL	.000***
4. Closure Flexibility		54 62 34	51 53 46	EEEEEEEEEEEEEEEEEEEEE MMMMMMMMMMMMMMMMMMMMMM LLLLLLLLLLLLLL	.000***
1. Non-Verbal Reasoning	*PROFESSIONAL HIERARCHY*	73 73 73	56 56 56	EEEEEEEEEEEEEEEEEEEEEEEEEEE MMMMMMMMMMMMMMMMMMMMMMMMMM PPPPPPPPPPPPPPPPPPPPPPPPPPPP	.682
2. Word Fluency		79 84 58	58 60 52	EEEEEEEEEEEEEEEEEEEEEEEEEEEEEEEEEEEE MMMMMMMMMMMMMMMMMMMMMMMMMMMMMMMM PPPPPPPPPPPPPPPPPPPPPPP	.000***
3. Vocabulary		79 73 62	58 56 53	EEEEEEEEEEEEEEEEEEEEEEEEEEEEEEEEE MMMMMMMMMMMMMMMMMMMMMMMMMM PPPPPPPPPPPPPPPPPPPPPPPPPP	.000***
4. Closure Flexibility		66 58 73	54 52 56	EEEEEEEEEEEEEEEEEEEEEEEEEE MMMMMMMMMMMMMMMMMMMM PPPPPPPPPPPPPPPPPPPPPPPPPPPPP	.000***
1. Non-Verbal Reasoning	*SALES HIERARCHY*	66 46 50	54 49 50	EEEEEEEEEEEEEEEEEEEEEEEEEE MMMMMMMMMMMMMMMMMM SSSSSSSSSSSSSSSSSSSS	.000***
2. Word Fluency		82 54 46	59 51 49	EEEEEEEEEEEEEEEEEEEEEEEEEEEEEEEEEEEE MMMMMMMMMMMMMMMMMMMMM SSSSSSSSSSSSSSSSSSS	.000***
3. Vocabulary		73 66 46	56 54 49	EEEEEEEEEEEEEEEEEEEEEEEEEEEEE MMMMMMMMMMMMMMMMMMMMMMMM SSSSSSSSSSSSSSSSSSS	.000***
4. Closure Flexibility		58 46 50	52 49 50	EEEEEEEEEEEEEEEEEEEEEEEE MMMMMMMMMMMMMMMMMM SSSSSSSSSSSSSSSSSSSS	.143
1. Non-Verbal Reasoning	*TECHNICAL HIERARCHY*	66 66 66	54 54 54	EEEEEEEEEEEEEEEEEEEEEEEEEE MMMMMMMMMMMMMMMMMMMMMMMMMM TTTTTTTTTTTTTTTTTTTTTTTTTTTTTTT	.166
2. Word Fluency		79 79 66	58 58 54	EEEEEEEEEEEEEEEEEEEEEEEEEEEEEEEEEE MMMMMMMMMMMMMMMMMMMMMMMMMMMMMM TTTTTTTTTTTTTTTTTTTTTTTTTTTTTTT	.000***
3. Vocabulary		79 69 66	58 55 54	EEEEEEEEEEEEEEEEEEEEEEEEEEEEEEEEE MMMMMMMMMMMMMMMMMMMMMMMMMMMM TTTTTTTTTTTTTTTTTTTTTTTTTTTTTTT	.005**
4. Closure Flexibility		50 54 66	50 51 54	EEEEEEEEEEEEEEEEEEEE MMMMMMMMMMMMMMMMMMMM TTTTTTTTTTTTTTTTTTTTTTTTTTTTTTT	.004**

** p < .01.   *** p < .001.

Centile Scale: 11   16   23   31   40   50   60   69   77   84   89 attempt to determine the relative contributions of the intellectual and behavioral measure in predicting the performance of higher-level personnel.

Special Aptitudes

The two special aptitudes assessed in the battery are creative potential and sales aptitude. The latter only applies to the Sales hierarchy. The group means for the sales aptitude score across the three levels of the hierarchy are: sales representatives, 50; middle managers, 52; and sales executives, 55. Sales executives are thus the highest scorers (a half-standard deviation above the mean) although direct selling is probably no longer part of their job.

Significantly increasing scores of creative potential across the levels of organizational functioning are shown for all hierarchies in Figure 5.4. These results indicate that potential for creative and innovative behavior is a characteristic of all top executives. However, it is also evident that it is of differential importance for the other occupational groups in the hierarchies. For example, in the Sales hierarchy creative potential is a requirement at all levels, since the average score for all occupational groups exceeds 50 (sales representatives, 51; middle managers, 53; executives, 54).

By contrast, in the Technical hierarchy, all but the executive group score below the mean. This is not surprising when one considers that the type of creativity measured here is characterized by subliminal reasoning and intuitive leaps to a solution, rather than by the application of deductive reasoning and systematic analysis in problem solution. Given this definition, it could be expected that highly qualified hard science professionals would also score below the mean, since their discipline is geared toward accurate measurement, systematic experimentation, and replication of results. Contrary to widely held opinion, therefore, high creative potential is not a uniformly desirable or even a necessary characteristic for occupational success.

It was mentioned in Chapter 4 that both Thurstone and Guilford viewed the potential for creative behavior largely as a personality characteristic and that, given a certain level of intelligence, there would be no linear relationship between creativity and intelligence. This view is supported by the fact that the correlations between the creativity and the four mental ability scores are in the low .1s. The highest correlation ($r = .15$) is with word fluency, and it seems reasonable that a capacity for creative thinking would have some relationship to the rapid generation of relevant verbal associations.

In addition to an overall score of creative potential, the Cree Questionnaire provides ten subscores for the factorially identified dimensions of

Figure 5.4
Occupational Group Means for Creative Potential in the Line,
Professional, Sales, and Technical Hierarchies

Category Scale	CS Scale	SS Scale	Normalized Standard Score Scale	Prob.
			37.5 40 42.5 45 47.5 50 52.5 55 57.5 60 62.5	
LINE HIERARCHY				
Creative Potential	62	53	EEEEEEEEEEEEEEEEEEEEEEEEEE	
	54	51	MMMMMMMMMMMMMMMMMM	.000***
	38	47	LLLLLLLLLLLLLLLL	
PROFESSIONAL HIERARCHY				
Creative Potential	58	52	EEEEEEEEEEEEEEEEEEEEEEEEE	.006***
	54	51	MMMMMMMMMMMMMMMMMMM	
	46	49	PPPPPPPPPPPPPPPPPP	
SALES HIERARCHY				
Creative Potential	66	54	EEEEEEEEEEEEEEEEEEEEEEEEEEE	
	62	53	MMMMMMMMMMMMMMMMMMMMMM	.009***
	54	51	SSSSSSSSSSSSSSSSSSSSSS	
TECHNICAL HIERARCHY				
Creative Potential	54	51	EEEEEEEEEEEEEEEEEEEEEE	
	46	49	MMMMMMMMMMMMMMMM	.020***
	34	46	TTTTTTTTTTTTTT	

```
                          11   16   23   31   40   50   60   69   77   84   89
                                               Centile Scale
```

* p < .05.   ** p < .01.   *** p < .001.

the creative personality. These dimensions portray the creative individual as one who, in the social environment, is dominant, likes to be a leader, and likes to entertain others. At the same time there is freedom from a need for social conformity allied with confidence. In the work environment, there is a preference for nonroutine and unstructured work settings, a need for autonomy, and dislike of close supervision. Ideas are produced best and most readily when working under pressure.

Some of the personal characteristics of the creative individual are an abundance of energy, restlessness, general haste, and impatience. They have a fast reaction time, are decisive and quick-thinking, and are capable of sustained and intense effort when their interest is aroused but may otherwise be rather sporadic workers. They generally have more outside interests than they can possibly satisfy.

Given these behavior characteristics, it could be expected that the Creativity score would show positive correlations with Extroversion ($r = .27$, $N = 2,468$, $p < .001$) and Emotional Responsiveness ($r = .33$, $N = 2,468$, $p < .001$) measured by the Temperament Comparator. These measures are described under the next heading of Personality Characteristics.

In a study by Srinivasan (1984), eight measures of creativity, which included three originally developed by Guilford and his associates (Unusual Uses, Consequences, Plot Titles), were used to develop High, Moderate, and Low creativity groups among 110 male engineers holding first-line supervisory positions in an industrial organization. Thereafter, one-way analyses of variance were run across these three creativity groups with Eysenck and Eysenck's (1970) scales for Extroversion, Neuroticism, and Psychoticism. There was no relationship between Neuroticism and Creativity but the Extroversion scale, as expected, was strongly related to Creativity ($F = 49.09$, d.f., 2, 107, $p < .01$). The additional interesting piece of information supplied by this study was that Creativity was also strongly related ($F = 57.87$, d.f., 2, 107, $p < .01$) to freedom from psychotic tendencies or, in other words, sound emotional health.

In the introduction to their study of creativity differences among managers, Chusmir and Koberg (1986) cite an impressive list of references attesting to the importance of creative and innovative behavior for managerial success. They claim, however, that previous empirical research neglected to measure creativity with more than one or two job-related attitudes or more than one managerial occupational category at a time. Chusmir and Koberg's results are particularly germane to our research since their samples consisted of 96 male and 60 female employees subdivided by levels of organizational functioning that corresponded to our first-line supervisory and middle-management groups. They related scores on creativity to a number of organization variables, four motivational needs as defined by McClelland (1961), and a personal characteristic of risk taking. Creativity was measured through administration of the Remote Associates Test (RAT) (Mednick, 1962). As its name implies, the test measures the ability to form remote or unusual word associations as, for example, relating the three stimulus words (cookies, sixteen, and heart) with the response word (sweet), which is the associative connective link.

Chusmir and Koberg present their results separately by gender for the two levels of organizational functioning. There were no significant gender differences in levels of creative thinking, a fact that has been confirmed by others (Kogan, 1974; Bolen & Torrance, 1978). Their results, in a broad sense, confirm McClelland's (1961) contention of the relationship between creativity and the need for the achievement and the need for power in the sample of male employees. The correlations between the creativity score and each of these motivational needs is positive for males at both levels of organizational functioning, and statistically significant with n Ach for first-line managers and with n Pwr for middle managers.

Female employees show a different pattern, with positive associations between creativity and the need for affilliation (n Aff) at both levels of organizational functioning, with a statistically significant relationship for first-line supervisors. Chusmir and Koberg suggest that the differences in the association patterns for men and women may be due to traditional socializations. Their results conform with ours in the experience and background area where we show some overlap but also some differences in the work motivations of men and women.

McClelland holds that the preeminent characteristic of successful entrepreneurs, defined as individuals who successfully start small businesses, is high n Ach. With the caveat that the reported research has generally been based on samples consisting predominantly or wholly of male subjects, this claim has been largely substantiated both in the United States and abroad in numerous studies (McClelland, 1961; McClelland & Winter, 1969; Wainer & Rubin, 1969; Singh, 1978; and Hundall, 1971). The relationship between the need for achievement and entrepreneurship has also been demonstrated by Hornaday and Aboud (1971) using conventional standardized tests rather than the projective tests used by McClelland and his associates. They found that the need for achievement, measured by the Edwards Personal Preference Schedule (Edwards, 1959); and leadership, independence, and lack of a need for support, measured by the Survey of Interpersonal Values (Gordon, 1960), differed significantly between entrepreneurs and men in general.

If we accept that the qualities of creativity, independence, lack of a need for support, and leadership have been shown to be associated with high n Ach, it is reasonable to agree with Rotter's view that individuals who have an internal locus of control, and are thus likely to believe that the outcome of a business venture will be influenced by their own efforts rather than uncontrollable circumstances, will have a high need for achievement (Rotter, 1966). Internal locus of control has also been related to successful entrepreneurship (Brockhaus, 1975; Borland, 1974).

Based on our own results and information obtained from the literature, we hypothesize that the variables in the managerial and professional test battery that are most likely to define the entrepreneurial personality are: Drive; Creativity; Internal Locus of Control; and Self-reliance, Extroversion, and Emotional Responsiveness, which are described below.

Behavior Characteristics

The Temperament Comparator provides scores on four behavioral dimensions: Extroversion versus Introversion, Emotional Responsiveness versus Emotional Control, Self-reliance versus Dependence, and Personal Insight. The occupational group means for these four dimensions are given for each level in the four hierarchies in Figure 5.5.

Figure 5.5 shows that the Self-reliance and Personal Insight dimensions behave similarly in all four hierarchies. The dimensions show increasing scores across levels with executives always being the highest scoring group except that middle managers have the same scores as their executives for Self-reliance and out-score them by one point on Personal Insight in the Professional hierarchy. The differences among the occupational groups means are significant in all but the Technical hierarchy, where the difference on Self-reliance approaches significance. It seems reasonable to assume, therefore, that these two attributes are important requirements for success in management positions.

The items that contribute to the Self-reliance dimension indicate that successful executives exhibit confidence and vigorous behavior and persistence in achieving difficult goals. They are decisive in decision making, regardless of whether or not they have group support for the decision, and are prepared to take responsibility for decision outcomes. Individuals at the low end of the continuum probably prefer managing by consensus to managing by directive and, in extreme cases, they would have difficulty in making decisions independently and would be oversensitive to the opinions of peers and subordinates.

Individuals who score high on Personal Insight have a firm self-image and are consistent and predictable in their interaction with others. The presumption is that consistent behavior fosters employee trust and that self-knowledge and self-acceptance facilitates meaningful interaction with others.

The Extroversion and Emotional Responsiveness dimensions behave differentially in the different hierarchies. One reason for this may be that for these dimensions, unlike the other measures in the test battery, a high score is not necessarily a "good" score. Rather, scores above and below the mean could represent a behavioral asset in different circumstances or conditions of operation, with the extremes at either end of the continuum representing unfavorable behavior characteristics.

The Line and Professional hierarchies show significantly increasing levels of extroversive and emotionally responsive behavior, with executives being the highest scoring groups. In the Sales hierarchy, the groups at all three levels score above the mean on these two dimensions. Favorable behavior for scores above the mean on this combination of variables would be generally warm and outgoing behavior combined with a fast reaction time and occasional impulsivity. The individual possessing these two characteristics will experience emotions deeply and express them easily. Under the right circumstances, the individual could act as a catalyst and engender enthusiasm in others. At the extreme end of the scale, this combination of dimensions could result in variable emotions, and mood swings that make behavior unpredictable and hamper persistence in goal achievement.

Executives in the Technical hierarchy score at about the mean on these two dimensions. The groups that consistently score below the mean on these two dimensions are the entry-level first-line supervisors, nonmanagement professionals, and the technical-specialist personnel. Moderately low scores on this combination of dimensions would describe individuals whose behavior is steady and consistent, who have temperate emotions,

Figure 5.5
Occupational Group Means for Temperament Factors and Personal Insight in the Line, Professional, Sales, and Technical Hierarchies

Category Scale		CS Scale	SS Scale	Normalized Standard Score Scale (37.5 40 42.5 45 47.5 50 52.5 55 57.5 60 62.5)	Prob.
1. Extroversion	LINE HIERARCHY	58 / 54 / 46	52 / 51 / 49	EEEEEEEEEEEEEEEEEEEEEEE / MMMMMMMMMMMMMMMMMM / LLLLLLLLLLLLLLLLLLLL	.005**
2. Emotional Responsiveness	LINE HIERARCHY	62 / 54 / 46	53 / 51 / 49	EEEEEEEEEEEEEEEEEEEEEEEEE / MMMMMMMMMMMMMMMMMMM / LLLLLLLLLLLLLLLLLL	.000***
3. Self Reliance	LINE HIERARCHY	69 / 66 / 50	55 / 54 / 50	EEEEEEEEEEEEEEEEEEEEEEEEEEEE / MMMMMMMMMMMMMMMMMMMMMMMM / LLLLLLLLLLLLLLLLLLLLLL	.000***
4. Pers. Insight	LINE HIERARCHY	62 / 54 / 34	53 / 51 / 46	EEEEEEEEEEEEEEEEEEEEEEEE / MMMMMMMMMMMMMMMMMMM / LLLLLLLLLLLLLL	.000***
1. Extroversion	PROFESSIONAL HIERARCHY	54 / 54 / 38	51 / 51 / 47	EEEEEEEEEEEEEEEEEEEEEE / MMMMMMMMMMMMMMMMMMM / PPPPPPPPPPPPP	.000***
2. Emotional Responsiveness	PROFESSIONAL HIERARCHY	54 / 50 / 42	51 / 50 / 48	EEEEEEEEEEEEEEEEEEEEEE / MMMMMMMMMMMMMMMMMM / PPPPPPPPPPPPPPPP	.001***
3. Self Reliance	PROFESSIONAL HIERARCHY	66 / 66 / 50	54 / 54 / 50	EEEEEEEEEEEEEEEEEEEEEEEEEE / MMMMMMMMMMMMMMMMMMMMMMMM / PPPPPPPPPPPPPPPPPP	.000***
4. Pers. Insight	PROFESSIONAL HIERARCHY	58 / 62 / 42	52 / 53 / 48	EEEEEEEEEEEEEEEEEEEE / MMMMMMMMMMMMMMMMMMMMMM / PPPPPPPPPPPPPPPPPP	.000***
1. Extroversion	SALES HIERARCHY	58 / 58 / 66	52 / 52 / 54	EEEEEEEEEEEEEEEEEEEE / MMMMMMMMMMMMMMMMMMMMMM / SSSSSSSSSSSSSSSSSSSSSSSSSS	.110
2. Emotional Responsiveness	SALES HIERARCHY	69 / 62 / 62	55 / 53 / 53	EEEEEEEEEEEEEEEEEEEEEEEEEEEE / MMMMMMMMMMMMMMMMMMMMMM / SSSSSSSSSSSSSSSSSSSSSSS	.455
3. Self Reliance	SALES HIERARCHY	58 / 50 / 42	52 / 50 / 48	EEEEEEEEEEEEEEEEEEEE / MMMMMMMMMMMMMMMMMM / SSSSSSSSSSSSSSS	..003**
4. Pers. Insight	SALES HIERARCHY	62 / 46 / 38	53 / 49 / 47	EEEEEEEEEEEEEEEEEEEEEEEE / MMMMMMMMMMMMMM / SSSSSSSSSSSSS	.000***
1. Extroversion	TECHNICAL HIERARCHY	50 / 58 / 50	50 / 52 / 50	EEEEEEEEEEEEEEEEEE / MMMMMMMMMMMMMMMMMMMM / TTTTTTTTTTTTTTTTTTTT	.349
2. Emotional Responsiveness	TECHNICAL HIERARCHY	54 / 54 / 46	51 / 51 / 49	EEEEEEEEEEEEEEEEEEEE / MMMMMMMMMMMMMMMMMMMM / TTTTTTTTTTTTTTTT	.270
3. Self Reliance	TECHNICAL HIERARCHY	69 / 54 / 58	55 / 51 / 52	EEEEEEEEEEEEEEEEEEEEEEEEEEEE / MMMMMMMMMMMMMMMMMM / TTTTTTTTTTTTTTTTTTTTTT	.072
4. Pers. Insight	TECHNICAL HIERARCHY	54 / 50 / 42	51 / 50 / 48	EEEEEEEEEEEEEEEEEEEE / MMMMMMMMMMMMMMMMMM / TTTTTTTTTTTTTTTT	.174

Centile Scale: 11   16   23   31   40   50   60   69   77   84   89

* p < .01.   *** p < .001.

and who can be relied upon in stressful situations. It seems reasonable that such behavior would be an asset in controlling and regulatory positions such as line supervisor, and in nonmanagement professional and technical positions that require careful and methodical work. Extremely low scores on these dimensions would result in over-control of emotional expression, either through inhibition or general lack of emotional response, together with over-cautiousness and a tendency to get into a rut.

Mean scores for the objective measures of reaction time and the ability to work under pressure obtained from The Press Test are given for the occupational groups at the three levels in all four hierarchies in Figure 5.6. It will be seen from the Prob. column in the figure that there are significantly increasing scores on all dimensions in all hierarchies. The ability to react fast and to maintain a high level of productivity under the pressure of distracting stimuli is characteristic of managers in all hierarchies. By contrast, the scores of first-line supervisors are the lowest obtained by any occupational group on the three parts of The Press Test. The reaction time scores are, in fact, too low to be plotted on the grid. At first sight, these results seem to contradict those obtained for first-line supervisors from the measures derived from the Temperament Comparator. It seems reasonable to expect individuals who show measured, steady, and consistent behavior to withstand the pressure of distracting stimuli and thus do well on Part III of The Press Test. In actual fact, it is the fast-reacting individual who can respond to distracting stimuli without being diverted from the main task. Individuals in regulatory and controlling positions who are rigidly systematic and orderly are likely to be unduly hampered by unexpected distractions and unable to achieve the degree of dissociation necessary to do well on Part III of The Press Test.

Personal-Emotional Adjustment

The last area of the test battery deals with the emotional health status of the individual. Scores on three factorially determined key adjustment factors and a measure of overall stress response are shown for the three levels of occupational groups in the four hierarchies in Figure 5.7. It should be noted that grids in the personal-emotional adjustment area of the test battery are on a different scale from the other tests. The reason for this is that the Emo Questionnaire is used as a screening procedure, and we are only concerned with scores that fall below a standard score of 40 on the grid. The vertical line on the grid is thus drawn at 40 rather than at the median score of 50, which applies to all other tests. Figure 5.7 shows consistent and significant increases in the level of response score (increasingly better scores) in all hierarchies. This is not interpreted to mean that executives operate under less pressure and stress, but rather that

Figure 5.6
Occupational Group Means for Reaction Time to the Verbal Stimulus,
Reaction Time to the Color Stimulus, and Reaction Time under
Distraction in the Line, Professional, Sales, and Technical Hierarchies

Category Scale		CS Scale	SS Scale	Normalized Standard Score Scale 37.5 40 42.5 45 47.5 50 52.5 55 57.5 60 62.5	Prob.
Part I. RT- Verbal Stimulus	*LINE HIERARCHY*	66 58 07	54 52 35	EEEEEEEEEEEEEEEEEEEEEEEEE MMMMMMMMMMMMMMMMMM L<--	.000***
Part II. RT- Color Stimulus		73 62 08	56 53 36	EEEEEEEEEEEEEEEEEEEEEEEEEEEE MMMMMMMMMMMMMMMMMM L<--	.000***
Part III. RT- Color with Distraction		76 69 18	57 55 41	EEEEEEEEEEEEEEEEEEEEEEEEEEEE MMMMMMMMMMMMMMMMMMMM LLLLL	.000***
Part I. RT- Verbal Stimulus	*PROFESSIONAL HIERARCHY*	66 76 58	54 57 52	EEEEEEEEEEEEEEEEEEEEEEEE MMMMMMMMMMMMMMMMMMMMMMM PPPPPPPPPPPPPPPPPPPPP	.000***
Part II. RT- Color Stimulus		79 79 62	58 58 53	EEEEEEEEEEEEEEEEEEEEEEEEEEEEEE MMMMMMMMMMMMMMMMMMMMMMMM PPPPPPPPPPPPPPPPPPPPPPP	.000***
Part III. RT- Color with Distraction		73 76 66	56 57 54	EEEEEEEEEEEEEEEEEEEEEEEEEE MMMMMMMMMMMMMMMMMMMMMM PPPPPPPPPPPPPPPPPPPPPPPP	.014*
Part I. RT- Verbal Stimulus	*SALES HIERARCHY*	73 58 54	56 52 51	EEEEEEEEEEEEEEEEEEEEEEEEEEEE MMMMMMMMMMMMMMMMM SSSSSSSSSSSSSSSSSSSS	.000***
Part II. RT- Color Stimulus		82 58 54	59 52 51	EEEEEEEEEEEEEEEEEEEEEEEEEEEEEEEE MMMMMMMMMMMMMMMMMM SSSSSSSSSSSSSSSSSSSS	.000***
Part III. RT- Color with Distraction		76 54 50	57 51 50	EEEEEEEEEEEEEEEEEEEEEEEEEEE MMMMMMMMMMMMMMMM SSSSSSSSSSSSSSSSSS	.000***
Part I. RT- Verbal Stimulus	*TECHNICAL HIERARCHY*	76 73 50	57 56 50	EEEEEEEEEEEEEEEEEEEEEEEEEEE MMMMMMMMMMMMMMMMMMMMMMM TTTTTTTTTTTTTTTTTTTT	.000***
Part II. RT- Color Stimulus		79 76 54	58 57 51	EEEEEEEEEEEEEEEEEEEEEEEEEEEEEEE MMMMMMMMMMMMMMMMMMMMM TTTTTTTTTTTTTTTTTTTTTT	.000***
Part III. RT- Color with Distraction		76 76 66	57 57 54	EEEEEEEEEEEEEEEEEEEEEEEEEEE MMMMMMMMMMMMMMMMMMMMMMM TTTTTTTTTTTTTTTTTTTTTTTTT	.043*

11 16 23 31 40 50 60 69 77 84 89

Centile Scale

* p < .05.   *** p < .001.

they have greater tolerance for stress. This interpretation is in accordance with the results obtained from the test of pressure tolerance.

Although some individuals failed the screening procedure (scored below a standard score of 40) on the key (Internal, External, and Somatic) adjustment factors, all occupational group means exceed 40. The only exception is for sales executives who score on the border for the External Adjustment Factor. This factor measures freedom from distorted per-

Figure 5.7
Occupational Group Means for Three Adjustment Factors and the Level of Response to Stressful Stimuli in the Line, Professional, Sales, and Technical Hierarchies

Normalized Standard Score Scale

Category Scale		CS Scale	SS Scale	25 27.5 30 32.5 35 37.5 40 42.5 45 47.5 50	Prob.
KI Internal Adjustment	*LINE HIERARCHY*	38 34 34	47 46 46	EEEEEEEEEEEEEEEEEEEEEEEEEEEEEEEEEEE MMMMMMMMMMMMMMMMMMMMMMMMMMMMM LLLLLLLLLLLLLLLLLLLLLLLLLLLLLLLLLLL	.627
KE External Adjustment		34 34 18	46 46 41	EEEEEEEEEEEEEEEEEEEEEEEEEEEEEEEE MMMMMMMMMMMMMMMMMMMMMMMMMMMM LLLLLLLLLLLLLLLLLLLLLLLLLLLL	.000***
KS Somatic Adjustment		42 34 27	48 46 44	EEEEEEEEEEEEEEEEEEEEEEEEEEEEEEEEEEEE MMMMMMMMMMMMMMMMMMMMMMMMMMMMMM LLLLLLLLLLLLLLLLLLLLLLLLLLLLLLLLL	.001***
LR (D) Level of Response		50 24 21	50 43 42	EEEEEEEEEEEEEEEEEEEEEEEEEEEEEEEEEEEEEEEE MMMMMMMMMMMMMMMMMMMMMMMM LLLLLLLLLLLLLLLLLLLLLLLLLLLLLLL	.000***
KI Internal Adjustment	*PROFESSIONAL HIERARCHY*	31 27 34	45 44 46	EEEEEEEEEEEEEEEEEEEEEEEEEEEEEE MMMMMMMMMMMMMMMMMMMMMMMMMMM PPPPPPPPPPPPPPPPPPPPPPPPPPPPPPPPPP	.166
KE External Adjustment		27 27 27	44 44 44	EEEEEEEEEEEEEEEEEEEEEEEEEEE MMMMMMMMMMMMMMMMMMMMMMM PPPPPPPPPPPPPPPPPPPPPPPPPPP	.870
KS Somatic Adjustment		27 27 34	44 44 46	EEEEEEEEEEEEEEEEEEEEEEEEEEE MMMMMMMMMMMMMMMMMMMMMMM PPPPPPPPPPPPPPPPPPPPPPPPPPPPPPPPPP	.293
LR (D) Level of Response		42 42 10	48 48 37	EEEEEEEEEEEEEEEEEEEEEEEEEEEEEEEEEEEEEE MMMMMMMMMMMMMMMMMMMMMMMMMMMMMMMMMMM PPPPPPPPPPPPPPPPPP	.000***
KI Internal Adjustment	*SALES HIERARCHY*	27 42 42	44 48 48	EEEEEEEEEEEEEEEEEEEEEEEEEEEE MMMMMMMMMMMMMMMMMMMMMMMMMMMMMMMM SSSSSSSSSSSSSSSSSSSSSSSSSSSSSSSSSSSS	.011*
KE External Adjustment		16 21 27	40 42 44	EEEEEEEEEEEEEEEEEEEEEEE MMMMMMMMMMMMMMMMMMMMM SSSSSSSSSSSSSSSSSSSSSSSSSSSS	.012*
KS Somatic Adjustment		24 34 34	43 46 46	EEEEEEEEEEEEEEEEEEEEEEEEE MMMMMMMMMMMMMMMMMMMMMMMMMMMMMM SSSSSSSSSSSSSSSSSSSSSSSSSSSSSS	.084
LR (D) Level of Response		38 16 16	47 40 40	EEEEEEEEEEEEEEEEEEEEEEEEEEEEEEEEEE MMMMMMMMMMMMMMMMMMMMMMM SSSSSSSSSSSSSSSSSSSSSSSS	.008**
KI Internal Adjustment	*TECHNICAL HIERARCHY*	31 27 38	45 44 47	EEEEEEEEEEEEEEEEEEEEEEEEEEEEEE MMMMMMMMMMMMMMMMMMMMMMMMMMM TTTTTTTTTTTTTTTTTTTTTTTTTTTTTTTTTTTTT	.010**
KE External Adjustment		27 27 27	44 44 44	EEEEEEEEEEEEEEEEEEEEEEEEEEEE MMMMMMMMMMMMMMMMMMMMMMMM TTTTTTTTTTTTTTTTTTTTTTTTTTTTTTTT	.859
KS Somatic Adjustment		27 27 34	44 44 46	EEEEEEEEEEEEEEEEEEEEEEEEEEEE MMMMMMMMMMMMMMMMMMMMMMMM TTTTTTTTTTTTTTTTTTTTTTTTTTTTTTTTTT	.489
LR (D) Level of Response		42 38 24	48 47 43	EEEEEEEEEEEEEEEEEEEEEEEEEEEEEEEEEEEEEE MMMMMMMMMMMMMMMMMMMMMMMMMMMMMMMM TTTTTTTTTTTTTTTTTTTTTTTTTTTT	.001***

* p < .05.   ** p < .01.   *** p < .001.

Centile Scale: 1 1 2 4 7 11 16 23 31 40 50

ceptions of the external world, from distrust of the motivations of others, and from tendencies to project the blame for perceived failures on others or circumstances out of their control. It should be noted that sales executives seem to feel the effects of stress more than their counterparts in other hierarchies since they are generally the lowest scoring group on all three adjustment factors. It should also be noted that in the Sales and Technical hierarchies, the Level III and middle-manager groups sometimes show significantly higher scores on the adjustment factors than their corresponding executives.

By contrast, in the Line hierarchy there were increasingly better scores across the three levels, with significant differences among the group means on the External Adjustment and Somatic Adjustment factors. In general, high scorers on the adjustment factors are free from unduly high levels of internal tension arising from feelings of inadequacy and unfocussed fear and anxiety (Internal Adjustment), have realistic perceptions of themselves in relation to the external world (External Adjustment), and are not suffering from vague physical complaints and feelings of depression that generally reflect long-term underlying emotional conflict (Somatic Adjustment).

COMMON AND UNIQUE ATTRIBUTES OF INCUMBENTS BY LEVEL AND HIERARCHY

In order to identify the attributes that were common and unique to incumbents in the different hierarchies at each level of organizational functioning, a procedure similar to that described in Chapter 3 was used to identify the common and unique job functions performed by incumbents.

At each level of functioning, attributes were identified for which at least one of the occupational groups had a mean normalized standard score of 54 or higher (on a standard score scale of 0 to 100), and the other occupational groups at the same level had normalized standard score values of at least 53 or more for the attribute. This procedure will identify the attributes that are both important and common to incumbents in the hierarchies at each level of functioning. Thereafter, to ensure that an important attribute was not overlooked, all remaining attributes at each level in each hierarchy with a normalized standard score of 53 or greater were listed. The two exceptions to these rules occur for two Level III occupational groups. One exception is a score of 52 for Active Relaxation Pursuits listed for line supervisors, since it is the highest score for that group. The second exception is a score of 52 for Reaction Time to Verbal Stimuli for the group of nonmanagement professionals, since this score is highly correlated with that for Reaction Time to Color Stimuli, which is listed for that group. The common and unique attributes for executives

Table 5.4
Test Battery Characteristics That Are Common and Unique to Level I Executive Groups

	Hierarchy			
	Line	Prof.	Sales	Tech.
Experience & Background				
Drive/Career Progress	59	57	56	56
Financial Responsibility	56	54	54	53
General Family Responsibility	60	60	56	55
Active Relaxation Pursuits	*53		*56	
Mental Abilities				
Non-Verbal Reasoning	54	*56	54	*54
Word Fluency	59	58	59	*58
Vocabulary	56	*58	56	*58
Closure Flexibility		54		
Aptitudes				
Creative Potential	53		54	
Sales Aptitude			55	
Behavior Characteristics				
Reaction Time – Verbal	54	*54	56	57
Reaction Time – Color	56	*58	59	58
Reaction Time – Distraction	57	*56	57	*57
Emotional Responsiveness	53		*55	
Self-Reliance	55	54		55
Personal Insight	53		53	

*Common to all levels in the hierarchy

at Level I in all hierarchies are given in Table 5.4, those for middle managers in Table 5.5, and for the Level III occupational groups in Table 5.6.

As could be expected from the results of the analysis of variance, Table 5.4 shows that there is considerable overlap in the attributes that characterize executives in all hierarchies at Level I. There are, however, some unique attributes listed for each hierarchy that suggests that there could be a loss in the prediction of performance if the Level I executives were treated as a homogeneous group.

The middle managers in the four hierarchies have, as is evident from

Table 5.5
Test Battery Characteristics That Are Common and Unique to Level II Middle Management Groups

	Hierarchy			
	Line	Prof.	Sales	Tech.
Experience & Background				
Drive/Career Progress	54	54	53	55
Leadership & Group Participation			53	
Prof. Work & Vocational Satisfaction		53		
Financial Responsibility		54		54
General Family Responsibility		55		53
Active Relaxation Pursuits	*53	54	*56	
Mental Abilities				
Non-Verbal Reasoning	54	*56		*54
Word Fluency	55	60		*58
Vocabulary	54	*56	54	*55
Closure Flexibility	53			
Aptitudes				
Creative Potential			53	
Behavior Characteristics				
Reaction Time - Verbal		*57		56
Reaction Time - Color	53	*58		57
Reaction Time - Distraction	55	*57		*57
Emotional Responsiveness			*53	
Self-Reliance	54	54		
Personal Insight		53		

*Common to all three levels in the hierarchy

Table 5.5, less overlap in the personal attributes measured by the test battery than the Level I groups. In the experience and background area, the only attribute that all four groups have in common is Drive, and the only mental ability listed for all four groups is the measure of English vocabulary.

As was the case with the functions performed by incumbents, there is also overlap, in each hierarchy, of attributes displayed by the Level I and II groups. In the experience and background area, with the exception of Active Relaxation Pursuits, the attribute values for the Level I executives are generally higher than those for the Level II middle managers. This can be seen by comparing Table 5.4 to Table 5.5. The higher scores for Level I executives may be partially due to age differences. There is also overlap across the two levels on the mental ability test as well as the scores for the behavior characteristics, but in these areas the executives do not score consistently higher than their respective middle managers.

It is evident from Table 5.6 that there is no test dimension that is common to all four occupational groups at Level III, although there is some similarity between the professional and technical–specialist groups. In general, the attributes show the same pattern of decreasing overlap across hierarchies as we observed for the job functions performed by the incumbents.

There are some attributes that are common to all levels of a hierarchy that could be considered characteristic of the heirarchy. These are marked with an asterisk in the three tables. The Line hierarchy has only Active Relaxation Pursuits common to all three levels. The Sales hierarchy has both Active Relaxation Pursuits and Emotional Responsiveness in common. The Professional and Technical hierarchies show the most similarity among incumbents at the three levels in the hierarchy with respect to both the mental abilities and the behavior attributes.

INTERPRETATION OF THE OCCUPATIONAL GROUP PROFILES

An attempt will be made to interpret the significant characteristics of individuals who could be expected to perform successfully in the various occupational groups. Apart from its academic interest, this information could be used by training departments to promote insight and understanding within an occupational group, or to help managers to understand the behavior characteristics, motivations, and objectives of their employees. The information could also be used in the selection process as a basis for the final employment interview, with or without knowledge of the applicant's objective measures obtained from the test battery. Since the Level III groups are the most disparate, these will be described first.

The First-Line Supervisor

In recent years, the key role of the first-line supervisor as responsible for the smoothness of day-to-day operations in the workplace, and as the link between workers and management, has been gradually eroded. In a long-term study of over 1,200 first-line managers in Australia, Gilmour

Table 5.6
Test Battery Characteristics That Are Common and Unique to Level III Entry-Level Groups

	Hierarchy			
	Line	Prof.	Sales	Tech.
Experience & Background				
School Achievement				53
Leadership & Group Participation			53	
Active Relaxation Pursuits	*(52)		*57	53
Mental Abilities				
Non-Verbal Reasoning		*56		*54
Word Fluency				*54
Vocabulary		*53		*54
Closure Flexibility		56		54
Behavior Attributes				
Reaction Time – Verbal		*(52)		
Reaction Time – Color		*53		
Reaction Time – Distraction		*54		*54
Extroversion	< 50		54	
Emotional Responsiveness	< 50		*53	

*Common to all three levels in the hierarchy

and Lansbury (1986) suggest four major factors responsible for restructuring the supervisory role in Anglo-American industrial organizations: (1) organizational changes, such as the introduction of growing numbers of technical specialists and professionals that have widened the gulf between the supervisor and the plant managers; (2) technical changes that have outmoded the technical skills of many first-line supervisors; (3) social changes that have produced a work force often with a different ethnic background or with higher levels of education than the supervisor, which serve to distance him or her from the work force; and (4) changes in industrial relations that have tended to concentrate more power and influence on the shop stewards (especially those representing strong unions) as the communicating link between workers and management. As a result of these changes, it is suggested that there are now two types of first-line supervisors with different career orientations: "One group of first line managers is younger and aspiring to a future career in the upper levels of management. The other group is older, having spent most of their working life on the factory floor, and consider their supervisory position as the apex of their careers" (Gilmour & Landsbury, 1986, p. 59).

In American institutions it has for many years been the practice to recruit (usually hard science) professionals on college campuses who are brought into the organization and enrolled in management development courses with the expectation that they will eventually manage the work force in the Line hierarchy. A clear example of this practice is seen in most highway divisions of departments of transportation, where every supervisory position is held by a qualified engineer. While this practice provides another career option for qualified professionals, it ensures that the immediate workshop or road supervisor will be of the type described by Gilmour and Landsbury who have no managerial aspirations. Indeed, the practice of importing professionals has essentially fractured the expected flow of upward movement in the Line hierarchy.

In the context of the STEP program, the first-line supervisory position as it will evolve in the future, or as it is presently represented by the supervisory group in our data base, is defined through the job analysis procedure that identifies the important functions to be performed in the position. Table 3.4 in Chapter 3 indicates that the major functions performed in the supervisory position concern the smooth flow of work operations, as indicated by high-importance values for the job functions of Coping with Difficulties and Emergencies and Promoting Safety Practices, and the immediate management of the work force, as indicated by the job function dimensions of Developing Group Cooperation and Teamwork and Supervisory and Personnel Practices.

At first glance, Table 5.6 seems to tell us little about incumbents in the first-line supervisory position except that they enjoy Active Relaxation Pursuits, since the remaining scores are all under the mean of 50. This is an artifact of norming the tests on the total higher-level population, thus ensuring that some members of the population will fall above and others below the mean. Although the supervisory-group scores are below the mean, the pattern of their relative strengths and weaknesses is as well defined as that of any other occupational group.

In the experience and background area of the test protocol (Figure 5.1), there are above average scores for Active Relaxation Pursuits and relatively high scores (which approach the mean) for School Achievement, Drive, and Leadership and Group Participation. If the educational background of the supervisor is graduation from high school or grade school, the attainment of the first rung on the Line managerial hierarchy is likely to be regarded as a self-actualizing achievement. The drive and leadership skills will be an asset in directing the work force.

With respect to the mental abilities (Figure 5.3), the highest score is 49 for deductive and analytical reasoning. The lowest score is for vocabulary but, optimally, all scores should fall in the range of at least 45 to 50. It should be remembered that since these tests are normed on the higher-level population, these scores represent at least an average level of general mental functioning in relation to the general population.

The supervisors differ most from managerial personnel in the behavioral area. Their objectively measured reaction time is so low that it cannot be plotted on the grid (Figure 5.6). Slow and considered behavior is their forte rather than rapid-fire response to stimuli. These results are in accordance with their average, or just below average, scores on the Extroversion and Emotional Responsiveness behavioral dimensions (Figure 5.5). These scores indicate that they are likely to be fairly cautious and considered in their approach to problem solving, and controlled and even tempered when dealing with employees. That below average scores on these dimensions are desirable is indicated in Table 5.6. Scores on these dimensions, should not, however, be excessively low since this will hamper interpersonal relations and distance the supervisor from the work group. Self-reliance is average in comparison with the higher-level population.

Creative potential is probably not an important consideration. Of greater importance would be adequate personal insight and a sound emotional health status, as indicated by scores on the key adjustment factors (Figure 5.7), which exceed the standard set in the screening procedure for emotional health.

Professionals

Young professional personnel with university credentials have more career options than any other occupational group. As indicated above, they may move into operational divisions in the Line hierarchy. Or, individuals with degrees in product areas such as chemistry and pharmacology, may move into the Sales hierarchy where they can use their special knowledge to promote product sales. Another option that was developed in the 1970s, and for reasons to be discussed later has been somewhat discredited, is the so-called "alternative career ladder," where highly qualified professionals advance in status and pay in their organizations without assuming management responsibility. Examples are a chief research scientist or corporate legal council.

Finally, there is movement up the Professional hierarchy as defined in our classification matrix where, after satisfactory service in professional or staff positions, the individuals move into management positions in the organization. The career path chosen by the individual will doubtless be influenced by many factors such as organizational structure, opportunity, perceived rewards, and possession of the skills and attributes that will facilitate successful performance in the position.

The functions performed by the individuals classified as professionals in our data base are described in Chapter 3 (Table 3.4). Objective Setting, and the Financial Planning associated with it, are characteristics at all levels in this hierarchy. At Level III, the Objective Setting will necessarily be at the project rather than the organizational level. Another function that occurs at all levels of the hierarchy is interdepartmental Coordination. Professionals, particularly in manufacturing organizations, will typically interact with departments responsible for the production, marketing, and sale of their products to inform themselves of the lines of research or product innovations that are likely to be responsive to market demands. Another of their functions is to represent their organizations in the scientific community by membership in professional societies and presentations at seminars and workshops. They are also responsible for the development of technical ideas and, in common with the two other entry-level groups, are concerned with Self-development and Improvement.

This group of young professionals has not yet shown the achievement in their personal lives or assumed the personal responsibility that would result in high scores in the experience and background area in Table 5.6. Indeed, the pursuit of higher degrees is quite likely to have resulted in a late start in generating significant earnings and in establishing a family. Their past achievements in the background area have been in academic settings and in preparing themselves for a career, as indicated by their scores (49) for both School Achievement and professional Work and Vocational Satisfaction, which are their highest on all of the background dimensions with the exception of Active Relaxation Pursuits (Figure 5.1).

Their outstanding assets are the intellectual ones of deductive and analytical reasoning and the visual perceptual skills. They also have a good grasp of classical English vocabulary (Figure 5.3). Having an above average level of creative potential is not an important consideration for individuals who will continue to work in a staff professional capacity. If, however, in an expanding organization it is expected that a fair number of the professionals will be promoted, care should be taken by the organization to ensure that there will be employees in the group who have sufficient creativity to facilitate performance in management positions.

The professionals are the highest scoring Level III group on the objectively measured reaction time and the ability to work under pressure (Figure 5.6). Furthermore, it is only in the Professional hierarchy that these characteristics are registered as important at all three levels. This seems to indicate that an essential requirement for successful performance in the Professional hierarchy is the ability to deal efficiently with a number of different stimuli as in multiple data processing.

Professionals have adequate insight and at least average Self-reliance. They tend to be reserved and not emotionally responsive. They are, in fact, the lowest scoring occupational group on the Extroversion and Emotionally Responsive dimensions (Figure 5.5). This cautious and considered behavior combined with emotional control will facilitate performance in positions that require close scientific measurements, replication of experiments, and attention to detail.

The professional group experiences considerable stress as indicated by their level of stress response (Figure 5.7). They are, however, able to cope with it successfully since they pass on the three key adjustment factors in the screening procedure for emotional health.

Sales Representatives

The sales representatives in the STEP data base generally sell industrial products. Included in such "products" are space in railroad cars and certain types of insurance. All sales representatives in the data base enjoyed a fair degree of autonomy in their work, did considerable traveling, and pursued their own customers. It was found that the different types of sales representatives mentioned showed considerable overlap in their skill and attribute profiles, which made it possible to identify the behavior characteristics that they had in common. These characteristics will not apply to sales representatives who largely provide a service, such as stocking shelves in supermarkets; across-the-counter sales people; or the one exception to product sales representatives that we have encountered, that of men selling cosmetics.

In defining the job functions of the sales representatives in Chapter 3 (Table 3.4), we found, predictably, that Handling Outside Contacts was one of the most important job functions. Furthermore, this function is important at all levels of the Sales hierarchy. Another avenue for outside contacts is representing the organization in the community as indicated by the high importance value for the Community/Organization Relations job function. The fact that Developing Technical Ideas emerges as an important function probably reflects the fact that many of the sales representatives held degrees in areas related to their products. Coping with Difficulties and Emergencies also seems to be an integral part of the job. These emergencies are likely to be related to problems of coordination, such as ensuring that marketing materials are available for new products or that deliveries are made to customers as promised, rather than workflow problems encountered by first-line supervisors.

Table 5.6 shows that one of the important attributes for sales representatives in the experience and background area of the test battery is Active Relaxation Pursuits. Indeed, this is an important attribute at all levels of the Sales hierarchy. Selling is generally regarded as a pressureful occupation, and engaging in physical activity and competitive sports may be one way of draining off tensions or of satisfying competitive instincts in a different arena. The sales representatives also have a surprisingly high score, which exceeds that of their executives, on Leadership and Group Participation (Figure 5.2). The assumption of leadership roles in social, community, or professional groups is probably yet another way of achieving visibility and establishing contacts outside of the organization.

The scores of the group of sales representatives on the mental ability tests are either just at or just below the mean of the higher-level population (Figure 5.3). Because of the way the tests were normed, this represents at least an average level of general mental functioning. However, it appears that the aptitudes and behavior attributes carry greater weight than the mental abilities in determining success in selling.

The Sales hierarchy is distinguished by being the only one in which mean scores for the potential for creative and innovative behavior are above average for the groups at all three levels (Figure 5.4). The dimensions of the creative personality include the ability to think intuitively, to be dominant in social situations, and to have a liking for autonomous work, all of which should facilitate performance in a sales position. Groups at all levels of the Sales hierarchy also have high scores for Emotional Responsiveness. In addition, the sales representative group scores high on Extroversion. Clearly, outgoing, emotionally responsive, and enthusiastic behavior, as described earlier in this chapter, is an asset for interpersonal relations and selling. As with all behavior dimensions, however, extreme scores are detrimental. Finally, adequate insight and a sound level of emotional health are desirable when introducing new members into the work force.

Technical Specialists

We observed in Chapter 3 that one function that was important at all levels of the Technical hierarchy was Financial Planning (Table 3.4), which could be expected since a sizeable number of employees in the hierarchy are drawn from financial institutions. In addition the technical specialists have, in common with sales representatives, both Handling Outside Contacts and Community/Organization Relations as important functions. This may be due to the fact that in many institutions, such as banks and accounting consulting agencies, the technical specialists do have client contacts and promote the services offered by the institution. A sense of cohesiveness, as indicated by emphasis on the Communications and Developing Teamwork functions, is also important in this hierarchy.

In the experience and background area of the test protocol, the Technical hierarchy is unique in that the groups at all levels score above the mean on the Financial Responsibility dimension (Figure 5.2). It is in accordance with the hypothesis concerning the ability of background data to predict future behavior and occupational choice that individuals who have demonstrated facility in handling their personal economy, as described earlier in this chapter, should gravitate toward employment in situations where they can increase their knowledge of investment strategies and other matters related to financial handling, and assume fiscal responsibility at the account, department, and later at higher levels in the organization.

The Technical hierarchy is also the only hierarchy in which occupational groups at all levels score above the mean on Professional Work and Vocational Satisfaction, although the Professional hierarchy approaches this with the lowest score being 49 for the nonmanagement professionals. The technical specialists are the highest scoring occupational group on School Achievement. This may be one of the few instances in which past school achievement will be shown to be related to later vocational success. Drive is average with respect to the higher-level population, and the group shows the usual high level of participation in Active Relaxation Pursuits. In general, the pattern of scores in the experience and background area of the last battery for the group of technical specialists presents a picture where past achievements in the early educational and later personal family environments have led to employment in harmonious occupational climates and satisfaction with their choice of a vocation.

Other characteristics of the technical specialists are "well-balanced" mental abilities, as indicated by a score of 54 on each of the mental ability tests (Figure 5.3). They have only an average reaction time and can be expected to work at a steady consistent rate and to maintain or even increase productivity under pressure (Figure 5.6).

Subliminal thinking and intuitive leaps to the solutions of problems are not their forte. Even the executives in the Technical hierarchy score no higher than 51 for creative potential (Figure 5.4). A high level of creative potential may even be a liability in this hierarchy since it is not apparently even a requirement for upward movement. In our personal experience in career counseling interviews, we have often encountered highly accomplished and very creative individuals who have felt restricted and stifled and been clear misfits in the traditional operations of the Technical hierarchy. If this is found to be the case, they can sometimes be more constructively employed in troubleshooting and other special assignments such as establishing new branch offices or markets.

In the behavioral area, technical specialists are above the mean in Self-reliance and, in common with the Professionals, show control over tendencies to impulsivity and the expression of emotions. As with all other occupational groups, adequate insight and a sound emotional health status are desirable.

Middle Managers

In order to avoid undue repetition, the attributes common to all middle managers will be described but reference will also be made to the attributes that are unique to the incumbents in each hierarchy.

We saw in Chapter 3 that there was some overlap between the executives and middle management groups on the steering and operational job functions but that the importance values for middle managers were at somewhat lower levels. The functions common to middle managers were those that stressed the nurturing of employees and the smoothness of operations in the immediate work group.

Just as the steering and operational functions (which are generally only performed by experienced executives) are at lower levels of importance for middle managers, so too are their scores in the experience and background area of the test protocol, which indicate past achievement and the assumption of responsibility in their personal lives. Table 5.5 shows that all middle managers show considerable Drive, with scores that approach the magnitude of a half standard deviation above the mean. Middle managers in the Professional and Technical hierarchies have above average scores (54) for Financial Responsibility in common. The Professionals are the only middle-management group that has a high score for Professional Work and Vocational Satisfaction. A high score for Leadership and Group Participation is unique to the Sales hierarchy. In general, Table 5.5 presents a picture in the background and experience area of the test protocol of "transitional" managers who have high drive, are assuming increasing responsibility in personal family and social environments, and who have some characteristics that are unique to their particular hierarchies.

Table 5.5 shows that there is increasing emphasis on the level of mental functioning with movement to the middle level of the hierarchies. In fact, in the Professional and Technical hierarchies, the mental ability scores of the middle managers are fairly similar to those of their corresponding executive groups, as shown in Table 5.4. In the Sales hierarchy, the only high mental ability score listed in Table 5.5 indicates a good grasp of English vocabulary. As though to compensate for their poorer showing on the mental abilities, sales is the only middle-management group that shows facility in intuitive thinking and substantial potential for creative and innovative behavior.

In the behavioral area, all but the sales middle managers show a fast reaction time and ability to work under pressure. Personal self-reliance is also beginning to make its appearance as an important managerial characteristic in the Line and Professional hierarchies. Emotional responsiveness, the warm and expressive behavior that facilitates interpersonal relations, is unique to the Sales hierarchy.

As with all occupational groups, an adequate level of personal insight and a sound emotional health status would be a requirement, especially in these middle management positions where there is emphasis on the supervision and development of the work force.

Executives

In Chapter 3 we saw that job functions that are of major importance for executives at Level I have narrowed, with concentration on the steering and operational functions of setting the overall objectives for the organization with the associated functions of decision making, financial planning, and organizational communications. Of somewhat lesser importance are functions that involve the development of the work force and the representation of the organization in the community.

Just as the job functions of top executives reduce in number but increase in importance, so too do the attributes common to all executives in the experience and background area of the test protocol reduce to three with scores that approach the level of one standard deviation above the mean (Table 5.4). These attributes are Drive/Career Progress and Financial and General Family Responsibility. High scores in these areas indicate self-actualization and the successful assumption of responsibility in the work, social, and personal family environments.

The need for an excellent level of mental functioning for all executives at Level I is indicated in Table 5.4 by high scores listed for three of the four mental ability tests in all four hierarchies. The highest scores are for language facility, covering both succinctness and ease of extemporaneous speech and breadth of vocabulary, which facilitates precision and subtlety in written and spoken language. In the Line and Sales hierarchies these intellectual assets are reinforced by potential for creative and innovative behavior. Sales executives also have a high level of sales aptitude.

In the behavioral area, all executives show a fast reaction time and an ability to maintain, or even increase, productivity under pressure. This rapid goal-oriented behavior is accompanied by high levels of self-reliance and decisiveness. In addition, sales executives are more emotionally responsive than the other executive groups.

The characteristics of successful managers identified by Ghiselli are in accordance with many that we have identified here. Ghiselli finds the most important characteristic to be leadership in the sense of the capacity to direct and guide the actions of others. Thereafter, he maintains that "The traits of intelligence, self-assurance, decisiveness, and the need for occupational achievement and self-actualization form a cluster of qualities which are somewhat less important for managerial talent than supervisory ability" (Ghiselli, 1971, p. 103). Ghiselli finds the ability to readily initiate necessary action and to see different solutions to problems, which might correspond to our potential for creative and innovative behavior, of even less importance for successful management. This result may be due to the fact that the managers in Ghiselli's sample are not classified by functional department. Our own results indicate that creativity is differentially important by hierarchy, being a strong requirement in the Line and especially in the Sales hierarchies, but of little importance in the Professional and Technical hierarchies. For the total group of executives, therefore, this could produce an average score for creativity.

Some measures in the managerial and professional test battery that were not included in Ghiselli's evaluation instrument show that there is increasing emphasis on personal insight with upward movement in the hierarchies, and high scores for this characteristic are registered in Table 5.4 for the Line and Sales executives. As for all occupational groups, a sound level of emotional health is desirable in top-executive positions.

Fortune 500 and Inc. 500 CEOs

We found in Chapter 3, in a study conducted by Moretti, Morken, and Borkowski (1989), that although groups of 35 each of Fortune 500 and Inc. 500 executives had some core job skills in common, the different organizational climates in which these two groups of senior executives functioned also produced some significant differences in some of the acquired job-function skill levels. Fortune 500 executives, from large established or structured organizations, had acquired job skills necessary for developing a stable work force and for representing the organization in the community. By contrast, Inc. 500 CEOs, in entrepreneurial organizations, were skilled in developing technical ideas, dealing with emergencies, and handling outside contacts.

The average scores for these two groups of executives, together with the Line executive norm, are given for the attributes measured on one version of the managerial and professional test battery in Table 5.7. The Prob. column in the table shows that, although the two groups of executives have a number of attributes in common, there are significant differences on eight of the attributes. Although both groups, expectedly, show a high level of drive to progress in their careers, the Fortune 500 group scores significantly higher on this dimension than their Inc. 500 counterparts. The Fortune 500 CEOs also scored significantly higher on group leadership skills and the successful handling of their personal finances. It should be mentioned, however, that the significantly higher scores of the Fortune 500 CEOs in the experience and background area are due partially to the fact that they are a somewhat older group.

Both groups have strong mental ability scores, although the highest score achieved by the Fortune 500 CEOs, which are also significantly

Table 5.7
A Comparison of the Skills and Attributes of Fortune 500 and Inc. 500 Chief Executive Officers

Attribute	Line Exec. Norm	Fortune 500	Inc. 500	Prob.
Drive/Career Progress	59	61	57	.013
Leadership	50	59	51	.0001
Financial Responsibility	56	56	54	.001
General Family Responsibility	60	62	60	
Non-Verbal Reasoning	54	52	56	
Word Fluency	59	54	55	
Vocabulary	56	64	60	.023
Creative Potential	53	57	63	.046
Extroversion	52	52	52	
Emotional Responsiveness	53	50	53	
Self-Reliance	55	51	49	
Personal Insight	53	51	51	
Reaction Time - Stress	57	49	56	.004
Internal Adjustment	47	45	41	.047
External Adjustment	46	45	44	
Level of Stress	50	49	44	.038

higher than that of their Inc. 500 counterparts, was for their breadth of English vocabulary. The highest score achieved by the Inc. 500 group, where they in turn significantly outscored the Fortune 500 executives, is for potential for creative and innovative behavior. This abundant creativity, combined with the high level of drive and above average scores for extroversive and emotionally responsive behavior, are some that were previously hypothesized to be indicators of entrepreneurship.

Both groups achieved the standards set in the screening procedure for emotional health. However, the Inc. 500 CEOs, working in the fast-growing entrepreneurial companies, experienced significantly higher levels of stress. This stress was largely due to internally generated tension arising from doubts about their adequacy to perform well and from generalized fear and anxiety, as indicated by the fact that they scored significantly lower than the 500 CEOs on the Internal Adjustment factor. These highly creative individuals are, however, realistic in their perception of the external world, accept responsibility for their failures, and are generally free from tendencies to projection or flights of unreality, as indicated by their score on the External Adjustment factor, which is within one point of that for Fortune 500 CEOs and two points of the Line executive norm. This is in accordance with Srinivasan's (1984) finding of a positive correlation between creativity and freedom from psychotic tendencies.

We have, throughout, stressed the desirability of a sound emotional health status for incumbents in all occupational groups, but it would be particularly important when hiring for positions in which individuals are likely to be subjected to stress, such as positions that involve competitive selling or positions of responsibility in fast-developing entrepreneurial organizations.

In this chapter we have identified and defined the skills and attributes measured by the test battery that differentiated across the levels in the four management hierarchies and also identified the common and unique attributes of incumbents by level and hierarchy. The information gained was used to develop behavior profiles thought to portray successful performers in the key occupational groups. In Chapter 6, which deals with the validity of the STEP program, the relationship between the identified characteristics and actual performance on the job is investigated.

6

The Reliability and Validity of the STEP Measurement Systems

Discussion of the reliability of a measurement system often precedes the presentation of validity evidence, since the reliability of a measure represents the upper bound of its validity. Theoretically, the validity coefficient should not exceed the reliability estimate since the latter represents all but the error variance associated with the measure.

In the STEP program the concern is not so much with the reliabilities of the individual dimension scores, which are given for the sixteen job function dimensions in Chapter 2 and for the predictive measures of the test battery scores in Chapter 4, but rather, the concern is with the derived composite Job Skill Assessments (JSAs) and estimates of Potential for Successful Performance (PSP) presented in the final STEP report for the individual. These composite scores will be defined in Chapter 7, which describes the applications of the STEP program. Suffice it to say here that the JSA reported for any of the twelve key positions in the four, three-rung managerial hierarchies is the average of the individual's MP-JFI—Ability scores for those functions that have been identified as important for overall successful performance in the position. Similarly, the PSP for any level of functioning in any managerial hierarchy is the weighted average of the individual's scores on the tests that have been identified as valid predictors of performance in the position.

RELIABILITY OF THE COMPOSITE SCORES

The formula used in the calculations was one developed by Mosier (1943) for determining the reliability of a weighted composite. The formula is derived from the standard deviations, reliabilities, and intercorrelations among the scores contributing to the composite. Application of the formula produced the information given in Table 6.1 for the JSAs and in Table 6.2 for the PSPs.

Tables 6.1 and 6.2 provide some important information about both sets of composite scores. First, the reliabilities are at acceptably high levels. Second, the magnitudes of the standard errors of measurement provide assurance that the rules of thumb applied in Chapter 7 represent sufficiently stringent standards for determining significance between dimension scores in profile comparisons.

THE VALIDITY OF THE STEP MEASURES

The demonstration of the relationship between the qualification (or test) measures and performance on the job, generally referred to as validation of selection or promotion procedures, was a continuing research thrust of the Human Resources Center of The University of Chicago for almost two decades. Since the enactment of the Civil Rights Act of 1964, with its Title VII aimed at establishing nondiscriminatory employment practices, validation procedures have been subject to the requirements of a series of governmental guidelines. In the 1970 Equal Employment Opportunity Commission (EEOC) "Guidelines on Employee Selection Procedures," the emphasis was on entry-level positions, where there are a large number of applicants. The trend was toward separate validations for each organization and, under certain prescribed conditions, within each group by race, sex, or conditions of employment. The 62 validity coefficients (described later) were for specific occupational groups, sometimes subdivided by race and sex, and derived from the performance criterion validation procedure required by the 1970 "Guidelines."

It soon became apparent that this approach was not practical when dealing with racially and sexually mixed employee populations operating in differently structured work contexts. The suggestion of multiunit validation studies in the 1970 EEOC "Guidelines" received increasing emphasis in the 1974 Amendment to the U.S. Office of Federal Contract Compliance (OFCC) Order on Employee Testing Procedures and the 1978 "Uniform Guidelines on Employee Selection Procedures." Under certain conditions it was now possible to combine similar jobs in geographically separated work environments in one validation, or even more generally, to apply the results of a validation for a particular job in one organization to a similar job in another organization which had not participated in that validation. A necessary condition was that a job analysis demonstrate that the functions to be performed and the requirements of the relevant jobs be essentially similar.

The 1978 "Guidelines" provided further flexibility in validation requirements by their acceptance of three types of validation procedures and

Table 6.1
Reliability Estimates (rxx), Standard Deviations (Sx), and Standard Errors of Measurement (Se) of the Job Skill Assessments (JSAs) Derived from the MP-JFI—Ability

Level		Line	Prof.	Sales	Tech.
I	rxx	.80	.79	.81	.77
	Sx	4.20	4.18	4.28	3.99
	Se	1.88	1.92	1.87	2.29
II	rxx	.84	.81	.83	.83
	Sx	4.09	4.16	4.42	4.12
	Se	1.62	1.81	1.82	1.70
III	rxx	.83	.76	.79	.70
	Sx	4.85	4.54	4.66	4.09
	Se	2.00	2.22	2.14	2.24

their encouragement of responsible research. However, the "Guidelines" still did not provide a feasible approach to validations of higher-level positions where the functions performed are not immediately observable; sample sizes are typically small; and, at top levels, clearly similar positions may be held by no more than two or three people. Yet it is placement in these higher-level positions that is often critical for the organization's future. Because of these considerations, and the view expressed by many professionals (Guion, 1976; Dunnette, 1976) of the necessity of general principles and theories in establishing a science, a long series of research studies was undertaken to develop a more generalized validation approach for higher-level positions.

Table 6.2
Reliability Estimates (rxx), Standard Deviations (Sx), and Standard Errors of Measurement (Se) of the Estimates of Potential for Successful Performance (PSPs) Derived from Managerial and Professional Test Battery Scores

Level		Line	Prof.	Sales	Tech.
I	rxx	.91	.90	.88	.89
	Sx	3.23	3.57	4.24	3.47
	Se	.97	1.13	1.47	1.15
II	rxx	.90	.91	.88	.88
	Sx	3.51	3.77	4.39	3.72
	Se	1.11	1.13	1.52	1.29
III	rxx	.88	.90	.87	.90
	Sx	3.41	3.29	4.22	3.35
	Se	1.18	1.04	1.52	1.06

One objective of the studies was to investigate the assumptions underlying what is known in the literature as "component validity." The major assumption is that specific functions that have been clearly identified through job analysis require the same human abilities, skills, and attributes for their successful performance, regardless of organizational or institutional setting. Another approach taken was to investigate the ability of the job-function and test-battery scores, singly and in combination, to predict the earnings of incumbents within each hierarchy and at each level of functioning. The newest thrust in the validation research was to validate the derived composite JSA and PSP scores in specific occupational settings. The performance criterion validations are discussed below.

PERFORMANCE CRITERION VALIDATIONS

The results for 62 validation studies for specific occupational groups, conducted between February 1963 and April 1979 by the Human Resources Center of The University of Chicago, are given in Baehr (1984b). All of the studies were concurrent performance criterion validations. In other words, test scores and performance indices were collected independently for employees in the particular occupational groups and various statistical procedures were employed to determine the correlation between these two sets of measures.

The Criterion Measures

The criterion measures used were either supervisory assessments of performance, implemented by the researchers and obtained through use of the paired comparison technique, or objective indices of performance obtained from company records.

The Paired Comparison Technique (P.C. Index)

Although no subjective technique can completely eliminate the effects of personal bias or the constant errors of measurement, experience with the paired comparison (PC) technique indicated that use of the technique minimized these errors and yielded best results for a wide variety of occupations.

The technique requires the supervisor to compare each employee in the group he or she is qualified to rate with every other employee, and to make the judgment as to which member of each pair is doing the better job overall. The result is a scaled ranking of all individuals in that group. On the basis of this ranking, a "performance index" is assigned to each employee. Two or more raters' results for each employee are aver-

Figure 6.1
Illustration of Possible Consistent and Inconsistent Responses in the Use of the Paired Comparison Technique

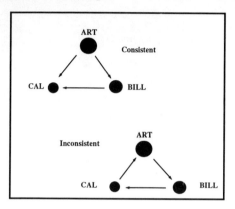

aged to provide the final index of that employee's performance. This final index is known as the Paired Comparison Index (P.C. Index).

As an internal check, a measure of the consistency of the ratings made by each individual rater can be calculated. The concept of consistency is illustrated in Figure 6.1. For example, if a rater indicates that Art is doing a better job than Bill and that Bill is doing a better job than Cal, then, to be consistent, the rater should say that Art does better than Cal. If Cal is chosen over Art, there is an inconsistency (Kendall, 1955). Too high a level of inconsistency suggests that the rater is either not using clear-cut criteria in making judgments or is not really very familiar with the employees being rated.

When several raters have rated the same individuals, it is also possible to obtain a measure of the similarity of their judgments, or the extent to which they are in agreement in their ratings. Any rater who deviates markedly from the others may have provided unreliable ratings. There are thus three measures to be derived from the PC technique:

—the PC rating or index,

—the measure of rater consistency, and

—the measure of inter-rater similarity or agreement.

Table 6.3 shows the number and cumulative percentage of consistent judgments, made by individual raters, and of similar judgments, made by two or more raters, using the paired comparison technique for performance appraisal in 20 performance criterion validation studies. The table

Table 6.3
**Cumulative Percentage of Consistent and of Similar Judgments Made by
Raters in 20 Validation Studies**

Percentage Scale	Consistent Judgments		Similar Judgments	
	Total	Cum. %	Total	Cum. %
100	43	26.4		
95 – 99.9	85	78.5		
90 – 94.9	20	90.8	1	1.2
85 – 89.9	7	95.1	11	13.9
80 – 84.9	4	97.5	13	29.1
75 – 79.9	0	97.5	14	45.3
70 – 74.9	2	98.7	29	79.1
65 – 69.9	0	98.7	9	89.5
60 – 64.9	2	100.0	7	97.7
55 – 59.9			2	100.0
Total	163		86	

shows that 90.8% of the raters made 90% or more consistent judgments
and that 26.4% of the raters actually made 100% consistent judgments.
Only one rater, with 39.6% consistent judgments, was dropped from the
studies. It is clearly easier for any individual rater to be internally consistent than to be making judgments for each pair of employees that are
similar to those made by some other rater for those employees. Nevertheless, the results for similarity of judgment are surprisingly good with
79.1% of the raters having more than 70% of their judgments in common
and 29.1% having more than 80% of their judgments in common. Only one
rater, with 48.7 percent similar judgments, was dropped from the studies.
Overall, these results demonstrate a degree of stability not often encountered in subjective assessments of performance.

Objective Indices of Performance

Objective performance indices were used in addition to the supervisory assessments where possible. Unfortunately, they were generally
available for only one occupational group, that of sales representatives
(Level III in the Sales hierarchy). It was sometimes possible to obtain
multiple indicies of performance. For example, in a performance criterion validation study for a sample of 101 sales representatives (Baehr,
1979b), the following objective measures were recorded: (1) total sales
in dollars, (2) number of new accounts, (3) percentage value of new ac-

counts, (4) number of accounts lost, (5) percentage value of lost accounts, (6) number of service calls, (7) number of sales calls, and (8) percentage increase in sales. Since these measures were clearly interrelated and overlapping, they were factor analyzed and the resulting three clearly interpretable and linearly independent factors were used as criteria in the study. The factors were defined, respectively, as New Sales Effectiveness, Sales Efficiency, and Overall Sales Performance.

Two additional criterion measures were obtained for this group of sales representatives based on the Managerial and Professional Job Functions Inventory (MP-JFI) that was described in Chapter 2. The MP-JFI was used to obtain, independently, the importance of the functions performed in the position and the sales representatives' self-assessed ability to perform them. The summed ability scores for a sales representative, with and without weighting by the importance value for the function, were used as separate criterion measures. It is of interest to note that the multiple correlations obtained for these two measures (.60 and .62, respectively) were as high or higher than those obtained with either subjective or objective criteria. It also appeared that weighting the summed ability scores did not increase the obtained validity coefficient.

The Validity Coefficients

In the early years of the study, small sample sizes precluded the use of multiple regression analysis. Instead, the researchers assigned each subject in the study a single index based on their interpretation of the test battery results, which represented the Potential for Successful Performance in the position. Product moment correlations were then calculated between the PSPs and the paired comparison performance indices. In early 1963, these correlations were a modest .3, but with greater experience with the test battery the correlations increased to .5 and above by the end of the year.

The 62 occupational groups in the validation studies were classified with respect to the 12 key positions in the 4 managerial heirarchies. As a result, 9 validations based on 2 groups of chemical lab technicians, 4 groups of skilled hourly workers, and 3 groups of grocery clerks were excluded from further consideration. The result of the classification is shown in Table 6.4. Of the 53 groups in Table 6.4, a further 9 were dropped because of small sample sizes. The remaining 44 studies had sample sizes ranging from 26 to 240 with a mean of 111. The obtained validity coefficients were normally distributed and ranged from .31 to .90 with a mean of .62. The majority of the validity coefficients are multiple correlations, and it should be noted that in some instances they are overestimates since they were not corrected for shrinkage. Nevertheless, the compelling evidence is that, regardless of the type of criterion measure used or the

Table 6.4
Classification of Occupational Groups That Participated in the Validation Studies

Level	Line	Prof.		Sales	Tech.	Total
I			3*			3
II	2	–		3	1	6
III	6	6		25	7	44
Total	8	6	3	28	8	53

*Executives from all hierarchies were combined in the validations

type of validity coefficient calculated, strong positive correlations between the test battery and independent measures of performance were obtained.

Although the magnitudes of the validity coefficients were satisfactory, a troubling circumstance, evident in Table 6.4, was that the bulk of these performance criterion validations (44 out of 53, including studies with small sample sizes) occurred at Level III of the four hierarchies. Typically, it is at this level that large numbers of employees perform essentially the same functions (as in a sales force) thus making it feasible to perform validations in accordance with the governmental "Guidelines." Occasionally, validations were also possible at the Level II of the hierarchies (6 out of 53). The three validations conducted at Level I were possible only by combining the executives from all hierarchies at that level in the organization. The unfeasibility of traditional validation procedures for higher-level positions led to a search for more generalized approaches to validation.

JOB COMPONENT VALIDATION STUDIES

In contrast to performance criterion validation studies where the object is to predict overall performance on the job, in job component studies the object is to predict performance on the individual important components of the job. In other words, an attempt is made to establish significant relationships between the predictors and successful performance of identified job functions. Earlier in this chapter it was shown through analyses of variance that the pattern of significant differences for the job functions and for the predictors measured by the test battery were very similar across levels of functioning and across hierarchies. In other words, when there were a number of significant changes in the functions performed on the job, there were corresponding changes in the

Table 6.5
Stepwise Multiple Correlations Obtained in the Prediction of MP-JFI
Importance and Ability Measures by Scores from the Test Battery

Job Functions		Importance	Ability
		(N = 157)	(N = 234)
1.	Objective Setting	.58 ***	.55 ***
2.	Financial Planning	.46 ***	.51 ***
3.	Work Procedures & Practices	.34 **	.38 ***
4.	Interdepartmental Coordination	.21 *	.48 ***
5.	Dev. Technical Ideas	.56 ***	.58 ***
6.	Decision Making	.61 ***	.60 ***
7.	Developing Teamwork	.38 ***	.46 ***
8.	Coping with Emergencies	.18	.39 ***
9.	Promoting Safety	.44 ***	.46 ***
10.	Communications	.43 ***	.63 ***
11.	Dev. Employee Potential	.49 ***	.35 ***
12.	Supervisory Practices	.33 **	.42 ***
13.	Self-Development	.47 ***	.62 ***
14.	Personnel Practices	.35 **	.37 ***
15.	Comm./Org. Relations	.45 ***	.52 ***
16.	Handling Outside Contacts	.42 ***	.55 ***

* $p < .05$, ** $p < .01$, *** $p < .001$

abilities, skills, and attributes of the employees who performed them. This was seen as providing presumptive evidence of component validity. An attempt is made here to actually determine the extent to which the individual job functions could be predicted by the measures in the test battery.

The scores from the managerial and professional test battery were used in a stepwise regression, separately, against each of the MP-JFI Importance and Ability measures. The results given in Table 6.5 show that all but 1 of 16 Job function Importance measures have statistically significant correlations, with 11 of the 16 being significant at or beyond the .001 level of confidence. The results are even better for the Ability measures where all correlations are significant at or beyond the .001 level of confidence.

Stepwise regressions were also run for the 23 STEP predictor scores in the test battery against the MP-JFI Importance and Ability measures. These correlations were generally smaller than those given in Table 6.5.

The PSP predictor correlations ranged from .15 to .47 with a mean of .32 for the Importance measures and from .18 to .54 with a mean of .36 for the Ability measures. However, with the exception of the .15 correlation, all are still statistically significant and the majority are significant at or beyond the .001 level of confidence. Apart from the fact of a small number (23) of available predictors in this series of regressions, a possible explanation for the reduction in the magnitudes of the correlations is that the PSP predictors were selected largely on the basis of the results of the traditional validations that use the criterion of overall job performance, and that the individual job functions are differentially important for overall performance in the different occupational groups. The higher correlations obtained from the use of all test battery scores are probably a better estimate of the true relationships among the test and job function measures.

It is noteworthy that in both series of regressions the self-assessed Ability measures were better predicted. These results support the use of carefully obtained self-assessments such as those obtained by the MP-JFI, which uses a forced distribution response technique. The average of the 16 product moment correlations between corresponding importance and Ability measures was .52 for the Line hierarchy, .52 for the Professional hierarchy, .61 for the Sales hierarchy, and .55 for the Technical hierarchy.

In reviewing the results of the regressions against the job functions, it was noted that many of the selected predictors made intuitive sense, for example, high Ability scores in Financial Planning were obtained by individuals who had high scores on financial and general family responsibility, analytical reasoning, vocational satisfaction, and who were controlled rather than impulsive. A few more examples are high Ability scores in Coping with Difficulties and Emergencies was shown by individuals who had a fast reaction time, were creative, worked well under pressure, and were socially independent. Finally, high Ability in Handling Outside Contacts was shown by individuals who were socially at ease, had professional/successful parents, were dominant in social situations, and had a positive social orientation.

A further investigation of possible predictors for performance of the job functions was made by running multiple regressions of scores from each area of the test battery, separately, against the MP-JFI Importance and the MP-JFI Ability measures. All of the test areas proved to be useful predictors of performance and the ultimate objective is to construct a matrix that will link job functions and personal skills and attributes. With such a matrix it would be possible to develop a test battery for any position for which an MP-JFI Importance profile was available that could be implemented without additional validation. This procedure must, however, await further research.

THE PREDICTION OF EARNINGS

In contrast to the performance criterion validation studies, which were done independently for the twelve key occupational groups, using different employee populations and criterion measures, the object here was systematic validity studies by level and hierarchy based on the total data base and using the same performance criterion. After some consideration, it was decided that for these subjects, who were employed in different occupational specialities in different parts of the United States, a measure of the current earnings of the individuals would be the most feasible indication of their worth to their respective organizations.

Hilton and Dill (1962), in an attempt to improve on absolute salary as a criterion and to adjust for some of the effects of age, tenure, occupational speciality, and geographic location, used salary growth expressed as the average annual percentage increase in salary. However, rather unexpectedly, the results of their study indicated that although salary growth had some useful properties, absolute salary was better predicted. They concluded (Hilton & Dill, 1962, p. 158) that, in their experience, "the use of peer ratings, supervisory ratings, measures of administrative responsibility, and indices of organizational attainment all have deficiencies which are sufficiently serious to justify the use of salary as an alternative measure despite its imperfections."

The measure used in the present study was current earnings, which consisted of current salary plus earned incentive pay or bonus. Corporate bonus was not included since it is usually only available to top-level executives and is not so much an indication of personal merit as of organization profitability. (The bonus of some executives in our study was in millions of dollars.) The measure of earnings was corrected for successive cost-of-living increases over the twelve-year period (1975 to 1987) of data collection. The salary information was obtained from a confidential personal data sheet completed by the subjects at the time the test battery was administered.

The STEP program produces three sets of measures that can reasonably be expected to predict current earnings. The importance of the functions performed by the individual, as measured by the MP-JFI importance scores, should reflect earnings based on the same philosophy that underlies job evaluation procedures, that is, that some functions are of greater worth to organizations and thus more highly remunerated than others. For example, setting objectives for the organization may be regarded as being more important for the success of the organization than promoting safety attitudes. It follows from this assumption that if the particular functions performed are an indication of earnings, then the ability to perform the important functions in a position, measured by the MP-JFI Ability scores, should be at least as good if not a better indicator of earning capacity. Finally, since relationships have been established between the ability to perform the functions and the individual's skills and attributes, as measured by the test battery, the test battery scores should also be related to earnings.

The intention was to run stepwise multiple regressions of each of the three sets of scores obtained from the STEP program (job function importance and ability scores and test battery scores) against the earnings criterion. It was considered, however, that use of the total number of measures in the test battery in the regressions would result in a disproportionately large number of predictors for the number of subjects, especially when the total sample was sectioned by hierarchy and level of functioning. Preliminary regressions were, therefore, undertaken for measures from each area of the test battery against earnings. The results indicated all areas were able to predict earnings, quite often with substantial multiple correlations. However, it was thought that the correlations obtained in the regressions of experience and background measures against salary (ranging from .51 to .85) could be spuriously high and due, in part, to related measures that contribute to both the test score and the earnings criterion. After consideration, only 12 measures were selected from the test battery for use in the regressions. The predictors were the four specific tests of mental ability; the overall scores for creative potential obtained from the Cree Questionnaire; the composite scores for Extroversion, Emotional Responsiveness, Self-reliance, Excitability, Social Orientation, and Personal Insight obtained from the Temperament Comparator; and the Level of Stress Response obtained from the Emo Questionnaire. The references for the tests and the definitions of the dimensions are given in Chapter 4. Use of only 12 out of a possible 74 measures constitutes a rather stringent test of the predictive ability of the test battery.

Regression of the STEP System Measures Against Earnings

Stepwise regressions were run separately for the Importance, Ability, and the 12 test battery scores against earnings. For each set of predictors, the total sample was divided into approximately equal halves to provide a hold-out sample for the calculation of cross-validity coefficients. The regressions were run for the overall group of employees, for each of the four managerial hierarchies, and for each level of organization functioning. These results are shown in Table 6.6. Severe restriction in sample sizes precluded the running of regressions for the 12 occupational groups.

Table 6.6 shows for the total group substantial and significant primary with well-maintained cross-validity coefficients for all three sets of pre-

Table 6.6
Stepwise Multiple Regressions and Cross-Validity Coefficients of MP-JFI Importance and Ability Scores and Test Battery Scores Against Earnings

| | | Overall | Level | | | Hierarchy | | | |
			I	II	III	Line	Prof.	Sales	Tech
MP–JFI – Importance									
Primary	R	.31***	.23*	ns	.62***	.39***	.20*	.64***	.34***
	N	420	162	218	36	127	158	25	100
Cross	R	.29***	-.02	–	.35*	.46***	.03	-.09	.35
	N	411	143	225	33	117	156	27	102
MP–JFI – Ability									
Primary	R	.42***	ns	.20**	.40***	.63***	.35***	.25*	.32**
	N	577	158	252	162	184	179	90	113
Cross	R	.48***	–	.05	.17*	.54***	.26***	.34***	.21*
	N	580		225	163	204	158	75	114
Twelve Test Scores									
Primary	R	.42***	.34	.28	.30	.51***	.42*	.67**	.56*
	N	400	132	158	112	156	115	58	71
Cross	R	.42***	.27**	.15*	.11	.50***	.20*	.20	.00
	N	400	113	173	114	178	105	56	69

ns = nonsignificant, near zero primary correlations.

* $p < .05$, ** $p < .01$, *** $p < .001$

dictors. However, the Ability measures and test scores appear to be somewhat better predictors than the importance measures. Essentially the same results are obtained for each of the four hierarchies, with the test scores being generally the best predictors, followed by the Ability and then the Importance measures. The results of the regressions by level are less consistent except possibly for the Importance and Ability measures at Level III. It was shown in Chapter 3 that the functions performed by executives at Level I were very similar in all hierarchies and that there was also considerable overlap in the functions performed by middle managers at Level II. The somewhat inconsistent regression results obtained by level may be due to the lack of variability in the functions performed by executives and middle managers compared with those performed by Level III employees, who represent four different occupational groups.

In general, the results of this series of regressions indicate that all three of the measures obtained from the STEP measurement systems can predict earnings. The best predictions are consistently made by the test battery scores and job skill measures, which are the basis for the individual's report of STEP program results described in Chapter 7.

Comparison of Cognitive and Personality Measures as Predictors of Performance

The question was raised in Chapter 4 concerning the relative ability of the cognitive and behavioral measures to predict performance. The 400 subjects in Table 6.6, for whom test scores and earnings were available, were used in a study by Baehr and Orban (1987) to determine the significance of the incremental variance accounted for by the personality measures over and above that accounted for by the cognitive measures and vice versa.

Regressions were run against performance (as represented by earnings) separately for the cognitive measures, the personality measures, and the combination of measures for the total group, the three levels, and the four hierarchies. The results indicate that the best prediction of performance was obtained from the combination of measures. Furthermore, when applied to the total sample, the tests of incremental validity demonstrated that both types of measures significantly increased validity. The results also supported the conventional view that, because of preselection on cognitive ability in higher-level positions, the personality measures would be better predictors than the cognitive measures for these positions. Examination of the multiple correlations obtained in the three regressions by level indicated that it was only at Level I that the correlation for the personality measures ($r = .26$, $N = 245$, $p < .05$) and the incremental variance accounted for by these measures was significant ($F = 2.26$, $d.f.$, 2, 243, $p < .05$). Conversely it was only at Level III that the correlation with the cognitive measures reached the .001 level of confidence ($r = .29$, $N = 226$, $p < .001$). These results demonstrate, once again, the validity of the test battery measures and also the importance of including both cognitive and personality measures in the test battery.

PREDICTION OF PERFORMANCE BY ESTIMATES OF POTENTIAL AND JOB SKILL ASSESSMENTS

In the validation studies described thus far, the predictors have been individual scores obtained from the test battery or Individual Ability and Importance measures. The predictors in the studies described here are the composite scores: the estimate of Potential for Successful Performance and the Job Skill Assessment are derived, respectively, from the two measurement systems that underlie the STEP program. The PSPs are the weighted average of the individual's test scores that validation research has shown to predict performance for the respective occupational groups. Similarly, the JSAs are the average of the individual's assessed ability levels on the functions that previous research has identified as being important in the particular position.

Although a considerable body of evidence attesting to the reliability and validity of the STEP measures has been accumulated, there are additional requirements for legal compliance if the STEP program and the composite scores are to be used in an organization without further validation. The "Uniform Guidelines on Employee Selection Procedures" (1978) defines three requirements for the use of criterion-related validity from other sources.

Demonstration of the Transportability of a Validated Test Battery

The three requirements for what is often referred to as the demonstration of the transportability of a validated test battery are (1) the demonstration of acceptable procedures and obtained validity evidence in the original studies, (2) the demonstration that the jobs for which the selection procedures are to be used closely match those in the original study with respect to major work behaviors as shown by job analyses in both contexts, and (3) that the procedures be applied to essentially similar employee populations and that there be evidence of test fairness in the original studies. Considerable care has been taken to ensure that these conditions are satisfied by users of the STEP program. Since the validity evidence for the STEP rests, in part, on 44 criterion-related validation studies, the validity evidence has been reviewed in detail (Baehr & Moretti, 1985) with respect to the requirements of the "Technical Standards

(14B)" and "Documentation (15)" sections for criterion-related studies in the "Uniform Guidelines" and is available for users on request.

The requirement of similarity between the functions performed in the jobs on which the validations were based and prospective new user's jobs is addressed through the prerequisite of a job analysis for the implementation of the STEP program for any position. In addition to on-site visits and interviews with knowledgeable organization personnel, the major vehicle for the job analysis is the job function importance profile developed for the position through use of the MP-FJI. This procedure is described in more detail in Chapter 7. Suffice it to say here that the profile represents an operational definition of the job in question that is compared with the profiles developed on national samples of employees for each of the twelve key positions in the managerial hierarchies. The comparison is made through the use of a computerized profile comparison procedure (Orban, 1985). If a match is identified, then the test battery that has been validated for that position can be used. If there is no match, a new validation should be undertaken.

The third "Guideline" requirement for the use of previously obtained validity evidence is that the new user's employee populations be similar to those used in the original validation and that there had been a demonstration of test fairness in the original validation. London House has addressed this issue by continuing studies of adverse impact. Data bases are maintained for all users and adverse impact studies are undertaken when requested or when samples of sufficient size have been collected. To date, such studies have produced no evidence of adverse impact against any protected group by race or sex. Results of the adverse impact studies have been reported, in part, in Baehr and Moretti (1985).

Although these procedures ensure legal compliance, it is still of professional interest, and sometimes also a preference of the new user, that the validity of the estimates of potential and job skill be demonstrated for positions in the organization for which the STEP program is to be used.

Revalidation of the PSPs and JSAs

The revalidation of the PSPs and JSAs is actually a form of cross validation. However, this is a more stringent test than traditional cross validation, which is usually based on a holdout or subsample of the same group of employees used for the calculation of the primary coefficients, whereas the PSPs and JSAs are applied to different samples of employees who hold similar positions in different organizations and locations. The results of some preliminary revalidation studies are summarized below.

Three Levels of Management In a Mid-Sized Bank

In an early human resource planning and development project conducted in a mid-sized bank (Baehr, 1978), it was possible to compare the effectiveness of PSPs used in the STEP program, which were based on previously established national standards, with those of PSPs based on the regression equation obtained in a concurrent performance criterion validation study for a defined occupational group in the bank. The details of the study were as follows:

Sample Size. The job analysis identified three occupational groups in the Technical hierarchy: Level I ($N=4$), Level II ($N=11$) and Level III ($N=43$).

Predictors. PSPs were calculated for all employees based on both the relevant national normative samples and the specific validation conducted for the largest (Level III) group.

Criterion Measures. Paired comparison performance appraisals made by their immediate supervisors were conducted separately for each of the three groups.

Obtained Validity Coefficients. A correlation of .44 ($N=43$, $p<.002$) was obtained for the specific validation compared with a correlation of .35 ($N=43$, $p<.014$) using the predetermined national standards used in the STEP program.

Conclusions. The coefficient obtained from the bank's specific validation study was slightly (greater by .09) but not significantly better than the validity coefficient of the PSPs based on the national standards for Level III in the Technical hierarchy. However, the PSPs from the specific validation could be used only at Level III and have no value for predicting potential for promotion since they have a nonsignificant correlation when applied to employees at the two higher levels in the hierarchy. By contrast, the PSPs based on the relevant national standards established for each level maintain the same levels of validity across the three levels of the Technical hierarchy ($r=.35$, $N=58$, $p<.003$). A further disadvantage of the specific validation is that its effectiveness is strongly affected by the level of performance of the employee group on which it is based. If it is a poor performing group, this could result in the selection of poor quality or even inappropriate personnel.

Managers of Professionals in a Heavy Industry Organization

This study (Moretti & Allen, 1988) was conducted as a preliminary to the use of the STEP program for the selection and development of two levels of managers of professional engineers in a heavy industry organization. The details of the study were as follows:

Sample Size. A total of 83 higher-level employees in a heavy industry manufacturing company were classified as Level I ($N=27$) and Level II ($N=56$) in the Professional hierarchy.

Predictors. PSPs and JSAs were calculated for all employees based on the relevant national standards used in the STEP program.

Criterion Measures. An organization psychologist and the employees' supervisors rated the performance of all Level II middle managers on the 16 MP-JFI job functions. A composite index was obtained by averaging the ability ratings on the functions identified as important at Level II in the Professional hierarchy.

Obtained Validity Coefficients. A significant product moment correlation was obtained between PSPs and the criterion ($r=.37$, $N=56$, $p<.017$). A regression of both PSP and JSA scores against the performance criterion produced even better prediction ($r=.46$, $N=56$, $p<.026$).

Contrasted groups validity was established when statistically significant differences were obtained between Level I and Level II managers on both the PSP ($F=4.42$, d.f., 26, 55, $p<.05$) and JSA ($F=7.84$, d.f., 26, 55, $p<.01$) scores, with Level I being the higher scoring group.

Conclusion. The study demonstrates validity of both potential and skills scores used in the STEP program at Levels I and II of the Professional hierarchy.

Sales Representatives in the Petroleum Industry

The purpose of this study conducted by Elliott, Wilson, and Moretti (1990) was to determine the validity of the PSPs in the present position and also for the next higher position in the hierarchy.

Sample Size. A total of 42 territory managers from a major petroleum industry were classified as Level III (sales representatives) in the Sales hierarchy.

Predictors. PSPs were calculated for all sales representatives, based on the relevant STEP norms, for all three levels in the Sales hierarchy.

Criterion Measures. Supervisory ratings of performance in the present position and of promotability were obtained for the most recent two years and an average calculated for each type of rating to provide greater stability.

Obtained Validity Coefficients. A high correlation was found between supervisory ratings of performance and PSPs for the present position ($r=.50$, $N=42$, $p<.001$). A strong correlation was also found between supervisory assessments of promotability and PSPs for the next higher (middle manager) position ($r=.42$, $N=42$, $p<.003$).

Conclusions. The study demonstrates the validity of the PSPs derived from the STEP program both for assessed performance in the present position and for promotability to the next higher position in the hierarchy.

Theater Managers in the Entertainment Industry

A study was undertaken by Brady, Elliott, and Adams (1990) to test the validity of PSPs calculated for theater managers in the entertainment industry.

Sample Size. A total of 54 managers were classified as Level III in the Line hierarchy.

Predictors. PSPs were calculated for all managers based on the national standards for Level III in the Line hierarchy.

Criterion Measures. Supervisory assessments of performance were made for all managers using the London House University Series Performance Evaluation Form and the group divided into the top 35% and bottom 35% of performers based on the composite performance rating.

Obtained Validity Coefficients. The means and standard deviations of the PSPs were calculated for the high- and low-performing subgroups of managers. A t-test showed that there was a significant difference between the mean PSP scores of the subgroups ($t = 1.78$, $p < .05$).

Conclusions. The results indicate that there is a positive relationship between STEP potential estimates and performance at Level III in the Line hierarchy.

Although the studies that have just been described are based on rather small samples of employees, in aggregate the results indicate significant relationships between the STEP program estimates of potential for successful performance based on national standards and independently obtained performance indicies for employees in all four hierarchies. These studies represent the logical culmination of over two decades of validation research in the course of the development of the STEP program. Participating organizations are encouraged to revalidate the STEP composite scores in the particular organization setting in which they will be used, and it is expected this type of validation study will soon be available for all the occupational groups in the four managerial hierarchies covered by the STEP program.

Selection and promotion, and associated validation research, are two major but by no means the only applications of the STEP program. Chapter 7 describes a wide array of applications for strategic human resource management.

NOTE

Portions of this chapter are abstracted from M. E. Baehr, *The Development and Validation of the Estimates of Potential for Successful Performance (PSP) of Higher-Level Personnel* (Chicago: The University of Chicago, Office of Continuing Education, 1984).

7

Implementation of the STEP Program for Strategic Human Resource Management

Melany E. Baehr and Donald M. Moretti

The STEP program was designed to facilitate a wide array of human resource management procedures applicable for higher-level professional, sales, technical, and management personnel described in Figure 1.1 in Chapter 1. These procedures include those relating to the job, such as job clarification and design; personnel procedures such as selection, promotion, performance appraisal, and career counseling; and organization-wide procedures such as succession planning and reassignment. The implementation of these procedures will be described later.

The information used to implement these procedures is obtained from the two professionally constructed measurement systems that underlie the STEP program. The job-analysis procedure is the anchor for the STEP program and a prerequisite for the implementation of any human resource application of STEP. The job analysis is implemented through the use of the Managerial and Professional Job Functions Inventory (MP-JFI)—Importance, which is described in detail in Chapter 2. The instrument is used to identify the relative importance of the functions to be performed in the position for overall successful job performance. The MP-JFI, with a different response mode, is used to determine the respondent's perceived level of ability in each of the identified job functions. This procedure is described in Chapter 3. The development of a managerial and professional test battery to measure the qualifications (abilities, skills, and attributes) of the individual is described in Chapter 4, and its validity is investigated in Chapter 6. The test battery is available in three different formats to efficiently implement some of the different human resource management applications described in the following section.

HUMAN RESOURCE APPLICATIONS

A listing of a number of human resource management procedures that can be implemented through the use of objective information obtained from the STEP program measurement systems is given below. Thereafter, the steps for their implementation and the data that they provide are described briefly for the most often used procedures.

Procedures Relating to Specific Positions
>   1. Job Description
>   2. Job Clarification

Personnel Procedures
>   3. Training Needs Assessment
>   4. Selection
>   5. Promotion
>   6. Career Counseling and Planning
>   7. Outplacement Counseling

Organization Procedures
>   8. Performance Appraisal Systems
>   9. Succession Planning/Management Continuity
>   10. Strategic Reorganization/Reassignment

JOB DESCRIPTION

Definition

There will probably always be a need for traditional job descriptions that provide information on fiscal responsibility, major areas of accountability, and reporting relationships. The objective in this procedure, however, is to identify the relative importance of the functions to be performed for overall successful performance and to break them down into their component parts for purposes of job orientation and on-the-job training.

STEP Modules Required

1. Job analysis package that consists of an administration manual and 10 Managerial and Professional Job Functions Inventory (MP-JFI)—Importance booklets.

Procedure

1. Analysis of the job through the administration of the MP-JFI—Importance to a minimum of 5–10 well-functioning incumbents and/or their supervisors or other personnel familiar with the position.

Information Obtained

Using a first-line supervisory position as an example, the information obtained would be as follows:

1. Composite MP-JFI job function importance profile produced from the ratings made by incumbent first-line supervisory personnel.

2. Composite MP-JFI item importance profiles for each function produced from the ratings made by incumbent first-line supervisory personnel.

3. Composite MP-JFI job function importance profile for the first-line supervisory position produced from the ratings made by middle managers rating the first-line supervisory position.

4. Item importance profiles for each function produced from ratings made by middle managers. If a computerized profile comparison program shows no significant differences between profiles (1 and 3) then,

5. Combined (first-line supervisors and middle managers) composite MP-JFI job function importance profile for the first-line supervisory position. This profile is illustrated in Figure 7.1.

6. Combined composite item importance profiles for each of the job functions as illustrated for the Supervisory Practices job function in Figure 7.2.

7. Results of the computerized comparison of the combined composite MP-JFI job function importance profile with the normative profiles of national samples of employees in each of the twelve key positions, including the first-line supervisory position and the two management positions in the Line hierarchy.

Implementation

The job description for a position is obtained from an analysis of the information provided by the procedures described above and an interpretation of the identified importance functions for the job and the items that contribute to them. The following information was obtained for the supervisory position shown in Figure 7.1.

1. The computerized comparison of the composite job function profiles of the incumbent supervisors and their managers indicated that there were no significant differences between them. In other words, the supervisors and their managers assigned the same priorities to the functions to be performed. A mutual understanding and agreement between job incumbents and their managers provides a sound foundation for future performance appraisal and on-the-job training. If the empirical tests had shown that the profiles for the two groups differed significantly, then job clarification procedures, as described in the following section, would have been required.

2. The comparison of the agreed-upon composite job-function Impor-

Figure 7.1
Agreed-Upon Composite Job Function Importance Profile for the First-Line Supervisory Position Together with the National Standards for First-Line Supervisors (L), Middle Managers (M), and Executives (E) in the Line Hierarchy

	SS Scale	Profile Grid (57.5 40.0 42.5 45.0 47.5 50 52.5 55.0 57.5 60.0 62.5)	Rank
ORGANIZATION			
1. SETTING ORGANIZATIONAL OBJECTIVES Formulating the overall mission and goals of the organization and setting short and long-range objectives which are significant and measurable.	42	NNNNNNN — L — M — E	16
2. FINANCIAL PLANNING AND REVIEW Making economic decisions and managing capital assets; establishing a budget and controls to assure that the budget is met.	46	NNNNNNNNNN — L — ME	13
3. IMPROVING WORK PROCEDURES AND PRACTICES Analyzing, interpreting, and evaluating operating policies; initiating and formulating improved procedures and policies.	56	NNNNNNNNNNNNNNNNNNNNNNNN — L M E	5
4. INTERDEPARTMENTAL COORDINATION Understanding and coordinating the problems and work activities of different departments within the organization.	49	NNNNNNNNNNNNNNN — L E M	8
LEADERSHIP			
5. DEVELOPING AND IMPLEMENTING TECHNICAL IDEAS Originating technical ideas and designs; translating technical ideas into feasible solutions to organizational needs.	45	NNNNNNNNNN — EM L	15
6. JUDGEMENT AND DECISION MAKING Analyzing incomplete information to make decisions; acting upon decisions concerning resource and work force allocation.	48	NNNNNNNNNNNNN — L ME	10
7. DEVELOPING GROUP COOPERATION AND TEAMWORK Encouraging and building work group relations that will lead to better exchange of ideas, more open communication and higher morale.	55	NNNNNNNNNNNNNNNNNNNNNNN — LME	6
8. COPING WITH DIFFICULTIES AND EMERGENCIES Working efficiently under pressure; effectively handling unexpected problems, day-to-day crises and emergency situations.	58	NNNNNNNNNNNNNNNNNNNNNNNNNNN — E M L	4
9. PROMOTING SAFETY ATTITUDES AND PRACTICES Taking responsibility for the identification and elimination of job safety and health hazards.	62	NNNNNNNNNNNNNNNNNNNNNNNNNNNNNNNN — E M L	2
10. COMMUNICATIONS Monitoring and improving both external communication channels and internal upward and downward lines.	46	NNNNNNNNNN — L M E	13
HUMAN RESOURCES			
11. DEVELOPING EMPLOYEE POTENTIAL Evaluating employees' present performance and potential in order to create opportunities for better use of their abilities.	65	NNNNNNNNNNNNNNNNNNNNNNNNNNNNNNNNNNNNNNN — L M E	1
12. SUPERVISORY PRACTICES Clarifying subordinates' job functions and responsibilities and motivating employees while maintaining discipline and control.	60	NNNNNNNNNNNNNNNNNNNNNNNNNNNNNN — E M L	3
13. SELF DEVELOPMENT AND IMPROVEMENT Formulating self-improvement goals; using feedback from others to help assess one's own strengths and weaknesses and coordinating personal career goals with organizational needs.	48	NNNNNNNNNNNNN — E M L	10
14. PERSONNEL PRACTICES Ensuring that the organization adheres to federal equal opportunity and affirmative action requirements and implementing special recruiting and training programs for minority applicants.	53	NNNNNNNNNNNNNNNNNNNN — EM L	7
COMMUNITY			
15. PROMOTING COMMUNITY-ORGANIZATION RELATIONS Staying informed on community, social, economic, and political problems and their relevance and impact upon the organization.	47	NNNNNNNNNNNNN — L M E	12
16. HANDLING OUTSIDE CONTACTS Promoting the organization and its products to outside contacts and clients and properly conveying the organization's relationship with them.	49	NNNNNNNNNNNNNNN — LM E	8

11% 16% 23% 31% 40% 50% 60% 69% 78% 84% 89%

Interpretation. The supervisory profile in this organization is generally similar to that of the national norm for first line supervisory positions denoted by an "L" on the grid.

Figure 7.2
Item Importance Profile for the Supervisory Practices Job Function in the Line Hierarchy

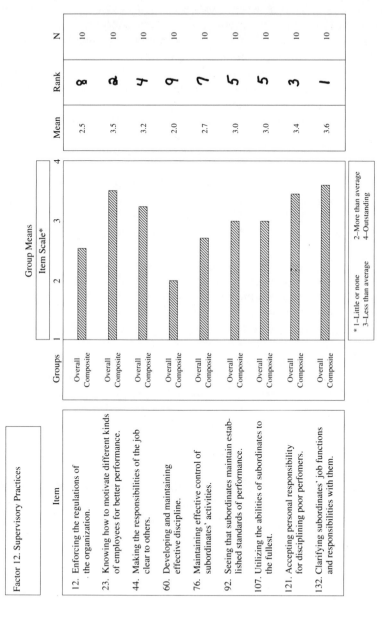

Factor 12. Supervisory Practices

Item	Groups	Group Means Item Scale*	Mean	Rank	N
12. Enforcing the regulations of the organization.	Overall Composite		2.5	8	10
23. Knowing how to motivate different kinds of employees for better performance.	Overall Composite		3.5	2	10
44. Making the responsibilities of the job clear to others.	Overall Composite		3.2	4	10
60. Developing and maintaining effective discipline.	Overall Composite		2.0	9	10
76. Maintaining effective control of subordinates' activities.	Overall Composite		2.7	7	10
92. Seeing that subordinates maintain established standards of performance.	Overall Composite		3.0	5	10
107. Utilizing the abilities of subordinates to the fullest.	Overall Composite		3.0	5	10
121. Accepting personal responsibility for disciplining poor perfomers.	Overall Composite		3.4	3	10
132. Clarifying subordinates' job functions and responsibilities with them.	Overall Composite		3.6	1	10

* 1–Little or none   2–More than average
  3–Less than average   4–Outstanding

167

tance profile with those with the twelve key positions in the STEP program indicated that the composite profile most resembled that of first-line supervisors in the Line hierarchy. This meant that the organization's first-line supervisors were functioning at the same level as first-line supervisors in other comparable industrial organizations.

3. As an aid for identifying the most important functions performed in the position, the functions are rank-ordered with respect to their importance score in the column on the right-hand side of the page in Figure 7.1. Greatest consideration should be given to the six highest-ranked factors since their importance scores are all 55 or greater. In other words, their importance scores are at least a half standard deviation above the mean. The functions that are seen as important for the first-line supervisory position can be classified into two general categories, those dealing with day-to-day operations and those dealing with the development of the work force. A listing of the important functions, and their contributing items, that fall into these two general categories are shown, respectively, in Figure 7.3 and 7.4.

4. The important job functions can be further interpreted by translating the generic items in the MP-JFI into specific activities performed in the position through focus group discussions. Two techniques that have proved useful in conducting such discussions are "brainstorming" to loosen up the group and produce a large number of specific activities, followed by the use of the critical incident technique to produce examples of good and poor performance of the activity. The systematically classified specific job activities provide the basic information for on-the-job training and the development of curricula for group-training programs. The activities can also be used, as will be shown later, in the development of job-analysis-based, customized performance appraisal procedures.

JOB CLARIFICATION

Definition

In our experience, it happens all too frequently that employees and their supervisors have very different concepts of the priorities of the employee's job, which results in significantly different job function profiles. This has obvious and serious consequences for employee productivity and morale and for performance appraisal. The purpose of the job clarification process is to provide quantitative information and a procedure for developing understanding and agreement among supervisors and employees concerning the priorities of the employee's job.

STEP Modules Required

1. MP-JFI—Importance booklets for employees in the position and their supervisors.

Figure 7.3
Important Factors Dealing with Day-to-Day Operations

FACTOR 3 -- Improving Work Procedures and Practices (9 items)

DEFINITION -- Analyzing, interpreting, and evaluating policies; initiating and formulating improved procedures and policies within the organizational structure; insuring that new procedures are installed smoothly.

ITEMS

3.	Interpreting policies and rules of the organization to others.
19.	Evaluating the effectiveness of organization structure for implementing procedural innovations.
35.	Reviewing the organization's operations in order to initiate needed improvements.
51.	Analyzing operating policies to determine their relevance to the current work situations.
67.	Consulting with others to ensure that new procedures are installed smoothly.
83.	Recommending changes in established policies whenever needed.
98.	Identifying and analyzing the cause of organization problems.
113.	Developing and maintaining a general interest in innovation and needed change.
127.	Formulating new work procedures as technology and regulatory policies change.

FACTOR 9 -- Promoting Safety Attitudes and Practices (9 items)

DEFINITION -- Taking responsibility for the identification and elimination of job safety and health hazards; promoting and communicating safety practices and regulation to employees; investigating possible job-related accidents and illnesses.

ITEMS

9.	Promoting constructive attitudes toward on-the-job safety and health.
25.	Identifying and eliminating safety and health hazards in the work place.
41.	Seeing that work schedules are compatible with safety.
57.	Taking responsibility for the safety record of the group.
73.	Recognizing the effect of the physical work environment on attitudes toward safety.
89.	Communicating health and safety rules and regulations to employees.
104.	Investigating accidents and illnesses that could be job related.
118.	Encouraging employees to use personal protective equipment.
130.	Training employees in safe work practices.

FACTOR 8 -- Coping With Difficulties and Emergencies (8 items)

DEFINITION -- Efficiently working under pressure; effectively handling unexpected problems, day-to-day crises, and emergency situations; quickly analyzing operation breakdowns and setting priorities for action.

ITEMS

8.	Coping with unexpected work and production problems.
24.	Recognizing priorities for action in emergencies.
40.	Working efficiently under pressure.
56.	Handling dangerous or emergency situations.
72.	Making on-the-spot decisions in order to meet production deadlines.
88.	Informing others about standard emergency procedures.
103.	Resolving day-to-day crises that arise in the work situation.
117.	Analyzing the causes of breakdowns in operations with a minimum of delay.

Figure 7.4
Important Factors Dealing with the Development of the Work Force

---

FACTOR 7 -- Developing Group Cooperation and Teamwork (10 items)

DEFINITION -- Encouraging and building work group relations which will lead to better exchange of ideas, improved decision-making, more open communication, higher morale, and a sense of purpose; recognizing destructive problems and conflicts within the work group.

ITEMS

7.	Leading the way in building cooperative relationships within the work group.
23.	Being alert to the level of morale in the work group.
39.	Building a sense of pride and purpose in the work group.
55.	Fostering the attitude that the group must solve many of its own problems.
71.	Encouraging the work group to make its own decisions and to communicate them to the supervisor.
87.	Encouraging others to exchange relevant ideas and experiences among themselves.
102.	Encouraging subordinates to develop positive attitudes toward the organization.
116.	Helping to build cooperative relationships within the work group.
129.	Recognizing emotional problems within the work group.
138.	Effectively solving conflicts within the work group.

FACTOR 11 -- Developing Employee Potential (9 items)

DEFINITION -- Evaluating emplyees' present performance and potential in order to create opportunities for better utilization of their abilities; examining and responding to employee dissatisfactions; assisting others in overall career development.

ITEMS

11.	Creating opportunities for subordinates to improve their performance.
27.	Rewarding good work appropriately.
43.	Reassigning individuals for better utilization of their abilities.
59.	Fairly determining an individual's potential for increased responsibility.
75.	Evaluating the work performance of others.
91.	Examining employee dissatisfactions and taking appropriate action.
106.	Making judgements about the qualifications and potential of others.
120.	Evaluating the decision-making ability of others.
131.	Assisting others in developing long-range career plans.

FACTOR 12 -- Supervisory Practices (9 items)

DEFINITION -- Clarifying subordinates' job functions and responsibilities; motivating employees while maintaining discipline and control; seeing that subordinates maintain established standards of performance and accepting personal responsibility for those who do not.

ITEMS

12.	Enforcing the regulations of the organization.
23.	Knowing how to motivate different kinds of employees for better performance.
44.	Making the responsibilities of the job clear to others.
60.	Developing and maintaining effective discipline.
76.	Maintaining effective control of subordinates' activities.
92.	Seeing that subordinates maintain established standards of performance.
107.	Utilizing the abilities of subordinates to the fullest.
121.	Accepting personal responsibility for disciplining poor performers.
132.	Clarifying subordinates' job functions and responsibilities with them.

Procedure

1. Administration of the MP-JFI—Importance to all employees in the position and to their supervisors.

Information Obtained

1. Composite job function and item importance profiles for the group of supervisors.
2. Job function and item importance profiles for the group of employees.
3. Job function and item importance profiles for each employee in the position.
4. After clarification, composite job function and item importance profiles for the combined group of incumbents and supervisors.

Implementation

A preliminary step to the clarification procedures is to determine whether or not there is a significant difference between the two profiles as a whole through the use of the computerized profile comparison program. If there is no significant difference, the incumbent and supervisor profiles can be combined in a composite profile that serves as an operational definition of the position. When the profiles are significantly different, they should not be combined until the clarification procedure has been completed.

The first step in the clarification procedure itself is to identify the functions for which the incumbent and supervisor groups have significantly different importance scores. The significance of the difference can be judged in relation to the standard error of measurement of the job-function scores that are given in Chapter 6. Since the standard errors of measurement vary slightly from one job function to another, the following guidelines (which are stringent enough to ensure significant differences) are provided for the practical implementation of the results.

Comparison

Two composite profiles	Five standard score points (one-half standard deviation)
A composite and an individual profile	Seven standard score points (about three-quarters standard deviation)
Two individual profiles	Ten standard score points (one standard deviation)

The second step is to compare, and to come to agreement on, the importance ratings of the items that contribute to the job function dimensions with significant differences. Given agreement on the item responses, it is possible to develop an "agreed upon" job function importance profile for the job. Job clarification often takes place in two different directions: *horizontal clarification* in which each individual employee compares his or her profile with the composite profile for the work group, and *vertical clarification* in which the relevant employee profile is compared with that of the supervisor or supervisory group composite. Vertical clarification can be done on a total, small-group, or on a one-on-one basis through meetings between the supervisor and the employee(s). The latter is often most effective but generally quite costly and time-consuming in large organizations. The total group procedure will work with motivated, high-morale employees but is sometimes used as a way for employees as a group to "get to" or attack an unpopular supervisor. A small-group procedure is often a good compromise.

An example of systematic differences in the perception of a Chief Executive Officer (CEO) and of his Executive Vice Presidents (EVPs) of the job priorities of the EVP position in a mid-sized bank setting is given in Figure 7.5.

Although there is agreement on the importance levels of Setting Organizational Objectives and Judgement and Decision Making, thereafter the EVP group continues to emphasize other organization-wide, high-level managerial functions such as Communications and Promoting Community-Organization Relations (indicated by a plus sign on the profile grid) whereas the CEO sees these functions as his prerogative and emphasizes, instead, the EVP functions that pertain directly to the job such as Improving Work Procedures, Developing Teamwork, and Supervisory Practices (indicated by a minus sign on the profile grid). As in other profile comparison procedures, the preferred method of resolving significant differences in job function importance scores is to examine and obtain agreement on the ratings made for the items that contribute to the job function score. Figure 7.6 shows ratings made by the CEO and the group of EVPs on the items that contribute to the Developing Group Cooperation and Teamwork factor. The item ratings are made on a four-point scale of 1 (little or no importance), 2 (below average importance), 3 (above average importance), and 4 (outstanding importance) in the MP-JFI booklet. Figure 7.6 shows the actual rating made by the CEO and, for the EVP group, the average scale rating for each item with its inter-quantile range.

Examination of the Difference column in Figure 7.6 indicates that the greatest differences (with the EVPs assigning lower importance values) occur for items 7, 116, 129, and 138. All of these items describe activities that require direct involvement with members of the work group. The salient example is item 129 (Recognizing emotional problems within the work group), which the EVPs unanimously rate as 1 or as being of little or no importance, whereas the CEO rates this item as being of above average importance. The two items (55 and 71) for which the EVPs have

Figure 7.5
Job Function Importance Profile for an Executive Vice President Position Produced from Ratings by the Chief Executive Officer (C) and a Group of Executive Vice Presidents (E)

	SS Scale	25 30 35 40 45 50 55 60 65 70 75	Rank
ORGANIZATION			
1. SETTING ORGANIZATIONAL OBJECTIVES	65	CCCCCCCCCCCCCCCCCCCCCCCCCC	2
Formulating the overall mission and goals of the organization and setting short and long-range objectives which are significant and measurable.	60	EEEEEEEEEEEEEEEEEEEEEEEEE	8
2. FINANCIAL PLANNING AND REVIEW	56	CCCCCCCCCCCCCCCCCCCCCCC	7
Making economic decisions and managing capital assets; establishing a budget and controls to assure that the budget is met.	50	EEEEEEEEEEEEEEEEEEE	8
3. IMPROVING WORK PROCEDURES AND PRACTICES	- 66	CCCCCCCCCCCCCCCCCCCCCCCCCCCCC	1
Analyzing, interpreting, and evaluating operating policies; initiating and formulating improved procedures and policies.	32	EEEEEEE	15
4. INTERDEPARTMENTAL COORDINATION	54	CCCCCCCCCCCCCCCCCCCCCC	8
Understanding and coordinating the problems and work activities of different departments within the organization.	57	EEEEEEEEEEEEEEEEEEEEEEEEE	5
LEADERSHIP			
5. DEVELOPING AND IMPLEMENTING TECHNICAL IDEAS	34	CCCCCCCC	14
Originating technical ideas and designs; translating technical ideas into feasible solutions to organizational needs.	40	EEEEEEEEEEE	12
6. JUDGEMENT AND DECISION MAKING	53	CCCCCCCCCCCCCCCCCCCCCC	9
Analyzing incomplete information to make decisions; acting upon decisions concerning resource and work force allocation.	50	EEEEEEEEEEEEEEEEEEE	9
7. DEVELOPING GROUP COOPERATION AND TEAMWORK	- 57	CCCCCCCCCCCCCCCCCCCCCCCC	6
Encouraging and building work group relations that will lead to better exchange of ideas, more open communication and higher morale.	45	EEEEEEEEEEEEEEE	11
8. COPING WITH DIFFICULTIES AND EMERGENCIES	36	CCCCCCCC	16
Working efficiently under pressure; effectively handling unexpected problems, day-to-day crises and emergency situations.	30	EEEEEE	16
9. PROMOTING SAFETY ATTITUDES AND PRACTICES	34	CCCCCCCC	14
Taking responsibility for the identification and elimination of job safety and health hazards.	39	EEEEEEEEEE	13
10. COMMUNICATIONS	46	CCCCCCCCCCCCCCC	12
Monitoring and improving both external communication channels and internal upward and downward lines.	+ 58	EEEEEEEEEEEEEEEEEEEEEEEE	4
HUMAN RESOURCES			
11. DEVELOPING EMPLOYEE POTENTIAL	61	CCCCCCCCCCCCCCCCCCCCCCCC	3
Evaluating employees' present performance and potential in order to create opportunities for better use of their abilities.	61	EEEEEEEEEEEEEEEEEEEEEEEEE	2
12. SUPERVISORY PRACTICES	- 61	CCCCCCCCCCCCCCCCCCCCCCCC	3
Clarifying subordinates' job functions and responsibilities and motivating employees while maintaining discipline and control.	48	EEEEEEEEEEEEEEEEE	10
13. SELF DEVELOPMENT AND IMPROVEMENT	48	CCCCCCCCCCCCCCCCC	11
Formulating self-improvement goals; using feedback from others to help assess one's own strengths and weaknesses and coordinating personal career goals with organizational needs.	51	EEEEEEEEEEEEEEEEEEEE	7
14. PERSONNEL PRACTICES	42	CCCCCCCCCCCC	13
Ensuring that the organization adheres to federal equal opportunity and affirmative action requirements and implementing special recruiting and training programs for minority applicants.	38	EEEEEEEEEE	14
COMMUNITY			
15. PROMOTING COMMUNITY-ORGANIZATION RELATIONS	61	CCCCCCCCCCCCCCCCCCCCCCCC	3
Staying informed on community, social, economic, and political problems and their relevance and impact upon the organization.	+ 75	EEEEEEEEEEEEEEEEEEEEEEEEEEEEEEEEEEEE	1
16. HANDLING OUTSIDE CONTACTS	51	CCCCCCCCCCCCCCCCCCC	10
Promoting the organization and its products to outside contacts and clients and properly conveying the organization's relationship with them.	56	EEEEEEEEEEEEEEEEEEEEEE	6

1%   2%   7%   16% 31% 50% 69% 84% 93% 98% 99%

Interpretation. The profiles represent systematic differences in the concept of the executive vice president position. The CEO emphasizes the skills that relate directly to the job such as Improving Work Procedures, Developing Teamwork, and Supervisory Practices (indicated by a minus sign) while the EVPs emphasize the organization-wide managerial skills of Communications and Promoting Community/Organization Relations (indicated by a plus sign).

Figure 7.6
Item Profile for the Developing Cooperation and Teamwork Function Produced from Ratings by the Chief Executive Officer (CEO) and a Group of Executive Vice Presidents (EVPs)

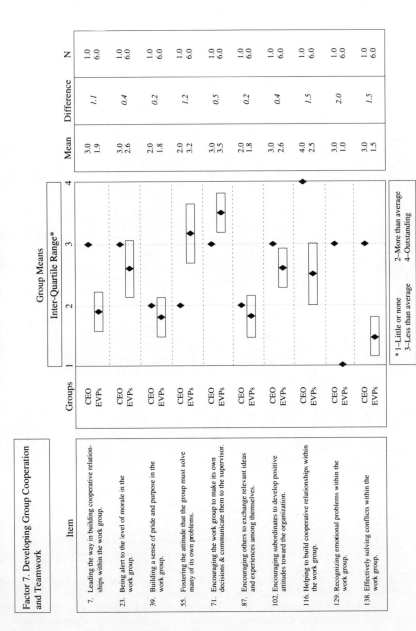

Factor 7. Developing Group Cooperation and Teamwork

Group Means

Item	Groups	Inter-Quartile Range*	Mean	Difference	N
7. Leading the way in building cooperative relationships within the work group.	CEO EVPs		3.0 1.9	*1.1*	1.0 6.0
23. Being alert to the level of morale in the work group.	CEO EVPs		3.0 2.6	*0.4*	1.0 6.0
39. Building a sense of pride and purpose in the work group.	CEO EVPs		2.0 1.8	*0.2*	1.0 6.0
55. Fostering the attitude that the group must solve many of its own problems.	CEO EVPs		2.0 3.2	*1.2*	1.0 6.0
71. Encouraging the work group to make its own decisions & communicate them to the supervisor.	CEO EVPs		3.0 3.5	*0.5*	1.0 6.0
87. Encouraging others to exchange relevant ideas and experiences among themselves.	CEO EVPs		2.0 1.8	*0.2*	1.0 6.0
102. Encouraging subordinates to develop positive attitudes toward the organization.	CEO EVPs		3.0 2.6	*0.4*	1.0 6.0
116. Helping to build cooperative relationships within the work group.	CEO EVPs		4.0 2.5	*1.5*	1.0 6.0
129. Recognizing emotional problems within the work group.	CEO EVPs		3.0 1.0	*2.0*	1.0 6.0
138. Effectively solving conflicts within the work group.	CEO EVPs		3.0 1.5	*1.5*	1.0 6.0

* 1–Little or none   2–More than average
    3–Less than average   4–Outstanding

slightly higher importance ratings both involve aspects of delegation of responsibilities and group autonomy.

The basic clarification needed in this situation is for the CEO and the EVPs to agree on the degree of authority and responsibility that resides in the EVP position and the extent to which functions that pertain directly to the job or to direct interaction with employees can be delegated by the EVPs. Thereafter, the agreed-upon functions to be performed by the EVPs and the degree of importance and responsibility assigned to each function, should be incorporated in the organizational job description for the EVP position.

IDENTIFICATION OF TRAINING NEEDS

Definition

The identification of training needs can be undertaken for (1) individuals for purposes of selection, promotion, individual development, or career counseling or (2) key occupational groups such as first-line supervisors, sales representatives, or supervisors of computer processing technicians, for example. The procedures are essentially similar except for the measures of dispersion (illustrated in Figure 7.7) obtainable for groups of employees. The job-analysis-based procedure described here provides training departments with an efficient and cost-effective way of determining the training needs of specialized personnel.

STEP Modules Required

1. Job analysis package for each targeted position.
2. MP-JFI—Ability booklets for employees in the position.

Procedure

1. Implementation of the job analysis procedure for the position.
2. Administration of the MP-JFI—Ability booklets to all employees in the position.

Information Obtained

1. Composite MP-JFI job function and item importance profiles for the position obtained from the job analysis.
2. MP-JFI job function ability profiles for each employee and a composite ability profile for the group as a whole, together with the dispersion of the employees' ability scores on each job function.

The information obtained through this procedure is presented for a group of field sales managers in Figure 7.7. The NNN line in Figure 7.7. is the performance standard established by the job analysis. The composite ability score for the group is plotted directly below the NNN line. The

Figure 7.7
Job Function Standard (NNN), Group Ability Score (····), and the Dispersion of Individual Employee Ability Scores for a Group of Field Sales Managers

Scale across: 25 30 35 40 45 50 55 60 65 70 75

Job Function	% Below Standard	SS Scale	Ability Score Distribution (with E/M/S markers)	CS Exceeds
ORGANIZATION				
1. SETTING ORGANIZATIONAL OBJECTIVES — Formulating the overall mission and goals of the organization and setting short and long-range objectives which are significant and measurable.	25.6%	49 / 47	1 1 1 5 2 27 24 53 11 21 (S M E)	38%
2. FINANCIAL PLANNING AND REVIEW — Making economic decisions and managing capital assets; establishing a budget and controls to assure that the budget is met.	35.9%	58 / 54	1 11 19 1 5 762 32 (EMS)	66%
3. IMPROVING WORK PROCEDURES AND PRACTICES — Analyzing, interpreting, and evaluating operating policies; initiating and formulating improved procedures and policies.	15.4%	50 / 51	2 1 3 3 4 9 4 7 2 1 3 (MS)	54%
4. INTERDEPARTMENTAL COORDINATION — Understanding and coordinating the problems and work activities of different departments within the organization.	17.9%	49 / 50	1 2 1 3 3 54 7 5 3 2 1 2 (M S E)	50%
LEADERSHIP				
5. DEVELOPING AND IMPLEMENTING TECHNICAL IDEAS — Originating technical ideas and designs; translating technical ideas into feasible solutions to organizational needs.	2.6%	40 / 44	1 21 2 34 38 22 13 11 1 1 (E M S)	27%
6. JUDGEMENT AND DECISION MAKING — Analyzing incomplete information to make decisions; acting upon decisions concerning resource and work force allocation.	28.2%	49 / 48	11 3 2 4 86 3 1 2 3 2 (S M E)	42%
7. DEVELOPING GROUP COOPERATION AND TEAMWORK — Encouraging and building work group relations that will lead to better exchange of ideas, more open communication and higher morale.	10.3%	54 / 57	1 135 3 2 56 36 1 1 (S M E)	76%
8. COPING WITH DIFFICULTIES AND EMERGENCIES — Working efficiently under pressure; effectively handling unexpected problems, day-to-day crises and emergency situations.	12.8%	46 / +52	1 4 2 3 4 3 5 5 2 4 1 1 1 (EM S)	58%
9. PROMOTING SAFETY ATTITUDES AND PRACTICES — Taking responsibility for the identification and elimination of job safety and health hazards.	2.6%	45 / 51	1 4 3 133 42 41113221 21 (E MS)	54%
10. COMMUNICATIONS — Monitoring and improving both external communication channels and internal upward and downward lines.	66.7%	57 / -45	111 1 33 4 5 44 53 41 (MS E)	31%
HUMAN RESOURCES				
11. DEVELOPING EMPLOYEE POTENTIAL — Evaluating employees' present performance and potential in order to create opportunities for better use of their abilities.	67.2%	64 / -52	1 3 126 49 21 1 111 (S E M)	58%
12. SUPERVISORY PRACTICES — Clarifying subordinates' job functions and responsibilities and motivating employees while maintaining discipline and control.	61.5%	59 / -51	12 73 24 32 3 22 (S)	54%
13. SELF DEVELOPMENT AND IMPROVEMENT — Formulating self-improvement goals; using feedback from others to help assess one's own strengths and weaknesses and coordinating personal career goals with organizational needs.	38.5%	51 / 48	11 11 254 23 2816 1 3 1 1 (E M S)	42%
14. PERSONNEL PRACTICES — Ensuring that the organization adheres to federal equal opportunity and affirmative action requirements and implementing special recruiting and training programs for minority applicants.	23.1%	56 / 55	7 2 3 61 43 1331 3 (S M E)	69%
COMMUNITY				
15. PROMOTING COMMUNITY-ORGANIZATION RELATIONS — Staying informed on community, social, economic, and political problems and their relevance and impact upon the organization.	17.9%	51 / 51	3 3 1 42 45 4 52 11 (M E S)	54%
16. HANDLING OUTSIDE CONTACTS — Promoting the organization and its products to outside contacts and clients and properly conveying the organization's relationship with them.	0.0%	51 / 56	22 2423 844 212 12 (EMS)	73%

Bottom percentile scale: 1% 2% 7% 16% 31% 50% 69% 84% 93% 98% 99%

NNN - Job Analysis Standard
•••••• - Group Composite Ability Score

E - Executive
M - Middle Manager
S - Sales Representative

This composite is based on 39 cases.

figures below the composite ability line show the range of the ability scores of the employees in the group and the number of employees whose ability scores fall at different points on the scale. (Any double-digit frequencies for larger groups are displayed vertically.) The numbers given in the first column on the grid are the percentage of employees whose ability scores fall significantly below the standard.

Implementation

1. Identification of the job functions on which sizable percentages of employees' ability scores are below the standard set by the job analysis. For this purpose, the usual rule of thumb of 7 standard score points for a significant difference between an individual and a composite score applies. The interpretation of a "sizable percentage" is a matter of organizational policy. Certainly 50%, or half of the employee group, falling below the standard would be a strong indication of a need for remedial training. However, some organizations may be concerned if no more than a quarter or a third of their employees fall below the standard.

2. Examination of the items that contribute to the identified dimensions and their translation from generic items to items that are specific to the position.

In Figure 7.7, the Communications, Developing Employee Potential, and Supervisory Practices job functions have, respectively, 66.7%, 87.2%, and 67.2% of employees who fall below the job analysis standard. In other words, there is a sizable percentage of employees who are deficient in the skills required for three functions that the job analysis has indicated are important for the position. Although this is not necessarily always the case, these three functions also have significantly lower group ability scores than the standard. On the other hand, although the Self-development and Improvement, Financial Planning and Review, and the Judgment and Decision Making factors do not show a significant ability difference for the group as a whole, they do have more than a quarter of the group of employees (38.5%, 35.9%, and 28.2%, respectively), significantly below the standard and could also be considered as indicating training needs.

An example of suggestions for curriculum development for training programs based on the measured abilities of national samples of employees is given in Baehr (1984a) and described in Chapter 3.

SELECTION TEST VALIDATION: STEP-V

Definition

The selection of new employees can be done for different purposes and under different conditions. The STEP test battery is available in different formats to implement the varying human resource needs. The STEP-

V is the only format for which a validation for a specific position is a prerequisite for implementation. Its use is indicated when there is a sufficient number of applicants or employees available to conduct a validation, which is most likely to occur at entry-level positions, and when it is desired to include specific skill or other trial tests in the battery that are judged to be particularly appropriate for the position. The strength of this procedure is that it produces a customized test battery specifically fitted for the position and may validate tests for future use in the STEP program. Some of the disadvantages are that the test battery can only be used for one position and will not provide estimates of potential for promotability. The procedure is applicable to either concurrent (based on personnel already employed in the position) or predictive (based on applicants for the position) validation studies. The steps in a concurrent validation are described below.

STEP Modules Required

1. Job analysis package.
2. A trial test battery that may contain some previously validated STEP tests and others that have been specifically chosen for the position.
3. Independently obtained measures of job performance for all employees (see a later section on performance appraisal).

Procedure

1. Implementation of the job analysis procedure for the position.
2. Administration of the trial selection test battery. (An option is to also administer the MP-JFI—Ability if the subjects have had previous job experience.)

Information Obtained

1. Results of the job analysis for purposes of providing an operational definition of the job and for identifying or developing the appropriate test battery. If the MP-JFI—Ability option is included, the job analysis will also provide a standard for the identification of individual- as opposed to group-training needs. This application is described later in this chapter.
2. A test battery score (obtained after regression of the test measures against performance) that represents the employee's estimated Potential for Successful Performance (PSP) in the position.
3. The employee's profile of scores on the identified valid measures in the trial test battery.
4. A validated test battery for the position.

Implementation

1. The administration of the validated test battery to applicants will produce PSPs that can be used to select high-potential employees.

2. The profiles of scores for employees can, if desired, be reviewed to determine possible developmental needs.

SELECTION AND/OR PROMOTION: STEP-S

Definition

STEP-S is recommended when selection is from candidates with little or no work experience but where potential for promotion is a consideration. An example of this situation would be the hiring of newly qualified (graduating) engineers with the expectation that a large proportion of these will be promoted from professional engineering to supervisory and, eventually, management positions.

STEP Modules Required

1. Job analysis package.
2. STEP-S test battery for the selected hierarchy.

Procedure

1. Implementation of the job-analysis procedure for the position.
2. Computerized statistical comparison of the obtained composite job function profile with that of the national normative samples for each of the twelve key positions in the STEP program in order to determine the best "fit." The hierarchy in which a key position's job-function profile most closely resembles that of the position described by the job analysis determines the selection of the test battery. (If no fit is found, a new validation can be undertaken as described in STEP-V).
3. Administration of the test battery validated for the positions in the selected hierarchy.

Information Obtained

1. Results of the job analysis (for purposes of determining the appropriate test battery).
2. A computerized report for each candidate that includes the following:

- One-page Summary of Results that provides an Estimate of Potential for Successful Performance for each of three positions in the selected hierarchy (illustrated in Figure 7.8).
- A STEP predictor profile that shows the applicant's score on all predictive test dimensions, together with the average scores of the national reference groups for the three levels of the hierarchy, as illustrated in Figure 7.9.

Figure 7.8
One-Page Summary of Results That Provides an Estimate of Potential for
Successful Performance for Each of the Three Positions in the
Professional Hierarchy

STEP PROGRAM INTERPRETATION

CONFIDENTIAL REPORT

The information in this report is confidential and must not be made known to anyone
other than qualified individuals employed by this employer, unless released by the
express written permission of the candidate. STEP scores should be considered in
the context of the candidate's total job qualifications.

This report presents the Evaluation of Potential
in the
Professional Hierarchy

LINDA HASTINGS
December 15, 1988
Battery No. 96000012

SUMMARY OF RESULTS

POTENTIAL ESTIMATES

Level	Score	Percent	Potential
Executive	53	62%	Desirable
Middle Mgr.	54	66%	Desirable
Professional	57	76%	Very Desirable

INTERPRETATION

Score Range	Percentile Range (exceeds)	Qualitative Description
39 or less	14% or less	Questionable
40 - 43	16% - 24%	Marginal
44 - 47	27% - 38%	Fair
48 - 52	42% - 58%	Good
53 - 56	62% - 73%	Desirable
57 - 60	76% - 84%	Very Desirable
61 or more	86% or more	Outstanding

Interpretation. The candidate is not only Very Desirable for a nonmanagement engineering
   position but has Desirable potential for later promotion to middle and upper management positions.

Implementation

1. Review of PSPs to select a group of applicants with high potential
for the position, a subgroup of which individuals also have potential for
promotion to the next higher position.

Figure 7.9
STEP Predictor Profile That Shows the Candidate's Scores on the Dimensions of the Managerial and Professional Test Battery and the National Norms for Professional (P), Middle Management (M), and Executive Personnel (E) in the Professional Hierarchy

E - Executive
M - Middle Manager
L - Line Supervisor

1% 2% 7% 16% 31% 50% 69% 84% 93% 98% 99%
••••••• Candidate's Score

Interpretation. The candidate matches or exceeds the norm for professional personnel on all dimensions, and often exceeds the norms for the two management positions.

2. Review of the test battery scores to determine possible avenues for the development of the individual, such as the language skills.

Since the STEP-S and STEP-ST program (described below) use the same test battery, some organizations have elected to use the STEP-ST with inexperienced candidates. Under these circumstances, the STEP-ST test battery is administered to obtain potential estimates for the hiring decision, and nine to twelve months later, the MP-JFI—Ability questionnaire is administered to establish training and development needs. This two-stage sequence of the STEP-ST program allows the newly hired individual to acquire job-related experience prior to assessing training needs for future growth.

SELECTION, PROMOTION, AND TRAINING: STEP-ST

Definition

STEP-ST is recommended when the level of acquired job skill and the identification of training needs are requirements over and above the level of potential for successful performance. An example of this situation would be the promotion of sales representatives to a sales middle-manager position. Sales representatives typically work on their own without the responsibility of supervising others or building teamwork or morale in the work group. The MP-JFI Supervisory Practices dimension has been identified as important by national samples of middle-management sales personnel, and the identification of training needs in this and related areas will facilitate efficient performance as a middle manager. Indeed, relevant job training is an asset for any type of employee but particularly when a job change involves movement from a nonmanagement to a management position.

STEP Modules Required

1. Job analysis package.
2. STEP-ST test battery for the selected hierarchy.
3. MP-JFI—Ability.

Procedure

1. Implementation of the job analysis procedure for the position and selection of the relevant test battery as described for STEP-S.
2. Administration of the selected hierarchy test battery together with the MP-JFI—Ability.

Information Obtained

1. Results of the job analysis (for purposes of determining the appropriate test battery).

2. A computerized report for each candidate that includes the following:

• One-page summary of results that provides, for each individual, an Estimate of Potential for Successful Performance and a Job Skill Assessment at each of the three levels of the selected hierarchy (illustrated in Figure 7.10).

• A STEP predictor profile that shows the applicant's score on all predictive test dimensions in the Sales hierarchy together with the mean scores of the national reference groups for the three levels of the hierarchy. (This is similar to that for the STEP-S program illustrated in Figure 7.9.)

• A job skill profile that shows the applicant's ability score on all job function dimensions of the MP-JFI together with the importance values for each dimension obtained from the job analysis for the position and the national normative standards for importance for each of the three levels of the hierarchy. This is illustrated in Figure 7.11.

Implementation

1. Review of each applicant's results to identify the employees who will be offered a position and, if necessary, to identify and address training needs for the new position.

2. Individual feedback of test results for purposes of identifying strengths, weaknesses, and training needs of newly hired or promoted employees is always advantageous. Feedbacks also fulfill a different but equally important function for the unsuccessful applicants for a position. The unsuccessful applicants are generally employees who have worked hard and who are well thought of in the organization or they would not have been considered for promotion. To leave them without information concerning the promotion decision as it pertains to them or about their future developmental or promotional opportunities is likely to result in resentful or dissatisfied employees who could adversely influence the morale of the work force. The feedback should emphasize developmental goals and possible ways in which they could groom themselves to take advantage of future promotional opportunities.

SELECTION, PROMOTION, TRAINING, AND CAREER COUNSELING: STEP-STC

Definition

Because of the somewhat greater time requirements and costs, STEP-STC is generally reserved for use with top-level personnel and key positions in the organization. The STEP-STC program has been used for human resource development as well as operational decision-making purposes. The most common operational application is selection for critical exec-

Figure 7.10

One-Page Summary of Results That Provides Potential Estimates and Job Skill Assessments for Each of the Three Positions in the Sales Hierarchy

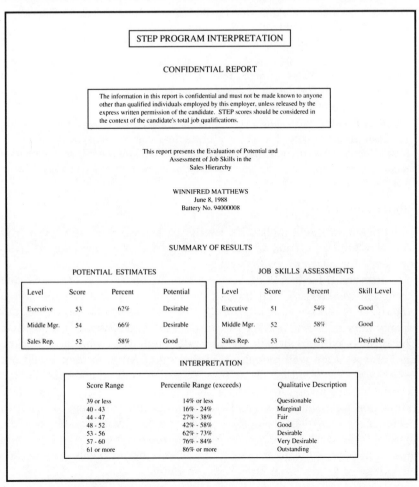

STEP PROGRAM INTERPRETATION

CONFIDENTIAL REPORT

The information in this report is confidential and must not be made known to anyone other than qualified individuals employed by this employer, unless released by the express written permission of the candidate. STEP scores should be considered in the context of the candidate's total job qualifications.

This report presents the Evaluation of Potential and Assessment of Job Skills in the Sales Hierarchy

WINNIFRED MATTHEWS
June 8, 1988
Battery No. 94000008

SUMMARY OF RESULTS

POTENTIAL ESTIMATES

Level	Score	Percent	Potential
Executive	53	62%	Desirable
Middle Mgr.	54	66%	Desirable
Sales Rep.	52	58%	Good

JOB SKILLS ASSESSMENTS

Level	Score	Percent	Skill Level
Executive	51	54%	Good
Middle Mgr.	52	58%	Good
Sales Rep.	53	62%	Desirable

INTERPRETATION

Score Range	Percentile Range (exceeds)	Qualitative Description
39 or less	14% or less	Questionable
40 - 43	16% - 24%	Marginal
44 - 47	27% - 38%	Fair
48 - 52	42% - 58%	Good
53 - 56	62% - 73%	Desirable
57 - 60	76% - 84%	Very Desirable
61 or more	86% or more	Outstanding

Interpretation. The candidate has Desirable potential and has acquired a Good level of job skill for a middle management position in the Sales hierarchy. She is a likely candidate for promotion and would soon become a proficient performer if she is given additional training in the relevant management functions.

utive positions, whether this be for candidates from outside the organization or through promotion from within. The development applications have taken place in organizational settings for top-management personnel, and in management development seminars for the purpose of self-development and career counseling. The latter application, which will include the rationale for the structure of the career counseling interview, together

Figure 7.11

A Sales Candidate's Job Skill Ability Profile (····) with the Job Analysis Standard for the Sales Representative Position (NNN) and the National Importance Levels for Sales Representatives (S), Middle Managers (M), and Executive Personnel (E) in the Sales Hierarchy

	SS Scale	25	30	35	40	45	50	55	60	65	70	75	Rank
ORGANIZATION								SM		E			
1. SETTING ORGANIZATIONAL OBJECTIVES — Formulating the overall mission and goals of the organization and setting short and long-range objectives which are significant and measurable.	- 40 / 49												16%
2. FINANCIAL PLANNING AND REVIEW — Making economic decisions and managing capital assets; establishing a budget and controls to assure that the budget is met.	56 / 58							EMS					73%
3. IMPROVING WORK PROCEDURES AND PRACTICES — Analyzing, interpreting, and evaluating operating policies; initiating and formulating improved procedures and policies.	50 / 50						MS		E				50%
4. INTERDEPARTMENTAL COORDINATION — Understanding and coordinating the problems and work activities of different departments within the organization.	- 52 / 49						MS		E				58%
LEADERSHIP						E	M	S					
5. DEVELOPING AND IMPLEMENTING TECHNICAL IDEAS — Originating technical ideas and designs; translating technical ideas into feasible solutions to organizational needs.	49 / + 40												46%
6. JUDGEMENT AND DECISION MAKING — Analyzing incomplete information to make decisions; acting upon decisions concerning resource and work force allocation.	53 / 49						S	M	E				62%
7. DEVELOPING GROUP COOPERATION AND TEAMWORK — Encouraging and building work group relations that will lead to better exchange of ideas, more open communication and higher morale.	57 / 54						S	E	M				21%
8. COPING WITH DIFFICULTIES AND EMERGENCIES — Working efficiently under pressure; effectively handling unexpected problems, day-to-day crises and emergency situations.	46 / 46						EM	S					34%
9. PROMOTING SAFETY ATTITUDES AND PRACTICES — Taking responsibility for the identification and elimination of job safety and health hazards.	51 / 45					E	M	S		S			54%
10. COMMUNICATIONS — Monitoring and improving both external communication channels and internal upward and downward lines.	56 / 57						MS	E					73%
HUMAN RESOURCES							S		E	M			
11. DEVELOPING EMPLOYEE POTENTIAL — Evaluating employees' present performance and potential in order to create opportunities for better use of their abilities.	- 53 / 64												62%
12. SUPERVISORY PRACTICES — Clarifying subordinates' job functions and responsibilities and motivating employees while maintaining discipline and control.	- 52 / 59						S		E	M			58%
13. SELF DEVELOPMENT AND IMPROVEMENT — Formulating self-improvement goals; using feedback from others to help assess one's own strengths and weaknesses and coordinating personal career goals with organizational needs.	58 / + 51						E	M	S				79%
14. PERSONNEL PRACTICES — Ensuring that the organization adheres to federal equal opportunity and affirmative action requirements and implementing special recruiting and training programs for minority applicants.	52 / 56						SM	E					58%
COMMUNITY							M	ES					
15. PROMOTING COMMUNITY-ORGANIZATION RELATIONS — Staying informed on community, social, economic, and political problems and their relevance and impact upon the organization.	53 / 51												62%
16. HANDLING OUTSIDE CONTACTS — Promoting the organization and its products to outside contacts and clients and properly conveying the organization's relationship with them.	53 / 51							EMS					62%

····· - Candidate's Ability Score
NNN - Job Analysis Standard

1% 2% 7% 16% 31% 50% 69% 84% 93% 98% 99%

Interpretation. The candidate has generally good job skills but has deficiencies (indicated by a minus sign) on the middle management functions of Developing Employee Potential and Supervisory Practices and on the executive Objective Setting function.

with outplacement procedures, will be discussed in Chapter 8. The procedure for implementation in an organizational setting is described here.

STEP Modules Required

1. Job analysis package.
2. Expanded STEP-STC test battery, sometimes including tests for all four hierarchies.
3. MP-JFI—Ability.

Procedure

1. Implementation of the job analysis procedure for the position (for the purpose of determining the appropriate test battery).
2. Administration of the expanded test battery together with the MP-JFI—Ability.

Information Obtained

1. Results of the job analysis of the key position for which a candidate is to be selected.
2. A computerized report for each individual that indicates the following:

- One-page summary of results that provides an Estimate of Potential for Successful Performance and a Job Skill Assessment for the individual at each of the three levels of the selected hierarchy, as illustrated in Figure 7.10 for the STEP-ST program.
- A STEP predictor profile that shows the individual's scores on all predictive test dimensions together with the mean scores of the national reference groups for the three levels of the hierarchy as illustrated for the STEP-S and STEP-ST programs in Figure 7.9.
- A job skill profile that shows the individual's score on all job function dimensions of the MP-JFI together with the importance values for each dimension obtained from the relevant job analysis as illustrated in Figure 7.11 for the STEP-ST program.
- Profiles of the underlying dimension scores of all multiscore tests. For example, in the Experience and Background area, only seven out of a total of sixteen scored dimensions appear in the predictor profile. Nevertheless, the remaining dimensions provide valuable information for career counseling such as the individual's adjustment to the early parental family and school environments, which is often indicative of adjustment in later life. The dimensions also provide information about, and the way in which, fiscal and family responsibility are handled in the personal family setting, including the two-career family. The generally accepted hypothesis is that individuals who have successfully assumed responsibility in one environment are likely to be responsible and successful in other environments.

Another example of the additional information obtained from the individual test profiles provided in the STEP-STC program is provided by the Cree Questionnaire. The Questionnaire produces an overall estimate of creative and innovative behavior reported on the STEP predictor profile. The overall estimate is the weighted sum of the individual's scores on thirteen behavior characteristics. A profile of the scores of the thirteen behavior characteristics that define the creative personality is provided, together with the normative group scores for the three levels of the selected hierarchy, as illustrated in Figure 7.12.

Figure 7.12 provides important information about whether or not the individual is dominant and a leader in social situations, whether or not he or she prefers an autonomous work environment, and the degree of the individual's work involvement. Information is also given about such personal characteristics as reaction time, energy level, and the rate of spontaneous production of innovative ideas. In general, the detailed test profiles that underlie the composite scores given in the predictor profile provide information on a variety of qualities that have been shown to facilitate effective leadership and efficient management.

For selected applications such as succession planning, self-development, career counseling, and outplacement, the STEP-STC can be administered and scored in any desired number of heirarchies. The summary page of information for scoring in all four hierarchies is illustrated in Figure 7.13. This summary presents an individual's estimate of Potential for Successful Performance and Job Skills Assessment at each level of the four managerial hierarchies, while highlighting in boldface the primary hierarchy and level as targeted by a job analysis of a given position. For example, in Figure 7.13, the individual is currently a sales representative (Level III in sales) so the potential estimates and job skill assessments are boldfaced for this primary position. In addition, the individual's potential estimates and job skill assessments are given for all levels of the remaining three hierarchies, permitting an evaluation of the individual's suitability for possible future positions for which he or she could be considered. This procedure is particularly valuable in career counseling and when there is a possibility of a career switch.

PERFORMANCE APPRAISAL

Definition

Psychometric performance appraisal techniques were first introduced in industrial organizations in the early 1920s. Because it is generally felt that knowledge of the employee's level of job performance is essential for efficient operation, a succession of appraisal techniques have been implemented ever since with rather less than more success. More recently, performance appraisal procedures have become the subject of governmental *Guideline* requirements and legal action as exemplified by

Figure 7.12
Candidate's Scores on the Underlying Dimensions of the Creative Personality Together with the National Standards for First-Line Supervisors (L), Middle Managers (M), and Executives (E) in the Line Hierarchy

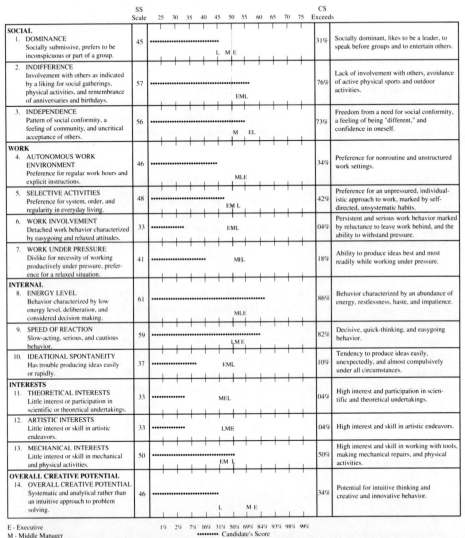

	SS Scale	25 30 35 40 45 50 55 60 65 70 75	CS Exceeds	
SOCIAL				
1. DOMINANCE Socially submissive, prefers to be inconspicuous or part of a group.	45	•••••••••••••••••••••••••• L M E	31%	Socially dominant, likes to be a leader, to speak before groups and to entertain others.
2. INDIFFERENCE Involvement with others as indicated by a liking for social gatherings, physical activities, and remembrance of anniversaries and birthdays.	57	••••••••••••••••••••••••••••••••••• EML	76%	Lack of involvement with others, avoidance of active physical sports and outdoor activities.
3. INDEPENDENCE Pattern of social conformity, a feeling of community, and uncritical acceptance of others.	56	••••••••••••••••••••••••••••••••••• M EL	73%	Freedom from a need for social conformity, a feeling of being "different," and confidence in oneself.
WORK				
4. AUTONOMOUS WORK ENVIRONMENT Preference for regular work hours and explicit instructions.	46	••••••••••••••••••••••••• MLE	34%	Preference for nonroutine and unstructured work settings.
5. SELECTIVE ACTIVITIES Preference for system, order, and regularity in everyday living.	48	•••••••••••••••••••••••••••• EM L	42%	Preference for an unpressured, individualistic approach to work, marked by self-directed, unsystematic habits.
6. WORK INVOLVEMENT Detached work behavior characterized by easygoing and relaxed attitudes.	33	•••••••••••••• EML	04%	Persistent and serious work behavior marked by reluctance to leave work behind, and the ability to withstand pressure.
7. WORK UNDER PRESSURE Dislike for necessity of working productively under pressure, preference for a relaxed situation.	41	••••••••••••••••••••• MEL	18%	Ability to produce ideas best and most readily while working under pressure.
INTERNAL				
8. ENERGY LEVEL Behavior characterized by low energy level, deliberation, and considered decision making.	61	••••••••••••••••••••••••••••••••••••••• MLE	86%	Behavior characterized by an abundance of energy, restlessness, haste, and impatience.
9. SPEED OF REACTION Slow-acting, serious, and cautious behavior.	59	•••••••••••••••••••••••••••••••••••• LM E	82%	Decisive, quick-thinking, and easygoing behavior.
10. IDEATIONAL SPONTANEITY Has trouble producing ideas easily or rapidly.	37	•••••••••••••••••• EML	10%	Tendency to produce ideas easily, unexpectedly, and almost compulsively under all circumstances.
INTERESTS				
11. THEORETICAL INTERESTS Little interest or participation in scientific or theoretical undertakings.	33	•••••••••••••• MEL	04%	High interest and participation in scientific and theoretical undertakings.
12. ARTISTIC INTERESTS Little interest or skill in artistic endeavors.	33	•••••••••••••• LME	04%	High interest and skill in artistic endeavors.
13. MECHANICAL INTERESTS Little interest or skill in mechanical and physical activities.	50	••••••••••••••••••••••••••••• EM L	50%	High interest and skill in working with tools, making mechanical repairs, and physical activities.
OVERALL CREATIVE POTENTIAL				
14. OVERALL CREATIVE POTENTIAL Systematic and analytical rather than an intuitive approach to problem solving.	46	••••••••••••••••••••••• L M E	34%	Potential for intuitive thinking and creative and innovative behavior.

E - Executive
M - Middle Manager
L - Line Supervisor

1% 2% 7% 16% 31% 50% 69% 84% 93% 98% 99%
•••••••• Candidate's Score

Interpretation. This candidate's overall creative potential (14) is only at the level of that of First Line Supervisors (L) and well below that of Line Middle Managers (M) and Executives (E). The contributors to the low overall score are low levels (below that of all three reference standards) of social dominance (1), work involvement (6), ability to work under pressure (7), and spontaneity in idea production (10).

Figure 7.13
One-Page Summary of Results That Provides Estimates of Potential for Successful Performance (PSP) and Job Skill Assessment (JSA) Scores for All Hierarchies and All Levels

London House   LH-STEP

Estimates of Overall Potential and Job Skills
BILL JOHNSON, Battery 0088001010, 08/27/90
ABC GENERAL #980001, Unit #0001

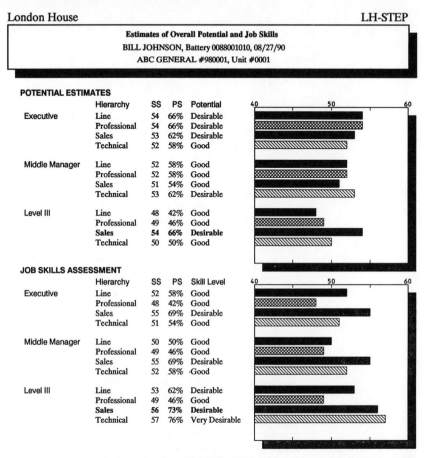

POTENTIAL ESTIMATES

	Hierarchy	SS	PS	Potential
Executive	Line	54	66%	Desirable
	Professional	54	66%	Desirable
	Sales	53	62%	Desirable
	Technical	52	58%	Good
Middle Manager	Line	52	58%	Good
	Professional	52	58%	Good
	Sales	51	54%	Good
	Technical	53	62%	Desirable
Level III	Line	48	42%	Good
	Professional	49	46%	Good
	Sales	**54**	**66%**	**Desirable**
	Technical	50	50%	Good

JOB SKILLS ASSESSMENT

	Hierarchy	SS	PS	Skill Level
Executive	Line	52	58%	Good
	Professional	48	42%	Good
	Sales	55	69%	Desirable
	Technical	51	54%	Good
Middle Manager	Line	50	50%	Good
	Professional	49	46%	Good
	Sales	55	69%	Desirable
	Technical	52	58%	·Good
Level III	Line	53	62%	Desirable
	Professional	49	46%	Good
	Sales	**56**	**73%**	**Desirable**
	Technical	57	76%	Very Desirable

Interpretation

Score Range	Percentile Range (exceeds)	Qualitative Description
39 or less	14% or less	Questionable
40 - 43	16% - 24%	Marginal
44 - 47	27% - 38%	Fair
48 - 52	42% - 58%	Good
53 - 56	62% - 73%	Desirable
57 - 60	76% - 84%	Very Desirable
61 or more	86% or more	Outstanding

Figure 7.14
Directions and an Illustrative Item for the Rating Scale Performance Evaluation

Evaluator's Name _____

Evaluator's Job Title _____

Company _____

Employee's Name _____

Employee's Job Title _____

Date _____

Directions

This rating form was designed for use in evaluating the performance of managers and professionals. It consists of 16 empirically derived job functions that are components of managerial and professional jobs.

For each job function, you will be asked to rate the manager or professional's performance on this dimension in comparison with your standard job requirements.

Example

Please circle the most appropriate response:

O. *Leadership Ability* -- Ability to take charge, to direct the work of others, and to persuade them to do the work in the way it should be done; ability to train others and also address a group of employees or a large audience.

(1)	(2)	(3)	(4)	(5)
Does not meet standard job requirements	Meets standard job requirements	Exceeds standard job requirements	Far exceeds standard job requirements	Does not apply
☐	☐	☐	☐	☐

In the example, the rater felt that the employee exceeded the standard job requirements for the "handling money" aspect of the job.

In these ratings, try to avoid three common errors:

1. *The "halo" error* -- This error occurs when the rater's overall impression of, or personal feelings about the person being evaluated are used as the basis for ratings, rather than carefully considering each aspect of performance separately. Rating a subordinate high on all dimensions because the subordinate is friendly and likeable is an example of this error; rating low on all dimensions because of problems in one area, such as attendance, is another.

2. *The leniency error* -- This error is made when all subordinates are rated at the high end of the scale. It's impossible for all employees to fall in the category of "far exceeds standard job requirements," yet some raters will give this rating to many or most subordinates. Though many managers are very good workers, we need to know which are more effective than others. Similar errors can be made by rating all subordinates as average or by using only the low end of the scale.

3. *Rating on anything but performance* -- Great care must be taken to make sure that factors such as physical attractiveness, race, sex, and age do not affect your ratings.

With these recommendations in mind, please rate the individual on the following aspects of a managerial or professional job:

Illustrative Item

The Individual:	(1) Does not meet standard job requirements	(2) Meets standard job requirements	(3) Exceeds standard job requirements	(4) Far exceeds standard job requirements	(5) Does not apply
1. *Setting Organizational Objectives* -- Formulating the overall mission and goals of the organization; setting short and long-range objectives which are significant and measurable and which incorporate future predictions; evaluating alternative structures for future organizational operations.	☐	☐	☐	☐	☐

Watson v. Fort Worth Bank & Trust (1988). Three standardized, job analysis-based performance appraisal techniques of increasing complexity are offered here.

Rating Scale Technique

STEP Modules Required

1. Job analysis package.
2. A London House University Series Performance Evaluation form for each employee to be evaluated. The 16 MP-JFI function titles (with accompanying definitions) provide the dimensions for the Performance Evaluation form. Instructions for using the 6-point rating scale and an illustrative item are given in Figure 7.14.

Procedure

1. Implementation of the job analysis procedure (for the position for the purpose of identifying the important functions to be performed).
2. Assessment by the supervisor (or preferably two or more supervisors) of the employee's level of ability on each of the job functions.

Information Obtained

1. Results of the job analysis.
2. The employee's profile of Ability scale values (competency levels) on each of the 16 job functions.
3. Overall assessment of the employee's ability based on the average of the scale values for the identified important functions (importance levels 50 or above). An alternative procedure is to weight the scale values by the job function importance levels before averaging.

Implementation

The overall assessment can be used as a performance criterion in test validation research or for some of the administrative purposes described below for the forced choice technique. The competency profiles can be used for employee development.

Forced Choice Technique

STEP Modules Required

1. Job analysis package.
2. MP-JFI—Ability booklet (one for each employee to be assessed by a supervisor, or two for each employee if self-assessments of performance are also required).

Procedure

1. Implementation of the job analysis procedure for the position (for the purpose of establishing the relative importance of the functions to be performed).

2. Assessment by the supervisor (or preferably by two or more supervisors) of the employee's level of ability on each job-activity item in the MP-JFI—Ability booklet. This assessment will be required of supervisors for each employee to be appraised and, if self-assessments are also desired, then

3. Self-assessment by employees of their perception of their level of ability on each job activity item, using the MP-JFI—Ability booklet.

Information Obtained

1. Results of the job analysis.

2. The employee's job function ability profile based on supervisory ratings (and on self-ratings, if desired).

3. The employee's item ability profiles based on supervisory ratings (and on self-ratings, if desired) for each job function.

4. Overall assessment of the employee's ability based on the average of the employee's job function ability scores (assessed by the supervisor and/or the employee) on the important job functions (importance levels 50 and above) identified through the job analysis. A job function ability profile is illustrated in Figure 7.15.

Implementation

The information can be used for both traditional objectives of performance appraisal: judgment followed by administrative action, and also for employee development.

1. *Administrative Action.* The supervisor's overall ability assessments can be used to determine merit increases and salary levels for an employee group. The overall supervisory ability assessment shown in the last row of Figure 7.15 is 51. For purposes of employee development, it is necessary to know the employee's assessed ability levels on the important functions as discussed below.

2. *Employee Development.* Procedures for employee development traditionally include an appraisal interview directed toward the identification of the employee's training needs and ways to address them. In the appraisal interview, the concern should be primarily with the employee's ability levels on the job functions with importance values of 50 or greater. In Figure 7.15, the job functions have been rank ordered with respect to the importance values obtained from the job analysis. Job functions with rank orders 1 through 7 (given in the right-hand column in the grid) would be of greatest concern.

Figure 7.15

Comparison of the Forced Choice Ability Ratings Made by the Supervisor (S) and the Employee (E) with the Job Analysis Importance Standard (NNN)

Item	SS Scale	Graph (25 30 35 40 45 50 55 60 65 70 75)	Rank
11. DEVELOPING EMPLOYEE POTENTIAL Evaluating employees' present performance and potential in order to create opportunities for better use of their abilities.	65 / 50* / 60	NNNNNNNNNNNNNNNNNNNNNNNNNNNNNN / SSSSSSSSSSSSSSSSSSSSS S / EEEEEEEEEEEEEEEEEEEEEEEEEE	1
9. PROMOTING SAFETY ATTITUDES & PRACTICES Taking responsibility for the identification and elimination of job safety and health hazards.	62 / 50* / 50*	NNNNNNNNNNNNNNNNNNNNNNNNNN / SSSSSSSSSSSSSSSSSSS S / EEEEEEEEEEEEEEEEEEE	2
12. SUPERVISORY PRACTICES Clarifying subordinates' job functions and responsibilities and motivating employees while maintaining discipline and control.	60 / 58 / 52*	NNNNNNNNNNNNNNNNNNNNNNNNNN / SSSSSSSSSSSSSSSSSSSSSSSSSSSSSS / EEEEEEEEEEEEEEEEEEEE	3
8. COPING WITH DIFFICULTIES & EMERGENCIES Working efficiently under pressure; effectively handling unexpected problems, day-to-day crises and emergency situations.	58 / 55 / 63	NNNNNNNNNNNNNNNNNNNNNNNN / SSSSSSSSSSSSSSSSSSSSSSSSS / EEEEEEEEEEEEEEEEEEEEEEEEEEEEEEEE	4
3. IMPROVING WORK PROCEDURES & PRACTICES Analyzing, interpreting and evaluating operating policies; initiating and formulating improved procedures and policies.	56 / 46* / 53	NNNNNNNNNNNNNNNNNNNNNNN / SSSSSSSSSSSSSSSSS / EEEEEEEEEEEEEEEEEEEE	5
7. DEVELOPING GROUP COOPERATION & TEAMWORK Encouraging and building work group relations that will lead to better exchange of ideas, more open communication and higher morale.	55 / 51 / 59	NNNNNNNNNNNNNNNNNNNNNN / SSSSSSSSSSSSSSSSSSSS / EEEEEEEEEEEEEEEEEEEEEEEEEEEE	6
14. PERSONNEL PRACTICES Ensuring that the organization adheres to federal Equal Opportunity and Affirmative Action requirements and implementing special recruiting and traning programs for minority applicants.	53 / 52 / 53	NNNNNNNNNNNNNNNNNN / SSSSSSSSSSSSSSSSSSS / EEEEEEEEEEEEEEEEEEE	7
4. INTERDEPARTMENTAL COORDINATION Understanding and coordinating the problems and work activities of different departments within the organization.	49 / 46 / 45	NNNNNNNNNNNNNN / SSSSSSSSSSSSSSSS / EEEEEEEEEEEEEE	8
16. HANDLING OUTSIDE CONTACTS Promoting the organization and its products to outside contacts and clients and properly conveying the organization's relationship with them.	49 / 52 / 52	NNNNNNNNNNNNNN / SSSSSSSSSSSSSSSSSSSSS / EEEEEEEEEEEEEEEEEEE	8
13. SELF DEVELOPMENT & IMPROVEMENT Formulating self-improvement goals; using feedback from others to help assess one's own strengths and weaknesses and coordinating personal career goals with organizational needs.	48 / 50 / 46	NNNNNNNNNNNNN / SSSSSSSSSSSSSSSSSS / EEEEEEEEEEEEEE	10
6. JUDGEMENT & DECISION MAKING Analyzing incomplete information to make decisions; acting upon decisions concerning resource and work force allocation.	48 / 48 / 52	NNNNNNNNNNNNN / SSSSSSSSSSSSSSSSSS / EEEEEEEEEEEEEEEEEE E	10
15. PROMOTING COMM.–ORGANIZATION RELATIONS Staying informed on community, social, economic and political problems and their relevance and impact upon the organization.	47 / 40 / 45	NNNNNNNNNNNNN / SSSSSSSSSSSS / EEEEEEEEEEEEEE	12
10. COMMUNICATIONS Monitoring and improving both external communication channels and internal upward and downward lines.	46 / 40 / 42	NNNNNNNNNNNN / SSSSSSSSSSS / EEEEEEEEEE	13
2. FINANCIAL PLANNING AND REVIEW Making economic decisions and managing capital assets; establishing a budget and controls to assure that the budget is met.	46 / 45 / 50	NNNNNNNNNNNN / SSSSSSSSSSSSSS / EEEEEEEEEEEEEEEEEE	13
5. DEVELOPING & IMPLEMENTING TECHNICAL IDEAS Originating technical ideas and designs; translating technical ideas into feasible solutions to organizational needs.	45 / 40 / 42	NNNNNNNNNNN N / SSSSSSSSSSS / EEEEEEEEEEEE	15
1. SETTING ORGANIZATIONAL OBJECTIVES Formulating the overall mission and goals of the organization and setting short and long-range objectives which are significant and measurable.	42 / 45 / 41	NNNNNNNNNN / SSSSSSSSSSSSSSSSS / EEEEEEEEEEE	16
OVERALL ABILITY RATINGS Supervisor / Employee	51 / 56	SSSSSSSSSSSSSSSSSSSSSS / EEEEEEEEEEEEEEEEEEEEEEEEEE	

*Significant difference between importance and ability rating.

1% 2% 7% 16% 31% 50% 69% 84% 93% 98% 99%

In order to set a positive tone in the appraisal interview, it could first be pointed out that the employee's ability levels as assessed by the supervisor (S) reach the required job analysis standard (N) on four of the seven important functions (12, 8, 7, and 14). Thereafter, the ability levels on factors 11, 9, and 3, where the supervisor's assessments of the employee's ability are seven standard score points below the importance standard, can be discussed. If the employee's self-assessment of ability (E) is available, it can be noted that the supervisor does not regard the employee as having a skill deficiency in Supervisory Practices (12), though the employee's self-assessment for ability is significantly low on this function. It can also be noted that the employee agrees with the low level of ability assessed for the Promoting Safety Attitudes and Practices function (9). This function may, thus, provide a good starting point for identifying training needs.

The preferred procedures for identifying training needs and, if necessary, resolving differences in the perceptions of the supervisor and the employee is to examine the item profiles for the relevant factors. The items profiles will resemble those illustrated in Figure 7.6 in the job clarification section. For the present purposes, the scores provided for each item will be the job analysis standard and its inter-quantile range, the supervisor's, and when available, the employee's self-assessments of ability. The translation of the generic MP-JFI items into items that describe actual activities performed in the position will pinpoint areas for on-the-job coaching and training.

The most complex of the three performance appraisal techniques described here involves, first, the translation of the generic items in the MP-JFI—Ability into the actual activities performed in a particular type of position in the organization, followed by psychometric procedures for scaling the activity items in developing a performance appraisal form.

Theoretically, any form of scaling technique could be used including the rating scale technique described previously to assess ability on the factors. Although straightforward, easy to implement, and generally liked by the assessors, the rating scale has the oft-cited disadvantage of being subject to the constant errors of measurement such as the errors of leniency (a tendency to make all ratings favorable), errors of central tendency, and to halo effects. One attempt to overcome these deficiencies, which appears to have been partially successful, was through the construction of Behavior Anchored Rating Scales (BARS), which peaked in the 1970s. Examples of these are a nationwide study by Campbell, Dunnette, Arvey, and Hellervik (1973) for the development of a scale for store managers and, in the private sector, the development of a scale for police officers (Landy & Farr, 1975).

In a further attempt to minimize the common errors in rating, Blanz and Ghiselli (1972) tested the applicability of the Mixed Standard Scale

(MSS) for rating managerial personnel in the United States. Both the authors and others who have compared the results of Behaviorally Anchored Rating and Mixed Standard Scale formats (Dickinson and Zellinger, 1980) find that the use of the MSS procedure significantly reduces halo effect and leniency error and has the further advantage of providing an internal measure of consistency or accuracy of ratings.

In constructing an MSS, each job function is measured by three items that represent, respectively, above average, average, and below average performance. These items are randomized in the appraisal form and the assessor has to indicate whether the performance of the employee being assessed is poorer, at the same level, or better than that described by the item. When calculating the performance score, the groups of three items are reassembled into what should be a Guttman scale. Unfortunately, for what seemed initially to be a significant advance in performance appraisal techniques, Saal (1979) and others have demonstrated that the mixed standard scales have unacceptable reliability when attempts are made to reconstruct the three-item Guttman scale underlying the performance dimension.

A technique that the author has found to be quite satisfactory follows the MSS procedure except that the performance dimension is stabilized through the use of six to nine items in the construction of the Guttman scale. The construction of such a scale is described below for well-trained sales representatives of chemical products.

Scaled Item Technique

STEP Modules Required

1. Job analysis package.

Procedure

1. Implementation of the job analysis procedure for the position (for the purpose of determining the important functions to be performed).

2. Focus group discussions by job incumbents and/or their supervisors to translate the generic MP-JFI items in the identified important functions into specific activities performed in the position.

3. Use of the activity items to construct six- to nine-item Guttman scales to represent each performance dimension identified in the job analysis. A detailed description of the construction of the Guttman scales cannot be undertaken here. Those who are interested in their construction are referred to Landy and Farr (1983) and to Edwards (1957). An example of a nine-item performance scale developed for the Handling Outside Contacts job function is shown in Figure 7.16.

4. Randomization of the scaled items from all behavior dimensions in

Figure 7.16
An Example of a Nine-Item Guttman Scale for the Handling Outside Contacts Job Function

Item		Performance Weight
4.	Handles customer complaints consistently and objectively by pinpointing the problem, reaching agreement on the remedy, and taking quick action to achieve results.	9.5
8.	Even when a customer is thought to be mistaken, avoids criticism unless a workable alternative can be suggested.	8.0
12.	Maintains a positive attitude toward servicing, seeing it as a form of reselling.	7.2
16.	Leaves names and phone numbers of a number of XYZ representatives with each customer.	6.0
20.	Makes customers feel important by finding out what kind of entertainment they like and arranging for it.	5.2
24.	Usually underestimates the entertainment budget.	4.0
28.	Sometimes gives customers incorrect information because facts have not been checked or information is not up to date.	3.4
36.	Is unsystematic and tardy about responding to telephone calls.	2.5
40.	Fails to routinely advise customers of new products and technology which are available.	1.1

a performance appraisal form, as illustrated in Figure 7.17. When using the form illustrated in Figure 7.17, the assessor merely has to indicate whether or not the employee exhibits the level of performance represented by the item.

Information Obtained

1. Results of the job analysis.
2. A work-oriented performance appraisal form specifically constructed for a particular type of position in the organization.

There is admittedly considerable time and effort involved in the construction of appraisal forms that consist of the random presentation of items scaled to represent poor to excellent performance on each important job function. The reward, however, is a job-analysis-based performance appraisal procedure that provides an estimate of the assessor's reliability or consistency, an overall assessment of the employee's performance, and specific job function information that can be used for em-

Figure 7.17
Example of an Appraisal Form Composed of Randomized Guttman-Scaled Items

Indicate with a check mark whether you consider that the employee does (yes) or does not (no) exhibit the level of performance indicated by the item.

Level of Performance

		NO	YES
1.	Ability to listen to conflicting reports from a customer and to sort out pertinent facts to deal with the situation.	___	___
2.	Keeps ahead of technological changes in our field and helps customers become aware of these changes and their impact on water treatment.	___	___
3.	Is able to lead or take charge when working with other salespersons or customers.	___	___
4.	Handles customer complaints consistently and objectively by pinpointing the problem, reaching agreement on the remedy and taking quick action to achieve results.	___	___
5.	Finds practical ways of dealing with customer problems which result in increased sales or service.	___	___
6.	Helps appropriate plant personnel identify and understand their water treatment problem in order to sell them the appropriate product.	___	___
7.	Is frequently sought out by other sales representatives for opinions and advice.	___	___
8.	Even when a customer is thought to be mistaken, avoids criticism unless a workable alternative can be suggested.	___	___
9.	Is able to judge future organizational needs through customer suggestions for product improvements.	___	___
10.	Prepares good reports: describing technical studies or justifying projects, etc.	___	___

ployee development and in the development of training program curricula.

SUCCESSION PLANNING AND REASSIGNMENT

Definition

Succession planning, reassignment, and the strategic reorganization of the organization's human resource require rather complex, organization-wide programs all of which cannot be adequately described within the context of this book. The basic procedure, however, from which the others flow is succession planning. An example is given here of a succession-planning project undertaken for a State Department of Transportation. A schematic organizational structure for the Highway Division of a State Department of Transportation, which indicates level of organizational functioning rather than reporting relationships, is shown in Figure 7.18. The numbers given in parentheses are the number of employees in each occupational group. The five District Engineers shown on the left of the figure direct the operations of the department and supervise the engineers employed in road construction and maintenance. The construction and maintenance engineers, in turn, supervise skilled trade and hourly personnel. In STEP terminology, the left side of Figure 7.18 represents the Line hierarchy and the right side of the figure, where Office Managers manage three levels of engineers engaged in the design of highways, bridges, tunnels, and the like, represents the Professional hierarchy.

A crisis occurred in the department when three of the five District Engineers (who are high-level executives in the department) either resigned or retired within a short period of time. Rather than simply reacting to the immediate crisis, the department decided to implement a succession-planning program in an attempt to prevent such crises from occurring in the future.

STEP Modules Required

1. A job analysis package for each of the eight occupational groups in Figure 7.18 and for the Chief Engineer position.
2. STEP-STC (or, if desired, STEP-ST) test batteries for all employees in the occupational groups.
3. MP-JFI—Ability booklets for all employees in the occupational groups.

Procedure

1. Implementation of the job analysis procedure for each of the eight occupational groups in Figure 7.18 and also for the Chief Engineer position (for the purpose of developing a job importance profile for each position).
2. Administration of the STEP-STC (or STEP-ST) and the MP-JFI—Ability booklets to all employees.
3. Computerized comparison of the occupational group job function importance profiles obtained from the job analysis with each of the national normative profiles for the twelve key occupations in the STEP program as described for the STEP-S procedure.
4. Preparation of a human resource data bank for the purpose of succession planning.

Figure 7.18
Schematic Organizational Structure for a State Department of Transportation

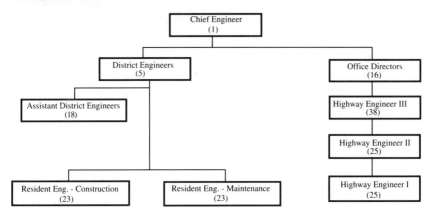

Information Obtained—Job Analysis

1. There were no significant differences in the job function importance profiles of Resident and Construction Engineers. Both groups supervise work crews of skilled and hourly personnel and the combined composite profile closely resembled that of Line II or middle-management personnel in the Line hierarchy.

2. The job function profiles of Highway Engineers I and II were similar enough to be combined. This was not unexpected since the groups contained fully qualified engineers performing similar professional work and were differentiated only by Civil Service tenure and pay scales. The composite job function profile best fitted that of nonmanagement professionals (Professional III) in the Professional hierarchy.

3. The Level III Highway Engineers have supervisory responsibility over the nonmanagement professionals and their composite job function profile identified them as functioning at Level II (Middle Managers) in the Professional hierarchy.

4. According to expectations, the composite District Engineer and Officer Director group job function profiles were classified, respectively, as Line Level I and Professional Level I.

5. The Chief Engineer job function profile resembled that of chief executive officers in the private sector.

6. There was no close fit for the Assistant District Engineer job function profile.

The last piece of information came as something of a surprise to the organization since the expectation had been that the Assistant District Engineer profile would most resemble that of the District Engineers, though possibly at a lower level of functioning, and that the most likely candi-

Figure 7.19
Average Job Function Importance Values for the District Engineer (D), Office Director (O), and Assistant District Engineer (A) Groups

CATEGORY SCALE	Diff	NS	Normalized Standard Score Scale	CS Exceeds
ORGANIZATION				
*1. Objective Setting		58	DDDDDDDDDDDDDDDDDDDDDDDDDDDDDDDDDDDD	79
		57	OOOOOOOOOOOOOOOOOOOOOOOOOOOOOOOOOO	76
	-9	49	AAAAAAAAAAAAAAAAAAAA	46
*2. Financial Planning		58	DDDDDDDDDDDDDDDDDDDDDDDDDDDDDDDDDD	73
		55	OOOOOOOOOOOOOOOOOOOOOOOOOOO	69
		56	AAAAAAAAAAAAAAAAAAAAAAAAAAAAAAAA	73
*3. Work Practices		55	DDDDDDDDDDDDDDDDDDDDDDDDDDDDDD	73
	+10	65	OOOOOOOOOOOOOOOOOOOOOOOOOOOOOOOOOOOOOOOOOOOO	94
		52	AAAAAAAAAAAAAAAAAAAAAAAAA	58
4. Coordination		49	DDDDDDDDDDDDDDDDDDDDD	46
	+10	59	OOOOOOOOOOOOOOOOOOOOOOOOOOOOOOOOOOOOOO	82
		49	AAAAAAAAAAAAAAAAAAA	46
5. Dev. Technical Ideas		42	DDDDDDD	21
	+9	51	OOOOOOOOOOOOOOOOOOOOOOOOOO	54
		45	AAAAAAAAAAAAA	31
LEADERSHIP				
*6. Decision Making		59	DDDDDDDDDDDDDDDDDDDDDDDDDDDDDDDDDDDDDD	82
		56	OOOOOOOOOOOOOOOOOOOOOOOOOOOOOOO	73
	-8	51	AAAAAAAAAAAAAAAAAAAAAAAAA	54
*7. Developing Teamwork		59	DDDDDDDDDDDDDDDDDDDDDDDDDDDDDDDDDDDDDD	82
	-6	53	OOOOOOOOOOOOOOOOOOOOOOOOOOO	62
	-8	51	AAAAAAAAAAAAAAAAAAAAAAAAA	54
8. Coping with Emergencies		44	DDDDDDDDDD	27
		46	OOOOOOOOOOOOOO	34
	+9	53	AAAAAAAAAAAAAAAAAAAAAAAAAAA	62
9. Promoting Safety		50	DDDDDDDDDDDDDDDDDDDDDD	50
		47	OOOOOOOOOOOOOOOO	38
	+6	56	AAAAAAAAAAAAAAAAAAAAAAAAAAAAAAAA	73
*10. Communications		51	DDDDDDDDDDDDDDDDDDDDDDDD	54
		53	OOOOOOOOOOOOOOOOOOOOOOOOOOO	62
		51	AAAAAAAAAAAAAAAAAAAAAAAAA	54
HUMAN RESOURCES				
*11. Developing Employee Potential		61	DDDDDDDDDDDDDDDDDDDDDDDDDDDDDDDDDDDDDDDDDD	86
	-5	56	OOOOOOOOOOOOOOOOOOOOOOOOOOOOOOO	73
	-8	53	AAAAAAAAAAAAAAAAAAAAAAAAAAA	62
12. Supervisory Practices		50	DDDDDDDDDDDDDDDDDDDDDD	50
		49	OOOOOOOOOOOOOOOOOOOO	46
	+6	56	AAAAAAAAAAAAAAAAAAAAAAAAAAAAAAAA	73
13. Self-Development		47	DDDDDDDDDDDDDDDD	38
	-5	42	OOOOOOO	21
	-5	42	AAAAAAA	21
14. Personnel Practices		52	DDDDDDDDDDDDDDDDDDDDDDDDD	58
		52	OOOOOOOOOOOOOOOOOOOOOOOOO	58
	+5	57	AAAAAAAAAAAAAAAAAAAAAAAAAAAAAAAAAAA	76
COMMUNITY				
*15. Community Relations		62	DDDDDDDDDDDDDDDDDDDDDDDDDDDDDDDDDDDDDDDDDDDD	88
	-9	53	OOOOOOOOOOOOOOOOOOOOOOOOOOO	62
	-13	49	AAAAAAAAAAAAAAAAAAAA	46
16. Outside Contacts		48	DDDDDDDDDDDDDDDDDD	42
		46	OOOOOOOOOOOOOO	34
		45	AAAAAAAAAAAAA	31

Normalized Standard Score Scale: 37.5 40 42.5 45 47.5 50 52.5 55 57.5 60 62.5

Centile Scale: 11 16 23 31 40 50 60 69 77 84 89

* Level I Executive Functions

dates for the vacant District Engineer positions would be found in the Assistant District Engineer group. The actual situation was that the Office Director (Professional Level I) profile most resembled the District Engineer profile. This information did not, however, surprise the research team since empirical research has shown (see Chapter 3) that there is considerable overlap in the functions performed by Level I executives regardless of hierarchy. After the Office Directors, the composite profile for the Construction and Maintenance Engineers most resembled that of the District Engineers.

The job function importance profiles for the District Engineer, Office Director, and Assistant District Engineer positions are shown in Figure 7.19, which is a graphic representation of the similarities and differences in the functions performed by these groups of employees. The important job functions for high-level executives have been marked by an asterisk in Figure 7.19. When comparing the scores of the Assistant District Engineers and of the Office Directors with those of the District Engineers on these factors, it will be seen that the job function profile for the Assistant District Engineer position has significantly lower importance scores for five of the eight important executive job functions (factors 1, 6, 7, 11, and 15), as compared with three out of eight significant differences (factors 7, 11, and 15) for the Office Directors. The differences among these groups are also emphasized by an examination of the functions where the importance score exceeds that of the District Engineers. The Office Directors exceed the District Engineers on the clearly technical function of Developing Technical Ideas (5); Interdepartmental Coordination (4), which has been found to be characteristic of the professional hierarchy; and on Work Practices (3). The Assistant District Engineers, on the other hand, exceed the District Engineers on factors that deal with the direct supervision of the work force such as Supervisory Practices (12), Promoting Safety (9), Coping with Emergencies (8), and with personnel issues as exemplified by Personnel Practices (14).

The argument can be made (and the composite ability job profiles demonstrate) that employees develop job skills in the functions that they are called upon to perform. If this is the case, then Office Directors would be the presently best qualified successors for a District Engineer position. Perhaps, however, it is more important and fairer to ask whether or not Assistant District Engineers could readily acquire facility in the higher-level job functions if they were given the opportunity to do so. The most direct way of answering this question is through a comparison of the test battery scores of the two groups. The average scores of the two groups on 15 of the most predictive scores in the test battery for this hierarchy are shown in Figure 7.20. Figure 7.20 clearly indicates that the Assistant District Engineer group is significantly lower than the District Engineer group in some important characteristics that have been shown to be im-

Figure 7.20

Average Test Scores for the District Engineer (D), Office Director (O), and Assistant District Engineer (A) Groups

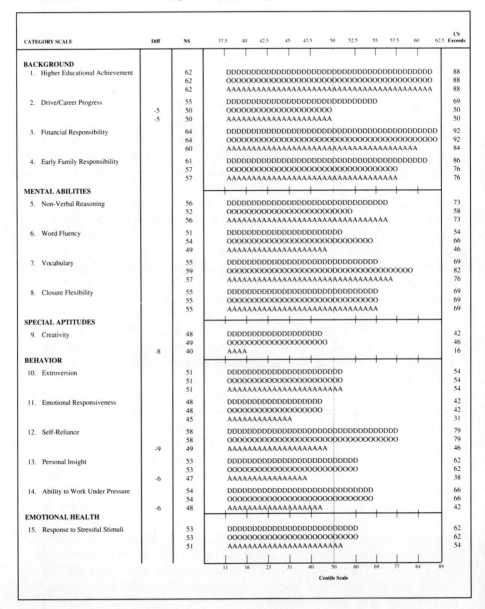

CATEGORY SCALE	Diff	NS	(Centile Scale chart)	CS Exceeds
BACKGROUND				
1. Higher Educational Achievement		62	DDDDDDDDDDDDDDDDDDDDDDDDDDDDDDDDDDDDDDDD	88
		62	OOOOOOOOOOOOOOOOOOOOOOOOOOOOOOOOOOOOOOOO	88
		62	AAAAAAAAAAAAAAAAAAAAAAAAAAAAAAAAAAAAAAAA	88
2. Drive/Career Progress		55	DDDDDDDDDDDDDDDDDDDDDDDDDDDDDD	69
	-5	50	OOOOOOOOOOOOOOOOOOOOO	50
	-5	50	AAAAAAAAAAAAAAAAAAAAA	50
3. Financial Responsibility		64	DDDDDDDDDDDDDDDDDDDDDDDDDDDDDDDDDDDDDDDDDDDDD	92
		64	OOOOOOOOOOOOOOOOOOOOOOOOOOOOOOOOOOOOOOOOOOOOO	92
		60	AAAAAAAAAAAAAAAAAAAAAAAAAAAAAAAAAAAAAAAA	84
4. Early Family Responsibility		61	DDDDDDDDDDDDDDDDDDDDDDDDDDDDDDDDDDDDDDDDD	86
		57	OOOOOOOOOOOOOOOOOOOOOOOOOOOOOOOOOOO	76
		57	AAAAAAAAAAAAAAAAAAAAAAAAAAAAAAAAAAA	76
MENTAL ABILITIES				
5. Non-Verbal Reasoning		56	DDDDDDDDDDDDDDDDDDDDDDDDDDDDDDDD	73
		52	OOOOOOOOOOOOOOOOOOOOOOOOOO	58
		56	AAAAAAAAAAAAAAAAAAAAAAAAAAAAAAAA	73
6. Word Fluency		51	DDDDDDDDDDDDDDDDDDDDDDD	54
		54	OOOOOOOOOOOOOOOOOOOOOOOOOOOO	66
		49	AAAAAAAAAAAAAAAAAAA	46
7. Vocabulary		55	DDDDDDDDDDDDDDDDDDDDDDDDDDDDDD	69
		59	OOOOOOOOOOOOOOOOOOOOOOOOOOOOOOOOOOOOOO	82
		57	AAAAAAAAAAAAAAAAAAAAAAAAAAAAAAAAAA	76
8. Closure Flexibility		55	DDDDDDDDDDDDDDDDDDDDDDDDDDDDDD	69
		55	OOOOOOOOOOOOOOOOOOOOOOOOOOOO	69
		55	AAAAAAAAAAAAAAAAAAAAAAAAAAAAAA	69
SPECIAL APTITUDES				
9. Creativity		48	DDDDDDDDDDDDDDDDDDD	42
		49	OOOOOOOOOOOOOOOOOOO	46
	-8	40	AAAA	16
BEHAVIOR				
10. Extroversion		51	DDDDDDDDDDDDDDDDDDDDDDD	54
		51	OOOOOOOOOOOOOOOOOOOOOOOO	54
		51	AAAAAAAAAAAAAAAAAAAAAAAA	54
11. Emotional Responsiveness		48	DDDDDDDDDDDDDDDDDDD	42
		48	OOOOOOOOOOOOOOOOOO	42
		45	AAAAAAAAAAAA	31
12. Self-Reliance		58	DDDDDDDDDDDDDDDDDDDDDDDDDDDDDDDDDDDD	79
		58	OOOOOOOOOOOOOOOOOOOOOOOOOOOOOOOOOOOO	79
	-9	49	AAAAAAAAAAAAAAAAAAA	46
13. Personal Insight		53	DDDDDDDDDDDDDDDDDDDDDDDDD	62
		53	OOOOOOOOOOOOOOOOOOOOOOOOO	62
	-6	47	AAAAAAAAAAAAAAAA	38
14. Ability to Work Under Pressure		54	DDDDDDDDDDDDDDDDDDDDDDDDDDDD	66
		54	OOOOOOOOOOOOOOOOOOOOOOOOOOOO	66
	-6	48	AAAAAAAAAAAAAAAAAA	42
EMOTIONAL HEALTH				
15. Response to Stressful Stimuli		53	DDDDDDDDDDDDDDDDDDDDDDDDD	62
		53	OOOOOOOOOOOOOOOOOOOOOOOOO	62
		51	AAAAAAAAAAAAAAAAAAAAAAAA	54

Scale (top): 37.5 40 42.5 45 47.5 50 52.5 55 57.5 60 62.5

Centile Scale (bottom): 11 16 23 31 40 50 60 69 77 84 89

portant for managerial success such as Drive/Career Progress (2), Creativity (9), Self-Reliance (12), Ability to Work Under Pressure (14), and Personal Insight (13), which facilitates Interpersonal relations.

It must be remembered, however, that these are group results and that there may be individuals within any of the groups who have the requisite qualifications for the District Engineer position. It was decided that all employees in the eight occupational groups would be regarded as potential candidates for a District Engineer position and would be included in the succession planning program.

Preparation for a Succession Planning Program

Estimates of Potential for Successful Performance and Job Skill Estimates were developed for all employees for the three levels in both the Line and Professional hierarchies. The six positions in these two hierarchies covered the possible vertical and lateral movements of this particular work force. A computerized human resource data bank that included the potential and skill estimates and other essential information about the employee was developed. Suggestions are given below for the content of such a data bank.

Personal Data

1. Identifying code number and the name of the employee.
2. Job-related educational history, fields of study, degrees earned, and total years of education.

Work History

3. Number of organizations in which employee was previously employed.
4. Years of relevant previous job experience.
5. Date of hiring and title of the first position held in the organization.
6. Dates of successive promotions and titles held in the organization.

Results of Evaluation Procedures

7. Results of the organization's regularly implemented performance appraisals in each position held in the organization.
8. Estimates of Potential for Successful Performance, updated as required for decision making or at two- to three-year intervals, obtained from the STEP program, together with scores on the predictor profiles.
9. Job Skill Assessments, updated as required for position moves or two- to three-year intervals, obtained from the STEP program together with skill levels on the sixteen MP-JFI functions.

Computer program software is available commercially for identifying employees who possess stated requirements for a given position in the organization or for classifying employees with respect to single or various combinations of the characteristics listed above. The implementation of this process in the Highway Division identified a number of candidates with excellent potential for the District Engineer position in the Office Director group and also some in the Assistant District Engineer group. The process also identified the focused experience and coaching required in the various job functions for full utilization of potential and high performance in the position for the selected candidates.

One important element in the utilization of higher-level personnel is a periodic review of the individual's strengths and weaknesses and the formulation of programs for training and development. This usually occurs at critical points in the individual's career with an organization, such as time of hire, at performance appraisals, when the individual is being considered for promotion or special assignment, and in the course of outplacement. The general context of the procedure is a career counseling conference. The structure of a career counseling conference, steps in its implementation, and the measured impact of a conference on participants in the program are described in Chapter 8.

8

The Career Counseling Conference

The career counseling conference described here is a blend between the standardized interpretation of profiled ability and interest measures and clinical or therapeutic procedures that often utilize projective tests and require considerable interpretation on the part of the counselor. The career counseling conference does, however, differ from these procedures in at least two significant respects. The first is that it is firmly anchored in an analysis of the job, and the second is that it employs the two STEP measurement systems that pertain, respectively, to the demands of the job and to the abilities, skills, and attributes of the individual. For effective interpretation and counseling, the counselor should have a strong background in behavioral theory and a sound knowledge of the relationships among the two measurement systems.

The career counseling conference can be used at any stage in the career of the individual. Some of its most frequent uses are for the selection and placement of individuals into key executive or professional positions in organizations, for selection among employed personnel for promotion into a management position, for counseling with a failing employee, and for outplacement. It has also been extensively used, either with individuals or on a small-group basis of ten to twenty employees, in organizational programs for self-directed development of higher-level personnel. The procedure for individuals is described below.

STRUCTURE AND CONTENT OF THE CAREER COUNSELING CONFERENCE

The career counseling conference can be based on the information from either the STEP-STC or the abbreviated STEP-ST program. The major difference between these programs is that the STEP-STC provides profiled scores of the behavioral dimensions of all tests in the battery, whether or not they contribute to the estimates of potential for successful performance. These additional dimension scores provide information about the individual's adjustment to the early developmental environments, the relationships in the personal family environment, and about relatively permanent behavior tendencies. This information helps to explain the later behavior of the individual and is very useful in a counseling situation.

Information Available for the Career Counseling Conference

The full array of information available for the career counseling conference is outlined below.

Work history and experience. Information about the individual's educational qualifications and previous work history is most efficiently obtained through use of a personal history questionnaire. The questionnaire can be completed either by mail or before the testing session. Other useful information that can be obtained from the questionnaire concerns the most and least liked aspects of the various positions held, the reasons for leaving a position, and the individual's perception of future career goals and objectives.

A profile of the individual's scores for the relative importance of the functions to be performed in the position and the job analysis standards with which to compare them (optional). The individual's concept of the job is determined through his or her use of the Managerial and Professional Job Functions Inventory—Importance. A comparison of the individual's Importance profile with established standards for the importance of the functions to be performed in the position provides useful information about the individual's concept of his or her job priorities. If the results of a job analysis are not available, the relevant national occupational group Importance standard can be used for the comparison. This procedure is optional but is included here in order to describe the full career counseling conference.

A profile of the individual's ability scores on the job functions and the job analysis standards with which to compare them. The individual's ability or competency levels are obtained through use of the Managerial and Professional Job Functions Inventory—Ability and the Importance levels from the job analysis. A comparison of the individual's ability scores with the relevant national occupational group standards makes it possible to obtain the individual's Job Skill Assessments (JSAs) at three levels of functioning in any selected hierarchy, as described in Chapter 7.

The individual's scores on the test battery and the national occupational group standards with which to compare them. The test scores can be obtained from either the STEP-STC or STEP-ST batteries. The occupational norms are the composite profiles of national samples of employees in the individual's present and possible future positions. Given the validity information concerning the test scores that best predict performance in the various positions, it is possible to develop estimates of Potential for Successful Performance (PSP) at each of the three levels of functioning in any selected hierarchy, as described in Chapter 7.

The Steps in the Career Counseling Conference

Although the career counseling conference is structured, with clearly defined objectives for its successive steps, it is not inflexible. The style of the particular counselor or the expressed needs and behavior of the individual seeking counseling may dictate different approaches or starting points. However, the steps described below provide a general framework within which the career counseling conference can be conducted. The structure of the process also ensures uniformity when a number of career counselors are involved. A full description of the successive steps in the procedure will be illustrated through the use of a case study of a "stopped career path." The successive steps in the career counseling conference are as follows:

1. Review of work history and experience.
2. Classification of the position by hierarchy and level.
3. Selection of relevant reference norms for the interpretation of test results.
4. Examination of the individual's concept of the relative importance of the functions to be performed on the job (optional).
5. Examination of the individual's job competencies and the identification of training needs for present and possible future positions.
6. Analysis of the individual's potential for successful performance and identification of strengths and weaknesses through the detailed interpretation of test results.
7. Discussion of career options and the possible consequences of each option.

INTERPRETATION OF THE RESULTS OF A CASE STUDY OF A STOPPED CAREER PATH

A very frequent career decision in the life of a qualified professional who has been successful in a professional capacity is whether or not to move to a position with managerial responsibility. There are at least two critical issues for the individual and the employing organization. First, is there real evidence of managerial potential and does the individual have the attributes and outlook that would facilitate effective interaction with management peers in the organization? Second, is there evidence of motivation to succeed in a management position or would the necessary withdrawal from the professional/technical aspects of the work cause undue frustration?

The first step into management for a professional usually involves the direction and coordination of the work of technical specialists or other professionals. The fail rate in this position is generally not too high since the job often requires some professional work, and, in addition, much of the managerial authority stems from professional reputation and expertise. It is nevertheless an important decision point since, unless the individual has the required managerial skills, he or she will be unable to progress to higher levels of management where there is increasing overlap in the managerial requirements of line managers and the managers of professionals.

It is at this stage, generally faced in the 30- to 40-year age bracket, where the individual finds him or herself passed over for promotion, sees the winding down of a previously "fast track" career, and faces the unpalatable prospect of a dead-end job for the remainder of his or her employment in the organization.

The job ability and test battery profiles discussed below are composites of "stopped career path" individuals who participated in career counseling conferences as part of the curriculum of the three-week management development seminars conducted by The University of Chicago. To facilitate the description of the career counseling procedure, the composite profile is referred to as that belonging to an individual called Max Westin.

Work History and Experience

The first step is a review of the individual's educational background and employment history. The responsibilities of the individual's present position are discussed along with the possibilities for upward or lateral movements in the organizational structure.

Mr. Westin's career progressed along traditional lines. After graduation from high school, he enrolled in a four-year mechanical engineering program at a state university. While at college he earned 50% of his tuition payments through mechanically oriented part-time and summer jobs. After graduation he was hired by the present organization as a nonmanagement professional, with the understanding that after gaining the requisite experience he would be enrolled in a management-training program and promoted to the first level of management.

Occupational Classification

At the conclusion of this section of the conference, a mutual decision is made concerning the classification of the individual's position with respect to a particular managerial hierarchy and the level of functioning within the hierarchy.

The classification of Mr. Westin's position is quite straightforward. As a university-qualified engineer he assumed a nonmanagement (Level III) position in the Professional managerial hierarchy. He then moved to a middle-level manager of professionals (Level II) position and has since been bypassed several times. He now wonders why he does not move into the executive ranks (Level I) in either the Line or the Professional managerial hierarchies.

Selection of the Relevant Reference Norms for the Interpretation of the Test Results

Next, the individual must indicate the occupational group reference norms to be used in the interpretation of the test results and the development of the PSPs. In addition to estimates of potential for the present position, the most common requests are for estimates of potential for the next higher position in the hierarchy. Except in the Line hierarchy, this involves a switch from staff professional, sales, or technical-specialist positions into management. Occasionally, the request involves a switch in hierarchy such as a chemical engineer considering a position involving the sale of chemical products.

Mr. Westin and the counselor agreed to the use of the two sets of reference norms for the interpretation of Mr. Westin's test results. These were the norms for the middle-management position (Level II), which he presently holds, and those of executive (Level I), the position to which he aspires in the Professional hierarchy.

Job Concept (optional)

Mr. Westin's concept of the priorities of the functions to be performed in his position is analyzed by comparing his job function Importance profile with the job function Importance standard obtained from the job analysis conducted for his middle-management position. If a job analysis is not available, the relevant national occupational group standard can be used in the comparison. The comparisons of Max Westin's MP-JFI Importance profile with the job analysis standard is shown in Figure 8.1.

An examination of the profiles in Figure 8.1 reveals, first, that the job analysis standard (represented by NNN on the profile) is very similar to the national occupational group norm for middle managers in the Professional hierarchy (represented by an M on the profile). On only three of the sixteen job function dimensions—(3) Improving Work Procedures, (16) Promoting Community/Organization Relations, and (8) Coping with Emergencies—do the differences be-

Figure 8.1
A Comparison of Max Westin's MP-JFI Importance Profile with the Job Analysis Standard

	SS Scale	25	30	35	40	45	50	55	60	65	70	75	CS Exceeds
ORGANIZATION													
1. SETTING ORGANIZATIONAL OBJECTIVES Formulating the overall mission and goals of the organization and setting short and long-range objectives which are significant and measurable.	63 64	•••••••••••••••••••••••••••••••P•••••M•••E NNNNNNNNNNNNNNNNNNNNNNNNNNNNNNN											90%
2. FINANCIAL PLANNING AND REVIEW Making economic decisions and managing capital assets; establishing a budget and controls to assure that the budget is met.	53 56	••••••••••••••••••••••••••••••EMP NNNNNNNNNNNNNNNNNNNNNNNNNNNN											62%
3. IMPROVING WORK PROCEDURES AND PRACTICES Analyzing, interpreting, and evaluating operating policies; initiating and formulating improved procedures and policies.	52 *60	•••••••••••••••••••••••••P••EM NNNNNNNNNNNNNNNNNNNNNNNNNNNNNN											58%
4. INTERDEPARTMENTAL COORDINATION Understanding and coordinating the problems and work activities of different departments within the organization.	54 55	•••••••••••••••••••••••••••••EMP NNNNNNNNNNNNNNNNNNNNNNNNNN											66%
LEADERSHIP													
5. DEVELOPING AND IMPLEMENTING TECHNICAL IDEAS Originating technical ideas and designs; translating technical ideas into feasible solutions to organizational needs.	46 47					EM		P					34%
						NNNNNNNNNNNNNNNNNN							
6. JUDGEMENT AND DECISION MAKING Analyzing incomplete information to make decisions; acting upon decisions concerning resource and work force allocation.	56 55	•••••••••••••••••••••P•••••M•••E NNNNNNNNNNNNNNNNNNNNNNNNNNNN											73%
7. DEVELOPING GROUP COOPERATION AND TEAMWORK Encouraging and building work group relations that will lead to better exchange of ideas, more open communication and higher morale.	55 58	•••••••••••••••••••••P•••••EM NNNNNNNNNNNNNNNNNNNNNNNNNNNNNN											69%
8. COPING WITH DIFFICULTIES AND EMERGENCIES Working efficiently under pressure; effectively handling unexpected problems, day-to-day crises and emergency situations.	41 *30	•••••••••••EM NNNNN						P					18%
9. PROMOTING SAFETY ATTITUDES AND PRACTICES Taking responsibility for the identification and elimination of job safety and health hazards.	46 47	••••••••••••EM NNNNNNNNNNNNNNNNNNNN						P					34%
		1%	2%	7%	16%	31%	50%	69%	84%	93%	98%	99%	

	SS Scale	25	30	35	40	45	50	55	60	65	70	75	CS Exceeds
10. COMMUNICATIONS Monitoring and improving both external communication channels and internal upward and downward lines.	56	••••••••••••••••••••••P•••••EM											73%
	52	NNNNNNNNNNNNNNNNNNN											
HUMAN RESOURCES **11. DEVELOPING EMPLOYEE POTENTIAL** Evaluating employees' present performance and potential in order to create opportunities for better use of their abilities.	55	••••••••••••••••••••••••P•••••EM											69%
	56	NNNNNNNNNNNNNNNNNNNNNNNNNNNN											
12. SUPERVISORY PRACTICES Clarifying subordinates' job functions and responsibilities and motivating employees while maintaining discipline and control.	53	••••••••••••••••••••••P•••••E•M											62%
	56	NNNNNNNNNNNNNNNNNNNNNNNNNNNNNN											
13. SELF DEVELOPMENT AND IMPROVEMENT Formulating self-improvement goals; using feedback from others to help assess one's own strengths and weaknesses and coordinating personal career goals with organizational needs.	46	•••••••••••••••••••EM	P										62%
	42	NNNNNNNNNNNNNNNN											
14. PERSONNEL PRACTICES Ensuring that the organization adheres to federal equal opportunity and affirmative action requirements and implementing special recruiting and training programs for minority applicants.	55	•••••••••••••••••••••••••••••P••ME											69%
	54	NNNNNNNNNNNNNNNNNNNNNNNNNNN											
COMMUNITY **15. PROMOTING COMMUNITY-ORGANIZATION RELATIONS** Staying informed on community, social, economic, and political problems and their relevance and impact upon the organization.	56	••••••••••••••••••••••••M•••••E•••P											73%
	58	NNNNNNNNNNNNNNNNNNNNNNNNNNNNNNN											
16. HANDLING OUTSIDE CONTACTS Promoting the organization and its products to outside contacts and clients and properly conveying the organization's relationship with them.	49	•••••••••••••••••••ME	P										46%
	50	NNNNNNNNNNNNNNNNNNNNNNN											

1% 2% 7% 16% 31% 50% 69% 84% 93% 98% 99%

* Significant Difference   NNN Job Analysis Standard
•••• Max Westin's Score
National Occupational Group Standards for : E-Executives, M-Middle Managers, and P-Professionals

211

tween these two standards approach the five standard score points required for a significant difference between two composite profiles. Furthermore, since coping with emergencies is not an important function for the position, this difference is of no consequence. The conclusion to be drawn is that the middle-management position in Mr. Westin's organization is at the same level of functioning as that of corresponding positions in similar organizations throughout the United States.

A comparison of Mr. Westin's Importance scores (represented by dotted lines on the profile) with the job analysis standard (represented by NNN on the profile) reveals that there are only two job functions where the difference reaches the seven standard score points required for significance when comparing an individual and a composite profile. The difference on Improving Work Procedures is indicated by a minus sign in the SS scale column, since Mr. Westin's score is below that of the job analysis standard, and by a plus sign on Coping with Emergencies, since the reverse situation exists here. The latter difference, however, is again trivial since this is not an important function for the position. The conclusion to be drawn here is that Mr. Westin has a very accurate concept of his job. He sees his job priorities in much the same way as do other middle managers in the Professional hierarchy. Whatever difficulties he may be experiencing on the job, therefore, are not due to a faulty conception of what has to be accomplished in the position.

When there are significant differences between an incumbent's job Importance profile and the job analysis standard, this is generally not because entirely different functions have been regarded as important, but more often because a larger number of functions have been regarded as important by the incumbent. When the additional functions are those that are important at lower occupational levels, the incumbent may have produced an accurate description of the job if he or she is employed in a small organization with less specialization in the functions performed. This would be especially likely if the incumbent's profile were compared with the national norms for the position rather than the job analysis standard. Given relevant norms, the inclusion of additional lower-level functions by the incumbent often indicates a failure to delegate previously performed functions in order to concentrate on the higher-level managerial functions required in the present position.

Job Competencies and the Identification of Training Needs

Training needs are identified by comparing the individual's MP-JFI—Ability scores with the job analysis Importance reference standard established for the position. If the results of a job analysis are not available, the individual's Ability scores may be compared with the relevant national occupational group standard for the position. In this instance, it is the middle management (M) standard for the Professional hierarchy. A comparison of Max Westin's MP-JFI—Ability profile with the job analysis standard is shown in Figure 8.2. It must be emphasized that the concern is not one of overall profile similarity but to determine if there are significant deficiencies in ability on the functions that have been identified as important for the position. Significant deficiencies have been indicated by a minus sign in Figure 8.2. A summary of the results of the comparison of Max Westin's MP-JFI—Ability scores and the job analysis standard is given in Figure 8.3.

The summary row in Figure 8.3 indicates that Mr. Westin has the necessary ability levels in some of the administrative, organization, and community job functions but that there are significant deficiencies in some of the middle management and also some of the executive functions. This pattern of abilities produced the Job Skills Assessments, which are ordinarily presented on the Summary of Results page of the STEP confidential report. For convenience, the Job Skill Assessments are reproduced below.

Level	Score	Percent	Skill Level
Executive	51	54	Good
Middle Mgr.	51	54	Good
Professional	54	66	Desirable

Mr. Westin is clearly still most competent in the professional job functions and has just better than average ability in the functions at the two managerial levels.

Potential for Successful Performance

The individual's test scores are compared with the relevant national occupational group test score means (standards) to identify strengths and weaknesses in the skills, abilities, and attributes that he or she can bring to bear in performing the job. Again, this is not an indiscriminate comparison on all of the test scores that comprise the test battery, but rather a comparison primarily of those test scores that have been identified through validation studies as important for performance in the given position. The comparisons for the most predictive test scores in the battery are shown in the Predictor Profile of the STEP Confidential Report. Max Westin's Predictor Profile in the Professional hierarchy is illustrated in Figure 8.4. If the STEP-STC program is used, the counselor has, in addition to the Predictor Profile, profiles of the dimension scores obtained from each individual test in the battery. A summary of Mr. Westin's identified strengths and weaknesses based on the complete STEP-STC report is given in Figure 8.5.

The particular pattern of strengths and weaknesses evident in Mr. Westin's test scores result in the estimates of Potential for Successful Perfor-

Figure 8.2
A Comparison of Max Westin's MP-JFI—Ability Scores with the Job Analysis Standard

	SS Scale	Scale (25–75) profile	CS Exceeds
ORGANIZATION			
1. SETTING ORGANIZATIONAL OBJECTIVES — Formulating the overall mission and goals of the organization and setting short and long-range objectives which are significant and measurable.	54 / − 64	P ... M E	66%
2. FINANCIAL PLANNING AND REVIEW — Making economic decisions and managing capital assets; establishing a budget and controls to assure that the budget is met.	55 / 56	EMP	69%
3. IMPROVING WORK PROCEDURES AND PRACTICES — Analyzing, interpreting, and evaluating operating policies; initiating and formulating improved procedures and policies.	60 / 60	P E M	84%
4. INTERDEPARTMENTAL COORDINATION — Understanding and coordinating the problems and work activities of different departments within the organization.	56 / 55	EMP	73%
LEADERSHIP			
5. DEVELOPING AND IMPLEMENTING TECHNICAL IDEAS — Originating technical ideas and designs; translating technical ideas into feasible solutions to organizational needs.	+ 56 / 47	EM ... P	73%
6. JUDGEMENT AND DECISION MAKING — Analyzing incomplete information to make decisions; acting upon decisions concerning resource and work force allocation.	43 / − 55	P ... M E	34%
7. DEVELOPING GROUP COOPERATION AND TEAMWORK — Encouraging and building work group relations that will lead to better exchange of ideas, more open communication and higher morale.	42 / − 58	P ... EM	31%
8. COPING WITH DIFFICULTIES AND EMERGENCIES — Working efficiently under pressure; effectively handling unexpected problems, day-to-day crises and emergency situations.	+ 44 / 30	EM ... P	27%
9. PROMOTING SAFETY ATTITUDES AND PRACTICES — Taking responsibility for the identification and elimination of job safety and health hazards.	53 / + 47	EM ... P	62%

Scale: 25 30 35 40 45 50 55 60 65 70 75

Percentiles: 1% 2% 7% 16% 31% 50% 69% 84% 93% 98% 99%

	SS Scale	CS Exceeds
10. COMMUNICATIONS Monitoring and improving both external communication channels and internal upward and downward lines.	− 40 / 52	16%
HUMAN RESOURCES **11. DEVELOPING EMPLOYEE POTENTIAL** Evaluating employees' present performance and potential in order to create opportunities for better use of their abilities.	− 48 / 56	42%
12. SUPERVISORY PRACTICES Clarifying subordinates' job functions and responsibilities and motivating employees while maintaining discipline and control.	− 44 / 56	27%
13. SELF DEVELOPMENT AND IMPROVEMENT Formulating self-improvement goals; using feedback from others to help assess one's own strengths and weaknesses and coordinating personal career goals with organizational needs.	46 / 42	34%
14. PERSONNEL PRACTICES Ensuring that the organization adheres to federal equal opportunity and affirmative action requirements and implementing special recruiting and training programs for minority applicants.	57 / 54	76%
COMMUNITY **15. PROMOTING COMMUNITY-ORGANIZATION RELATIONS** Staying informed on community, social, economic, and political problems and their relevance and impact upon the organization.	58 / 58	79%
16. HANDLING OUTSIDE CONTACTS Promoting the organization and its products to outside contacts and clients and properly conveying the organization's relationship with them.	54 / 50	66%

Scale: 25 30 35 40 45 50 55 60 65 70 75

Percentiles: 1% 2% 7% 16% 31% 50% 69% 84% 93% 98% 99%

− Significantly less ability than the standard
+ Significantly more ability than the standard
•••• Max Westin's Score
NNN Job Analysis Standard
National Occupational Group Standards for : E-Executives, M-Middle Managers, and P-Professionals

Figure 8.3
Summary of Max Westin's Job Skill Strengths and Weaknesses as Revealed by a Comparison of His MP–JFI—Ability Scores and the Job Analysis Standard

Job Skill Area	Salient Points	Implications
I. Organization	Has good ability on three of the four job functions in this area: Financial Planning, Improving Work Procedures, and Interdepartmental Coordination. Significantly low on Objective Setting.	May not yet have been exposed to, or have had the opportunity to participate in, the high level executive function of Setting Organizational Objectives.
II. Leadership	Ability profile deviates significantly from the job analysis standard on all six job functions in this area. Low scores for Decision Making, Developing Teamwork, and Communications. High scores for Technical Ideas, Coping with Emergencies, and Safety Practices.	The high scores in the clearly professional functions are not a drawback unless the professional functions are favored over the required management functions. Of greater concern are the low scores on Decision Making and Developing Teamwork which are requirements, respectively, for executive and middle management positions.
III. Human Resources	Significantly low ability scores on two of the four functions. These are: Developing Employee Potential and Supervisory Practices.	The two functions with low ability scores are both "group building" functions, which are important for his present middle management position.
IV. Community	Can satisfy the requirements of both functions in this area: Handling Outside Contacts and Promoting Community/Organization Relations.	These are strengths which could be utilized.
V. Summary	His strengths are in the administrative organization and community job functions. There are significant deficiencies in some of the middle management and executive functions.	Will need coaching in some of his present middle management functions and in higher-level functions if he is promoted. To aid his self-development, check the item responses for low ability factors. Also check the relevant test scores such as language skills (Communications) and behavioral attributes and emotional health for factors involving interpersonal relations.

mance, which are presented on the Summary of Results page of the STEP Confidential Report. For the convenience of the reader, this information is reproduced below.

Level	Score	Percent	Potential
Executive	50	50	Good
Middle Mgr.	50	50	Good
Professional	60	84	Very Desirable

Although this is not a universal occurrence, in Mr. Westin's case the corresponding potential estimates and the job skill levels shown previously are described very similarly at the three levels of the hierarchy.

Discussion of Career Options

Possible career options within the organization and, if necessary, outside the organization are discussed in the light of the estimates of potential and the identified strengths and weaknesses for the relevant positions. Further discussion centers around ways in which the identified strengths can be fully utilized, and identified weaknesses can either be remedied or compensated for.

There are a number of viable career options for Mr. Westin. He must, however, be brought to the realization that it is essential, for his present work efficiency and for his emotional health, that he make a deliberate career decision. Some viable alternatives are as follows:

1. *Move to a Level I managerial position.* His calculated potential for this position exceeds only 50% of the higher-level population (HLP). If such a move is made, therefore, he should have coaching and organizational support. In addition, he must be aware that this will, initially, create different kinds of emotional tensions.

2. *Deliberately elect to stay in his present position.* Mr. Westin is financially comfortable, has a nice home and a boat. If this decision is made, he may wish to seek fulfillment of other goals outside the organization.

3. *Move to a higher position in a smaller company with a more supportive environment.* This option may fulfill ego needs but should be carefully discussed with his family if the move involves relocation. As for the first alternative, relocation and a move to a new work environment will, initially, create different kinds of emotional tensions.

The move to a Level I position may, of course, not be offered to Mr. Westin if there are a limited number of such positions in the organization and better qualified employees who are available to fill them. Under these circumstances, Mr. Westin will not only need to be reconciled but ac-

Figure 8.4
Max Westin's Scores on the Predictive Dimensions in the Professional Hierarchy

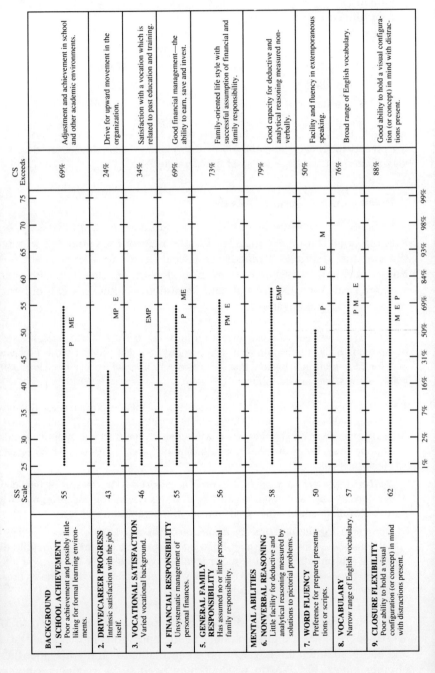

	SS Scale	25	30	35	40	45	50	55	60	65	70	75	CS Exceeds	
APTITUDES **10. CREATIVE POTENTIAL** Systematic and analytic approach to problem solving.	57						MP	E					76%	Intuitive thinking and potential for creative behavior.
TEMPERAMENT **11. PERSONAL INSIGHT** Inconsistency in self-ratings of behavior.	54						P	EM					66%	Demonstrated consistency in self-ratings of behavior.
12. EXTROVERSION Serious, persevering and consistent behavior.	47					P	ME						38%	Demonstrative, expressive and sometimes impulsive behavior.
13. EMOTIONAL RESPONSIVENESS Even-tempered, relaxed, undemonstrative behavior.	42					P	ME						21%	Emotionally responsive and enthusiastic behavior.
14. SELF-RELIANCE Group oriented behavior with emphasis on teamwork and group support.	43						P	M E					24%	Individually goal oriented and self-confident behavior.
EMOTIONAL ADJUSTMENT **15. LEVEL OF STRESS RESPONSE** Undesirably high level of stressful experiences.	45			P		M E							31%	Relatively low level of stressful experiences.
16. SOMATIC ADJUSTMENT Presence of physical complaints and depression, often associated with emotional conflict.	38				MEP								12%	Feeling of well-being and absence of physical complaints.
17. GENERAL ADJUSTMENT Apathy and general lack of enjoyment concerning everyday experiences.	44						EMP						27%	General buoyancy and healthy feelings of pleasure concerning everyday experiences.
		1%	2%	7%	16%	31%	50%	69%	84%	93%	98%	99%		

...... Max Westin's Score

National Occupational Group Standards for: E-Executives, M-Middle Managers, and P-Professionals in the Professional hierarchy

Figure 8.5
Summary of Max Westin's Strengths and Weaknesses in the Abilities, Skills, and Attributes Measured by the Managerial and Professional Test Battery

Area of Test Battery	Salient Points	Implications
I. Background and Experience	High achievement at school and as an adult. Successfully assumed personal family and fiscal responsibility. Has demonstrated acceptable leadership ability. The discrepancies in this area occur for the drive and vocational satisfaction scores which only exceed 24% and 34% of the Higher Level Population (HLP), respectively.	A generally achieving background. The low drive score does not indicate lack of ambition but rather that his career progress has not kept pace with that of his age peers. His lack of vocational satisfaction is probably a reflection of his feeling that he has been "passed over."
II. Mental Abilities	A very good level of general mental functioning which exceeds 76% of the HLP. Extremely high visual perceptual and reasoning skills. Word fluency is just average and below the executive standard.	The strong non-verbal skills are characteristic of well-functioning engineering professionals. The relatively low word fluency is a drawback and may contribute to the low score for Communications on the job skill profile.
III. Special Aptitudes	In addition to cognitive analytical skills he has creative potential which exceeds 76% of the HLP. He is independent in thought and action, has a high energy level, and works well under pressure.	His creative potential is one of his strengths which could be utilized in future job assignments or in the development of training programs.
IV. Temperament and Personality	Lacking in emotional responsiveness. Chief liability is lack of self-reliance. The latter is due largely to levels of decisiveness and self-confidence which only exceed 21% and 8% of the HLP, respectively.	Needs the support of a mentor or supervisor to help him to improve his self-confidence.
V. Personal-Emotional Adjustment	Has an undesirably high level of internal tension arising from feelings of inadequacy and anxiety. He is still able to maintain objectivity, and is coping, but at considerable personal cost.	In the interview, determine whether the stress is situational or of long duration. If the latter, is it a result chiefly of the work or of the home environment or both. What measures can be taken to relieve the stress?
Summary	He has an achieving past, intellectual assets, and creative potential. His liabilities are poor verbal skills, low self-reliance, and inner stress.	The inner tensions and emotional stress must be addressed before a career decision can be made. His options are to remain in his present position or to preceed to an executive position in the Professional hierarchy. In either case, he will need coaching and counseling.

tually to see some of the real advantages to staying in his present position if he is to remain productive there. Alternatively, he could engage in what is essentially outplacement counseling.

CASE STUDY INVOLVING SELECTION FROM AMONG HIGHLY QUALIFIED CANDIDATES

The main career issues in the "stopped career path" case study are whether or not the employee has a high enough level of potential and of acquired job skill to justify promotion to the executive level in the hierarchy and, should he be promoted, the kind and degree of training and organizational support that would be necessary to allow him to function effectively. A very different problem, which is often encountered when promoting into the few positions near the top of the organizational pyramid, is that of selecting from two or more highly qualified candidates.

It often happens that candidates for specialized, high-level positions are very similar with respect to their background, qualifications, and abilities. The present case study is based on real data for two candidates for the position of corporate legal counsel in a national insurance agency. Both candidates were in their forties, had established families, had completed bachelor and jurisprudence degrees at well-known universities, and had several years of experience in both nonmanagement professional and managerial positions. In order to preserve anonymity, the candidates will be referred to as David White and Sam Gove.

In addition to other information obtained in the course of the selection process, the results of the complete STEP-STC program were available for both candidates. The results are summarized here. The job skill assessments of the two candidates are shown in Table 8.1. Examination of Table 8.1 indicates that the candidates have comparable competency or skill levels for the executive position for which they are being considered and that Sam Gove has a slightly higher level of skill at the middle-management level. The summary of the job skill strengths and weaknesses is shown for the candidates, respectively, in Figures 8.6 and 8.7. Although the candidates' Job Skill Assessments are very similar, examination of Figures 8.6 and 8.7 shows that there are some differences in job skills that should be noted and, possibly, discussed in a personal interview. Both candidates have good Organization and Community Skills. There are some differences in the Leadership area, where David White has exceptional facility in Judgment and Decision Making but only average ability in Developing Teamwork, whereas Sam Gove's strength is Developing Teamwork. Sam Gove's ability in the "group-nurturing" Developing Teamwork function contributes to his "Very Desirable" Job Skill Assessment at the middle-management level of the hierarchy. One clear difference in job skills between the two candidates occurs for the Personnel

Table 8.1
Summary of the Job Skill Assessments of the Two Candidates in the Professional Hierarchy

David White			
Level	Score	Percent	Skill Level
Executive	57	76%	Very Desirable
Middle Manager	56	73%	Desirable
Professional	53	58%	Good

Sam Gove			
Level	Score	Percent	Skill Level
Executive	58	79%	Very Desirable
Middle Manager	59	82%	Very Desirable
Professional	51	54%	Good

Practices Function (which includes equal employment and affirmative action procedures), where Sam Gove is, rather surprisingly in view of his legal training, below average.

The potential estimates of the two candidates are shown in Table 8.2. Although both candidates have at least "Desirable" potential for successful performance, David White has consistently higher potential estimates at each level of the hierarchy. The reasons for the differences in the candidates' estimates of potential can be explained by comparing the summary of strengths and weaknesses shown for the candidates in Figures 8.8 and 8.9.

The candidates are almost identical with respect to their background and experience and very similar in their intellectual skills. The differences between the candidates surface in the special aptitude and temperament and personality areas of the test protocol. David White has an exceptional level of creative potential as compared with Sam Gove's above average level. David White also has an exceptionally high level of self-reliance combined with a perceptible absence of social skills. By contrast, Sam Gove has a good level of self-reliance but is also highly socially oriented and socially at ease. Finally, both candidates have a sound level of personal emotional adjustment.

The level of job skill will not be an important factor in making a choice between these two high-potential candidates since both are experienced and certainly bright enough to remedy any identified job skill deficiency. Rather, the choice is between an individual, represented by David White, who has some exceptional talents combined with personality characteristics that will require a particular type of working environment to allow

Figure 8.6
Summary of David White's Job Skill Strengths and Weaknesses as Revealed by a Comparison of His MP-JFI—Ability Scores and the Job Analysis Standard

Job Skill Area	Salient Points	Implications
I. Organization	Very high ability levels in Objective Setting and Improving Work Procedures. Exceeds only 31% and 38% of the HLP, respectively, on Financial Planning & Interdepartmental Coordination.	Has clear facility in the administrative and directive functions. Needs training in Interdepartmental Coordination. Low scores on Financial Planning not unusual in Professional hierarchy.
II. Leadership	His ability for Judgment and Decision Making exceeds 96% of the HLP but he has only average ability for Developing Teamwork.	Undoubted intellect, self-reliance, and decisiveness probably contribute to exceptional facility in Judgment and Decision Making. Average score for Developing Teamwork may reflect poor interpersonal skills.
III. Human Resources	Average ability in Developing Employee Potential. Exceeds 95% of the HLP in equal employment and affirmative action aspects of Personnel Practices.	Very well qualified in this area for a Corporate Legal Counsel position.
IV. Community	Exceeds 88% of the HLP in Promoting Community/Organization Relations.	A good representative for the organization in professional and community settings.
V. Summary	Overall, has a "Very Desirable" Job Skill Assessment at the executive level in the Professional hierarchy.	Clearly acceptable for the position and worth training in relatively low areas if these are important for the job.

Figure 8.7
Summary of Sam Gove's Job Skill Strengths and Weaknesses as Revealed by a Comparison of His MP-JFI—Ability Scores and the Job Analysis Standard

Job Skill Area	Salient Points	Implications
I. Organization	High ability levels in Objective Setting, Improving Work Procedures, and Interdepartmental Coordination. Low in Financial Planning.	Has generally good ability in the Organization job functions. Low scores on Financial Planning are not unusual in the Professional hierarchy.
II. Leadership	High ability, which exceeds 90% of the HLP, in Judgment and Decision Making and also above average ability in Developing Group Cooperation and Teamwork.	Has facility in both the intellectual and interpersonal job functions.
III. Human Resources	Very good ability to Develop Employee Potential but just below average on Personnel Practices.	The just below average score on the equal employment and affirmative action aspects of Personnel Practices should be probed in the personal interview.
IV. Community	Exceeds 86% of the HLP in Promoting Community/Organization Relations.	A good representative for the organization in professional and community settings.
V. Summary	Overall, has a "Very Desirable" Job Skill Assessment at the executive Level in the Professional hierarchy.	In addition to "Very Desirable" executive skills, he also has "Very Desirable" middle management group nurturing skills. Worth training in low areas. Generally impressive job skills.

Table 8.2
Summary of Potential Estimates of the Two Candidates in the Professional Hierarchy

David White			
Level	Score	Percent	Potential
Executive	61	86%	Outstanding
Middle Manager	60	84%	Very Desirable
Professional	57	76%	Very Desirable

Sam Gove			
Level	Score	Percent	Potential
Executive	55	69%	Desirable
Middle Manager	56	73%	Desirable
Professional	53	62%	Desirable

him to be fully productive; and a more down-to-earth Sam Gove with well-rounded abilities and the interpersonal skills that will facilitate adjustment to most working environments. In other words, in a corporate culture that stresses individual performance and creativity, David White could perform brilliantly while Sam Gove's performance is likely to be sound but unexceptional. On the other hand, in a more traditional or conservative work environment, Sam Gove is likely to be a highly valued, consistently good performer and David White probably frustrated in his work and at odds with his peers.

If these conditions are made clear to a prospective employer, the choice between the two candidates rests ultimately with the organization. The purpose of this case study, however, is to demonstrate that the ability to give a behavioral interpretation of a test protocol and the measures that contribute to the potential estimates considerably enhances the likelihood of sound human resource decisions.

PARTICIPANT EVALUATIONS OF THE CAREER COUNSELING CONFERENCE

The major concern thus far has been with the technical soundness of the STEP program, procedures for its professional implementation, and its compliance with the requirements of the "Uniform Guidelines on Employee Selection Procedures" (1978). However, elegant research design, empirically demonstrated validity, and professional acceptance are only one side of the coin. Unless the participants (who may have taken up to four hours to complete the tests and a further hour-and-a-half in the ca-

Figure 8.8
Summary of David White's Strengths and Weaknesses in the Abilities, Skills, and Attributes Measured by the Managerial and Professional Test Battery

Area of Test Battery	Salient Points	Implications
I. Background and Experience	Very high vocational satisfaction and drive to achieve. Successful assumption of personal family and fiscal responsibility. Demonstrated leadership skills. Good adjustment to early parental and school environments.	An extremely achieving past and maintains drive for future achievement. Good early adjustment facilitates emotional adjustment in later life.
II. Mental Abilities	A very good level of general mental functioning which exceeds 79% of the HLP. Good language and analytical skills. Relatively poor visual perceptual skills.	Greatest intellectual assets are the language skills and, in particular, breadth of English vocabulary. The language skills are essential for success in management. Visual perceptual skills less important for management than for success in engineering or hard science professional positions.
III. Special Aptitudes	Extremely high level of creative potential which exceeds 98% of the HLP. Extremely independent. Prefers an autonomous work environment. High energy level and maintains productivity under pressure.	Will only work well in an autonomous environment where there is scope for innovative and creative behavior. Will need constant challenge. May irritate peers. Will benefit from having a systematic assistant or secretary.
IV. Temperament and Personality	Good insight and a firm self image. Self-reliance exceed 99% of the HLP. Very decisive. Is not talkative and does not seek company.	Such high levels of self-reliance and goal directedness often associated with insensitivity to the needs of others. Check social attitudes and peer relationships in the personal interview.
V. Personal-Emotional Adjustment	A generally sound level of personal-emotional adjustment, though some internal tension. Is realistic in his perceptions and maintains a reasonably buoyant outlook.	Will cope well with the inevitably increased stress associated with increased responsibility or unexpected changes.
Summary	No deficiencies evident. Well-differentiated assets, some at very high levels.	Often difficult to find the right environment for exceptionally creative and self-sufficient people. If suitably placed, they are capable of brilliant performance.

Figure 8.9
Summary of Sam Gove's Strengths and Weaknesses in the Abilities, Skills, and Attributes Measured by the Managerial and Professional Test Battery

Area of Test Battery	Salient Points	Implications
I. Background and Experience	Very high vocational satisfaction and drive to achieve. Successful assumption of personal family and fiscal responsibility. Demonstrated leadership skills. Good adjustment to early parental and school environments.	An extremely achieving past and maintains drive for future achievement. Good early adjustment facilitates emotional adjustment in later life.
II. Mental Abilities	A very good level of general mental functioning which exceeds 73% of HLP. Good language and analytical skills. Relatively poor visual perceptual skills.	Greatest intellectual assets are the language skills and, in particular, breadth of English vocabulary. The language skills are essential for success in management. Visual perceptual skills less important for management than for success in engineering or hard science professional positions.
III. Special Aptitudes	Above average creative potential which exceeds 66% of the HLP. Work involved and works well under pressure.	Is receptive to creative ideas but probably prefers analytic to intuitive approach to problem solving.
IV. Temperament and Personality	Average insight and good level of self-reliance, which exceed 70% of HLP. Is self-confident and decisive. Highly socially oriented, seeks company, and is socially at ease.	A well balanced personality. Ability to lead but also has good interpersonal skills. Socially well adjusted.
V. Personal-Emotional Adjustment	A generally sound level of personal-emotional adjustment. Inclined to be over-serious but generally free of hampering tensions.	Generally sound and able to manage unexpected stress.
Summary	No deficiencies evident but also no exceptional assets. Consistently good scores on all predictive test dimensions.	Likely to take more conventional approaches and to demonstrate all-around good performance. Probably interact well with all levels of employees.

reer counseling conference) perceive the procedure as being genuinely useful to them, it is likely to be short-lived in either an organization or seminar setting. It seemed necessary, therefore, to determine participants' reactions to the career counseling conference in relation to their knowledge of themselves and their developmental and career goals.

The career counseling conference has, for over a decade, been an integral part of the annual, three-week residential management development seminars conducted by The University of Chicago. The seminar setting provided favorable conditions for a controlled investigation of the reaction of participants, since the seminars are always held in the same physical environment in Vail, Colorado, and the career counseling conferences are all conducted by uniformly qualified faculty members using a generally similar structure for the conference. Furthermore, each content area of the seminar is routinely evaluated by participants on the last day of the seminar. It was possible, therefore, to include in the evaluation a specially constructed questionnaire concerning the career counseling conference without disrupting the seminar agenda or intruding on participants' free time. The focus for the remainder of this chapter is an analysis of participant responses to the career counseling evaluation questionnaire.

Implementation of the STEP Program in the Seminar Setting

In order to conserve conferees' time during the seminar, the untimed behavior inventories and the MP-JFI for both Importance and Ability are mailed to registered participants and must be completed by a given time prior to the commencement of the seminar. The profiled results of participants' assessment of the relative importance of the functions to be performed in their position, and of their ability to perform them, are available during the first week of the seminar when individual learning contracts and goals are established. The faculty guide the participants through the procedure for identifying training needs, and this information helps participants determine which of the concurrent workshops offered during the second week of the seminar would be most beneficial for them.

The remaining tests in the managerial and professional test battery are administered on the first day of the seminar and the completed test booklets returned to London House for machine scoring and profiling. At the beginning of the second week of the seminar, faculty members provide each participant with an hour-and-a-half to two-hour career counseling conference. The evaluation of the different content areas of the three-week seminar is done on the final day of the seminar.

The Evaluation Questionnaire

A 22-item questionnaire with a "Yes," "?," or "No" response format was developed to evaluate the impact and effectiveness of the career counseling conference. The questionnaire contained two types of items. The first type consisted of general questions such as their reaction to the conference as a whole, their perceived usefulness of the conference for career planning, their understanding of the information provided about the job, and their opinion of the national standards used for the interpretation of results.

The second type of item was directed specifically toward the acquisition of the information that the participant was expected to obtain in given areas of the test protocol. The stem of each item was, "as a result of the career counseling conference and feedback of results from the STEP program I: ____" (followed by the item). A copy of the complete questionnaire is given in Appendix 8.1 at the end of the chapter.

The Subjects

The subjects were participants in the seminars conducted during the years 1981 through 1983. There was a total of 267 predominantly male participants, of whom 213 completed the evaluations, for an approximate return of 80%. Of the 213 participants, 82 were drawn from Level I positions, 100 from Level II positions, and the remaining 31 from Level III positions across the four managerial hierarchies.

Results of Participant Evaluations

The items that dealt with the overall career counseling procedure were analyzed for the total group of participants. For the items that probed the effects of feedback for specific areas of the test protocol, the responses were analyzed for subgroups of participants who had scored high (one-half standard deviation above the mean), and low (one-half standard deviation below the mean) on the relevant test in the battery. For example, the responses to the item "Know where there is a need to develop some aspect of my language skills" were analyzed separately for high- and low-scoring subgroups on the objective tests of Word Fluency (Human Resources Center, 1961) and the Bruce Vocabulary Inventory (Bruce, 1959), since these two tests measure different aspects of language skills.

For each item, the percentage of favorable responses was calculated for the high- and low-scoring subgroups on the test dimensions. The "Yes" is the favorable response for all the general reaction items. For the specific items, the "Yes" is the favorable response when it represents the hoped-for outcome of the career counseling procedure for a particular scoring subgroup. For example, the "Yes" is the favorable response to the item "Know where there is a need to develop some aspect of my language skills" for the low-scoring subgroup. It would not be of great concern if the high-scoring subgroups on the two language tests did not respond to the item in the affirmative. By contrast, the "Yes" is the hoped-for and favorable response to the item "See how I can better harness my creativity for the common effort" for the high-scoring group on the measure of overall creative potential, and one would not expect the low-scoring subgroup to derive this particular insight from the procedure. In short, one objective of the evaluation was to determine how, and the extent to which, high- and low-scorers in the various areas of the test protocol reacted to the career counseling conference.

Evaluations Made by the Total Group of Participants

Results for the items for which responses were analyzed for the total group of participants are shown in Table 8.3. The first, very general, item that deals with career advice and relates to the career counseling procedure as a whole has 74% favorable response from participants. The next three items deal with past achievements, self-image, and compensation for deficiencies. They are still fairly general but do have indirect reference to the norms used in the interpretation of test results. The favorable responses for this group of three items average about 82%. The last three items in Table 8.3 refer specifically to the occupational group norms used in the interpretation of the profiles. One of the three items, "Have meaningful standards of comparison for my strengths and weaknesses," refers to the occupational group norms used in the interpretation of the test results and the remaining two items refer, respectively, to the Importance and Ability levels of the norm group on the MP-JFI. The favorable response for this group of these items is higher than 90%. In general, the results given in Table 8.3 suggest that favorability of response increases with the specificity of the item.

Evaluations Made by High- and Low-Scorers on Selected Scores from the Test Battery

The results of the statistical analysis of the evaluations made by the high- and low-scoring subgroups are summarized below for the various areas of the test protocol.

Experience and Background

There were no significant differences between the percentages of favorable response of high- and low-scoring subgroups to the questionnaire items related to dimension scores obtained from the Experience and Background Inventory (EBI) (Baehr & Froemel, 1980). For example, there were no differences in the responses to Item 4 in the questionnaire, "Know

Table 8.3
Percentage of Favorable Responses Made by the Total Group of Participants ($N=213$)

Item No.		% Favorable Response
22	Useful input for career change or promotion	74
3	Realistic comparison on my past achievements with those of my age peers	77
21	Generally positive self-image reinforced	84
20	Know better how to compensate for deficiencies	85
19	Have meaningful standards of comparison for my strengths and weaknesses	95
1	Know how my concept of the job compares with that of others in similar positions	92*
2	Know my ability levels with respect to the important job functions	94*

*Based on 1984 and 1985 seminars since these items were not previously included in the questionnaire (N = 119)

the relative extent to which I assume leadership roles in group activities and the implications of this behavior," of the high- and low-scoring subgroups on the Leadership and Group Participation dimension of the EBI. Similarly, there were no differences in the response of the high-scorers (good parental family adjustment) and the low-scorers (poor parental family adjustment) on the Parental Family Adjustment dimension of the EBI to Items 5 and 6. These were, "Have a better idea of how early developmental experiences have shaped my life," and "Have a better perspective of my relationships with members of my parental family." Furthermore, the questionnaire items in this sensitive area of interpersonal family relationships show some of the lowest percentages of favorable response (e.g., 47% for the high- and 38% for the low-scorers for Item 6) of any items in the evaluation questionnaire.

Mental Abilities and Aptitudes

By contrast, this area of the test battery showed some of the most differentiated subgroup responses. For Item 8, "Know where there is a need to develop some aspect of my language skills," the low-scoring groups on the test of Word Fluency (Human Resources Center, 1961) gave 94% ($N=16$) favorable "Yes" responses as compared with 63% ($N=93$) for the corresponding high-scoring group. Similar results were obtained from the Bruce Vocabulary Inventory (Bruce, 1959) where the low-scorers gave 100% ($N = 19$) favorable responses as compared with 62% ($N = 114$) for the high-scorers. The difference between the word fluency groups was significant at the .01, and between the vocabulary groups at the .001, level of confidence.

High-scorers on the measure of overall creative potential obtained from the Cree Questionnaire (Thurstone & Mellinger, 1957/1985) gave a 68% ($N = 59$) favorable response to Item 9, "See how I can better harness my creativity for the common effort," as compared with only 44% ($N = 50$) for the low-scoring group, with a resulting difference that was significant at the .01 level of confidence. Conversely, it was the low-scorers on the measure of overall creative potential who gave a significantly higher percentage of favorable responses to Items 10 and 11 in the questionnaire, "See ways in which I can compensate for my own lack of creativity," and "See the advantage of utilizing the creativity of peers and subordinates." The actual percentages of the low- and high-scoring groups for the two items were, respectively, 64% ($N = 60$) versus 18% ($N = 60$), $p < .001$; and 88% ($N = 49$) versus 77% ($N = 61$), $p < .01$.

Measures in the Normal Range of Behavior

Three measures in the normal range of behavior used in the evaluations were derived from the Temperament Comparator (TC) (Baehr, 1957/1985). High-scorers on the Self-reliance dimension (individuals who are more self-reliant) gave a significantly higher percentage of affirmative responses than the low-scoring group to Items 12 and 13 in the questionnaire; these items deal with the perception of the self. They were "Have a better understanding of my own personality functioning," and "Have a clear picture of the image I portray to my supervisors and associates." The percentages for the high- and low-scoring subgroups on the two items were, respectively, 93% ($N = 88$) versus 80% ($N = 41$), $p < .05$; and 85% ($N = 88$) versus 76% ($N = 41$), $p < .05$. In addition, for the item dealing with an understanding of their personality functioning, high-scorers on the Personal Insight dimension give a higher percentage of affirmative responses (94%, $N = 78$) than the low-scoring group (84%, $N = 38$) resulting in a difference that was significant at the .05 level of confidence.

There is an interesting contrast in the responses to the two questionnaire items dealing with emotional responsiveness. For Item 15, "See the need to tone down my somewhat too volatile behavior," the responses are in the expected direction, with the high-scoring group on the Emotional Responsiveness dimension showing a higher percentage of affirmative responses (55%, $N = 68$) than the low-scorers (9%, $N = 47$) for a difference that was significant at the .001 level of confidence. On the other hand, Item 14, "Realize the effects on others of my too rigid control over spontaneity and responsiveness" receives an undifferentiated (46%, 52%) response from the two subgroups.

Screening Procedures for Emotional Health

The last part of the test protocol consists of scores in a screening procedure for emotional health obtained from the Emo Questionnaire (Baehr & Baehr, 1958/1986). The percentages of favorable responses of groups composed of individuals who had failed (scored below 40 on the standard score scale) compared with those who had passed on the Internal Adjustment factor, which is a measure of internal tension and stress, were in the expected direction for two questionnaire items. For Item 16, "Feel reassured that I am coping quite well in a tension filled world," the passing group has a higher percentage of affirmative responses (83%, $N = 139$) than the group of individuals who had failed (61%, $N = 57$), which resulted in a difference that was significant at the .001 level of confidence. Conversely, the group composed of individuals who had failed the screening procedure gave a higher percentage of affirmative response (65%, $N = 57$) to Item 17, "See the need for finding ways to discharge some of my emotional tensions," than the passing group (39%, $N = 139$), with a difference that was also significant at the .001 level of confidence. There was an undifferentiated (39%, 48%) response to Item 18, "See the need to avoid actions likely to induce further stress," which seems to imply a general acceptance of the fact that stress cannot be avoided.

Summary of the Statistical Analysis of Participant Evaluations of the Career Counseling Conference

The results for the general career items that were analyzed for the total group of participants are generally highly favorable and increase in favorability as the specificity of the item increases. The results suggest that participants appreciate having objective and relevant standards or norms with which to compare their test scores. These attitudes create a positive environment for self-directed development, on-the-job coaching, or formalized group-training programs. Indeed, in the evaluations made of the seminar as a whole, the career counseling conference has for many years been voted the most useful, or at least within the first three most useful, unit in the curriculum.

The remaining items in the evaluation questionnaire are directed toward specific measures in the test battery in order to investigate the relationship between a participant's score on a given test dimension and the favorability of his or her evaluation. There appears to be no relationship between scores on the experience and background test dimensions and the responses to the relevant questionnaire items. Furthermore, items dealing with interpersonal relations in the parental family get some of the lowest favorable responses of all items in the questionnaire. There are a number of possible reasons for this. Participants may perceive the items as being too "personal"; however, the items in the even more sensitive emotional health area do differentiate among the subgroups. A more likely reason is that participants do not perceive this area of the test results as being useful to them since it deals with past events, any long-range effects of which would not be remediable in this single-interview setting. These items are, nonetheless, useful to the counselor since the responses sometimes provide insight on behavioral problems presently being encountered by the participant.

The results in the area of mental abilities and aptitudes refute the suggestion sometimes made that the favorable evaluations of the career counseling conference are made largely by people with high scores on the test battery. Actually the reverse is the case, with some of the highest percentages of favorable response being for low-scoring groups on the two tests of language facility, where improvement in the scores could be expected to result from structured and assiduous efforts at self-improvement. The same is true also of low-scorers on creative potential when ways of compensating for a lack of creativity, through such means as harnessing the creativity of others or of adopting a team approach to management, are discussed in the conference. These responses suggest that participants both accept the test battery scores that relate to their abilities and the objectives of the career counseling conference. These objectives are to identify strengths and weaknesses for the purpose of utilizing the strengths and suggesting means for either improving deficiencies or of compensating for untrainable deficiencies.

Some interesting results are obtained for items relating to the Emotional Responsiveness test dimension in the normal range of behavior. The results suggest that the prevailing sentiment among higher-level personnel is that the individual should always give the impression of being in control and not make an overt display of emotion, since suggestions concerning some deleterious effects of a too-rigid control over spontaneity and responsiveness are rejected equally by the high- and low-scoring subgroups on the Emotional Responsiveness dimension. This notion is supported by the fact that the high-scoring subgroup on the Emotionality Responsive dimension shows a significantly higher affirmative response to the idea of toning down too-volatile behavior.

In the area of emotional health, participants who failed the screening procedure, which is an indication of high levels of internal tension, seemed to accept the diagnosis and to express a desire to find ways of discharging the tensions. If the tension is situational and caused, for example, by difficulty in working with a particular supervisor, the stress can sometimes be relieved by reordering the work environment. In cases of severe emotional problems or maladjustment, the counselor can do little more in a one-interview situation than to be supportive, not aggravate the situation, and, possibly, to recommend psychotherapy. On the positive side, participants who passed the screening procedure seemed to be reinforced in their belief that they were coping well in a tension-filled world.

This career counseling procedure is not widely applicable to the vocational counseling of high school students since it has been specifically developed for higher-level positions in business and industry. Its greatest strength is that it serves those key positions that are vital to an organization's future and that are often not amenable to traditional test validation procedures. The clearly defined framework for the counseling conference provides for uniformity in its use by different counselors. The uniform evaluations presented here are derived from sessions conducted by at least six different counselors. Even if the complete counseling procedure is not used, the objective data provided by the STEP program can serve as a useful input in any evaluation situation including individual career counseling; assessment centers; and personnel procedures for selection, placement, promotion, all of which have as their ultimate objective the orderly deployment of the human resource throughout the organization.

APPENDIX 8.1: CAREER COUNSELING EVALUATION QUESTIONNAIRE

As a result of the career counseling conference and feedback of the results on the STEP program I:

<u>CHECK ONE</u>

	Yes	?	No
1. Know how my concept of the important functions of the job compares with that of others in similar positions.	___	___	___
2. Know my ability levels with respect to the important functions of my job.	___	___	___
3. Can make a realistic comparison of my past record of achievements with that of my age peer group.	___	___	___
4. Know the relative extent to which I assume leadership roles in group activities and the implications of this behavior.	___	___	___
5. Have a better idea of how early developmental experiences have shaped my life.	___	___	___
6. Have a better perspective on my relationships with members of my parental family.	___	___	___
7. Can better judge my intellectual strengths and weaknesses.	___	___	___
8. Know where there is a need to develop some aspect of my language skills.	___	___	___
9. See how I can better harness my creativity for the common effort.	___	___	___
10. See ways in which I can compensate for my own lack of creativity.	___	___	___
11. See the advantage of utilizing the creativity of peers and subordinates.	___	___	___
12. Have a better understanding of my own personality functioning.	___	___	___

	Yes	?	No

13. Have a clear picture of the image I portray to my supervisors and associates.

14. Realize the effects on others of my too rigid control over spontaneity and responsiveness.

15. See the need to tone down my somewhat too volatile behavior.

16. Feel reassured that I am coping quite well in a tension filled world.

17. See the need for finding ways to discharge some of my emotional tensions.

18. See the need to avoid actions likely to induce further stress.

19. Have a realistic idea of my strengths and weaknesses with respect to some meaningful standards of comparison.

20. Know better how to cope with or compensate for some of my deficiencies.

21. Have had my generally positive image of myself reinforced.

22. Have had useful input for considerations with respect to a possible career change or promotion.

Name _____
(Optional)

237

9

The Challenges to Human Resource Management in the 1990s and Beyond

Brian D. Steffy and Melany E. Baehr

Speculating on the state of human resource management (HRM) in the year 2000 and beyond is not without its risks. Who in 1971 could have predicted the impact on the personnel function of equal employment opportunity, safety, and pension security legislation passed in that decade? This legislation, especially the Civil Rights Act as amended in 1972, forced managers to institute more professional job analysis procedures, as well as more reliable and accurate practices for hiring, promoting, and financially rewarding employees (Ledvinka, 1982). The personnel function was elevated in organizational stature as managers sought to ensure the legality of human resource (HR) practices and policies. Likewise, how many employers and employees in 1980 were as worried then as they are today about decreased career and earnings opportunities associated with the acquisition/merger wave, corporate restructurings, and downsizings witnessed during the eighties? During that decade approximately 500,000 white-collar jobs were eliminated and, within the managerial ranks, numerous middle-level management positions were cut in an effort to reduce bureaucratic overhead and control costs (Goldstein, 1988; Handy, 1990). Given these dynamic events over the past two decades, it must be assumed that HRM in the year 2000 cannot be predicted from a linear trend line extending from the present. It is much more probable that the HRM function will have to adapt to unexpected random shocks.

With this precaution in mind, this chapter identifies some of the dynamic forces currently in motion that may change the face of HRM. No attempt is made to provide a comprehensive list of specific forecasts; they can be found elsewhere (Goldstein, 1988; Handy, 1990; Hirsch, 1987). Instead, we first present a conceptual framework for evaluating the HRM function as an integrated system of policies and practices that govern organizations' employees. We then forecast subtle shifts in the HR system attributable to changes in the demand for and supply of labor, new institutional strategies and structures, and changing personal expectations. Recommendations are also made as to how the HR function might realign itself to obtain a motivated and committed work force in the face of declining opportunities for intraorganizational mobility and earnings. Finally, where appropriate, the role of the STEP progam in helping companies to adapt optimally to these trends is discussed.

A CONCEPTUAL TOOL FOR HUMAN RESOURCE MANAGERS

The mix of activities attributed to the HR function is best understood by recourse to an underused conceptual framework: internal labor market (ILM) analysis. Labor economists and industrial sociologists are somewhat familiar with this construct, although it may have the greatest utility for the personnel specialist. An organization's ILM is defined as the policies, practices, and procedures governing the allocation and evaluation of its work force (Doerigner & Piore, 1971). The ILM consists of those policies and practices instituted by management to ensure that, over the long run, the work force possesses the requisite skills, knowledge, abilities, and motivation to meet expected levels of job performance. It is a managerial tool for controlling labor costs. An organization's ILM can be delineated into at least five subsystems: (1) its *job system*, which defines the vertical, or hierarchical arrangement, and horizontal (job classes, divisions, national) configuration of jobs; (2) its *mobility system*, defined by the network of career paths that depict mobility into, through, and out of the job system; (3) its *compensation system*, which overlaps the job/mobility system and consists of decision rules and procedures for pricing jobs and differentially rewarding job-holders according to their performance and length of service; (4) its *training system*, which consists of a series of interventions and treatments to provide employees with the skills, knowledge, and abilities they lack, but are necessary to meet job demands; and (5) its *appraisal system*, which provides performance information to inform mobility, compensation, and training decisions. These five subsystems overlap and compliment one another and force us to appreciate the social and economic interdependencies of HR policies and practices.

CHANGES IN HUMAN RESOURCE SUBSYSTEMS

What changes can we expect in the management of the above HR subsystems? Below we outline the "conventional wisdom" and, perhaps, "new wisdom" regarding HRM. We focus most of our attention on managerial and professional/technical employees, since it is with these groups that the greatest changes are expected and for which the STEP program was developed.

Job-Mobility System

Conventional wisdom says that, whether we enter the organization in a managerial or nonmanagerial job class, we can expect to steadily move up the organization, enjoying greater status and earnings as we advance. We enter a port-of-entry position of a job class, moving vertically on what may be one of a number of job ladders within the job class. Perhaps we may move horizontally across job ladders or job classes, but the emphasis is on vertical and not horizontal mobility. Employees often possess knowledge of the job-mobility system. They may have expectations regarding the number of steps needed to advance from the port-of-entry to ceiling job in the job class, the probability of moving to the next job level in a given period of time, the length of time it typically takes to move from bottom to top, and the career consequences of moving horizontally to another ladder or job class. The rate of upward mobility would normally depend on the availability of positions created by attrition or expansion, the suitability of the employee's particular abilities and attributes for the functions to be performed in the position, and the level of relevant job skills that the employee has acquired in the course of progress to the present position.

Opportunity and specialized qualifications and training may not, however, be the major determinants of sustained upward mobility in rapidly changing job systems brought about by corporate restructuring and downsizing, themselves a consequence of mergers, acquisitions, and pressures to control costs in an increasingly competitive world economy. During the 1980s, and continuing into the 1990s, job systems have been thinned and flattened. Numerous white-collar, lower-level management and middle-level management jobs have been eliminated. Remaining jobs have been vertically loaded. For example, the responsibilities of remaining middle-management jobs have been broadened as these managers absorb part of the work load once done by those in the eliminated managerial jobs. Sudden and unexpected changes in organizations' job systems have placed an even greater burden on job analysis, which has been firmly established as a professional and legal prerequisite of most personnel procedures by successive governmental guidelines. The old classical job analysis procedures, based on the results of multiple interviews conducted by trained job analysts of incumbents at successively lower levels in the organization are now not only out-of-date but largely inoperable. This is due in part to the fact that the interview-based procedures often took a year or more to complete for a medium-sized organization alone. The results of such systems, which were expected to stay in place for some time, were descriptions of the requirements to be met for successive upward movement. They represented what industrial psychologists refer to as an enactment of a mechanistic-bureaucratic administrative paradigm (Perrow, 1986). Sudden and unexpected changes in an organization's job system requires a job analysis procedure that is professionally sound, preferably objective, and time- and cost-effective. Such a procedure would make it possible to monitor changes in position requirements with minimum effort and cost and could even be used to develop operational job descriptions for projected future positions. Here the viability of the Managerial and Professional Job Functions Inventory (Baehr, Lonergan, & Hunt, 1978) for current and future job analysis becomes clearer.

Apart from changing job structures, complete categories of jobs have been eliminated from organizations as employers close down entire departments, giving the work to outside consultants or temporary-service agencies. Japanese corporations have long recognized that externalizing jobs may reduce overhead and allow flexibility as business volume expands and contracts. If we add to these trends a slowing economy, hence fewer vacancies, mobility opportunities will become increasingly scarce. The fast-track may become the slow-track. Fewer promotions can be expected. Length of stay in most jobs will increase. The length of time required to move from the port-of-entry to ceiling job may increase. Most importantly, we should witness a slow shift in emphasis from vertical-oriented mobility to horizontal-oriented mobility.

The shift in emphasis to horizontal mobility may be both a necessary tactical realignment to changing strategic realities and, if effectively managed, a means of obtaining a motivated and committed work force, given increasingly scarce opportunities for vertical mobility. Horizontal mobility provides employees with an alternative set of opportunities; the opportunity to broaden their skills, knowledge, and abilities, thus making them more economically valuable to their current employer, as well as other employers. Human resource specialists suggest that we may see an increase in the following mobility practices and policies (Goldstein, 1988; Handy, 1990; Hirsch, 1987):

1. *Vertical loading:* employees will have more discretion and decision-making latitude as positions above and below them in the vertical hierarchy are eliminated.

2. *Job sharing:* employees may hold more than one position and any given position may be held by two or more individuals.

3. *Dual and spiral job ladders:* professional and technical employees may no longer have to enter the managerial ranks in order to enhance earnings and status but will be able to rise to higher levels of professional expertise without

assuming managerial responsibility. The concept of dual-career ladders was introduced over a decade ago and some HR specialists suggest that they have not been effective, although their failure may not be due to dual-ladder designs, but to not offering professional/technical employees the financial rewards offered to managers. For dual-job ladders to work, professional/technical employees may have to have access to the same perks, stock option plans, and profit sharing opportunities as managerial personnel (Raelin, 1987). Given these prerequisites, even more flexible arrangements may be common where professionals and managers rotate between juxtaposed dual ladders (i.e., the spiral job ladder).

4. *An increase in the rate of horizontal mobility:* in addition to increased movement across job ladders, national and international assignments may be treated as perks.

5. *Shrinking emphasis on formal job titles:* as the job-mobility system is flattened and decentralized, organizations will discourage the formation of "pecking orders," replacintg this culture with one based on the maintenance of community and collective-based decision making.

6. *Long-run vertical mobility:* employees will move up the job system, but it will be nonlinear. The "spiral" is perhaps the most correct metaphor describing an employee's career path. How far one moves upward and the rate of upward mobility will be a function, among other things, of the general competencies obtained through horizontal transfers.

Appraisal-Compensation-Training System

An organization's internal wage structure overlaps its job system. That is, wages are differentially assigned to jobs based upon the job's occupational content (job class, job ladder) and, within the job class, its vertical position along the job ladder. The higher wages for higher positions are attributed to increased discretion, risk, responsibility, effort, and skill requirements. Most organizations possess two internal wage structures: managerial and nonmanagerial. Among the nonmanagerial ranks, compensation and appraisal systems are usually more bureaucratically fixed and rigid. Conventional wisdom suggests that nonmanagerial employees are assigned to a job with fixed responsibilities and duties. Wage survey and job evaluation data inform compensation managers on the general pay parameters of the job class and the wages that should be attached to jobs hierarchically arranged within the job class. Merit ratings and seniority rules suggest how to differentially distribute rewards to employees working in the same job. These procedures will most likely remain intact, although, due to some thinning and flattening within the nonmanagerial job classes, we may see a corresponding flattening of the internal wage structure.

We should witness greater changes in pay policies and practices within the managerial and professional job classes. As the job-mobility system becomes more flattened and flexible, so will the internal wage structure. Subsequently, if we are to rationalize pay reward policies, they can no longer be based solely on vertical mobility or promotions. Otherwise, substantial pay raises will be infrequent. With an increasing emphasis on horizontal mobility, alternative mechanisms must be found for rationalizing rewards. Two suggestions have been offered. First, compensation specialists need to recognize and reward managers and professionals who, through horizontal mobility, cross-training, and other means, have developed a range of "general competencies." With an array of skills, knowledge, and abilities these employees may offer greater future service contribution value to the organization than those steadily moving up a specialized job ladder. "General competency" would need to be formally recognized as a job requirement if it is to be a component of a compensation system for a work force characterized as organic, flexible, and adaptable. "Pay-for-knowledge" (Milkovich & Newman, 1987) constitutes one approach for rewarding such employees. Similar practices are common among Japanese corporations (Ouchi, 1981). As in many Japanese firms, this means that the rate of earnings growth increases the longer one remains in the organization, since time is necessary in developing "general competencies."

If such policies are implemented, we should witness an increased emphasis on training requirements. The costs of training an entire higher-level work force in a wide array of competencies could become a serious consideration. It would seem to be more feasible to train for general competencies at managerial levels, where there is overlap in the functions to be performed, than at port-of-entry positions where there are often university-trained professional knowledge and skill requirements. A second approach to addressing the compensation issue is the strengthening of individual-based merit and bonus systems by differentially rewarding outstanding contributions. Merit-based rewards are particularly valuable because they allow pay increases without vertical movement. Individual merit and bonus systems allow the flexibility required for allocating rewards when the job-mobility system breaks down.

Finally, what are the implications for performance appraisal practices employed to base financial rewards. Conventional wisdom says that performance evaluations focus only on job-related, specific, observable, tangible, and quantifiable behaviors. Graphic-rating scales, behaviorally anchored rating scales, and behavioral observation scales implicitly assume such an approach. Given a possible shift in emphasis to general competencies similar across job classes and hierarchical levels, will conventional wisdom suffice? Perhaps organizations should modify or supplement traditional appraisal procedures so that current job performance is adequately rewarded, as well as the development of general competencies. To satisfy the professional and legal requirements of performance appraisal, the competencies would have to be clearly defined and their measurement quantified on a standardized scale. In the context of the STEP program, this would require that Job Skill Assessments be developed for individuals based on the identified important functions in the vertically and horizontally linked positions for which they could be considered.

IMPLICATIONS FOR HUMAN RESOURCE MANAGEMENT

It has, for many years, been generally accepted that the main role of the human resource function is to serve the overall objectives and mission of the organization (McGregor, 1960; Hambrick, Fredrickson, Korn, & Ferry, 1989). Recent economic forces and the restructuring due to mergers and downsizings have made it more difficult to fulfill this role both because of rapidly changing organization objectives and changes in the work force. Some claim that in the work force of the 1990s, the individual manager and professional is going to be more of a "free agent" (Hirsch, 1987). In other words, employees no longer believe in a long-term career with increasing rewards and security in a single corporation. As a result, they are taking more responsibility for their own careers by acquiring the job competencies that will make them attractive in the job market and allow them to seize the "main chance" without regard to company loyalty. To ensure the smooth and effective operation of the organization, the human resource function will not only face the challenge of motivating this rather disenchanted work force but will have to do so in the face of stringent competition among corporations for talented, high-potential individuals. Some suggestions are made for meeting these challenges.

Linking Human Resource Planning to the Strategic Business Planning Process

Although this has long been a hoped-for ideal, it has for many reasons been difficult to implement. One barrier to its implementation has been the traditionally reactive rather than proactive stance of the HR function (Andrews, 1987). Traditionally, the HR function has been called on to react to such organizational requirements as the need to hire an estimated number and type of personnel for the implementation of some organization objective, or to provide a replacement for an unexpected vacancy in a higher-level position, rather than to be part of the process that would make it possible to foresee such needs or provide for such contingencies. Another barrier has been that HR managers have not been accepted as equal members of the management team, but have often been accorded lower status and pay than their counterparts in other functional departments.

There are, however, strong indications of a change in attitude toward the HR function. In a survey investigating a range of business issues, including recommendations for transforming the HR function, sent to CEOs and senior executives in 20 countries, 78 percent of the 1,500 respondents felt that HR planning should be an intrinsic part of corporate strategy (Hambrick, Fredrickson, Korn, & Ferry, 1989). The same survey provided evidence of the growing importance of the HR function. When respondents were asked to rank 10 areas of expertise for the CEO of today and for the CEO of the year 2000, expertise in the HR area rose from a third to a second place ranking in importance for the CEO of the year 2000. Only expertise in strategy formulation was ranked higher.

HR specialists and managerial personnel will need to operate in close partnership to ensure the smooth functioning and profitability of the organization. HR specialists must be aware of the objectives of the organization and the HR planning that will be necessary to achieve them. Managerial personnel, on the other hand, must understand and support the HR procedures that have been designed to implement organization objectives. Ultimately, it is the managers who are responsible for the hiring, firing, training, and promotion of personnel.

Efficiency of the Human Resource Function

In the context of the overall profitability of the enterprise, HR managers should seriously consider the economic efficiency of their decisions. This point may seem obvious, yet many personnel scholars and practitioners design and implement a complex web of interdependent policies and practices without considering their net economic payoff (Steffy & Maurer, 1988). By definition, personnel activities are efficient, or economically productive, if the personnel expenses incurred lead to the acquiring and retaining of better performances, and this in turn translates into revenue flows such that the firm's total investment in wages and mix of policies and practices results in a rate of return equal to or exceeding some desired rate of interest (Steffy & Maurer, 1988; Thurow, 1970). Personnel subfunctions are economically interdependent. For example, decreasing the selection ratio (number hired to number of applicants) through increased recruitment investments should improve the validity of selection decisions, and hence the economic value of the firm (Steffy & Ledvinka, 1989). Selection investments may be viewed as a relatively inexpensive means of rank-ordering recruits according to those who require less training, socialization, and supervision, all of which are costly (Thurow, 1970). Improved recruitment, selection, and training, especially of lower-level personnel, may decrease costly counterproductive behaviors such as theft, absenteeism, accidents, injuries, malpractice, negligence, and ill-health (Jones, Barge, Steffy, Fay, Kunz, & Wuebker, 1988; Jones & Terris, 1991). "Efficiency wage theory" suggests that paying employees above market rates may actually control and decrease overall labor costs. A "lead" wage policy may attract better applicants who require less training, help sustain employee motivation and retention, and result in hiring a work force less predisposed to counterproductive behaviors (Steffy & Maurer, 1988).

Streamlining and Integrating Human Resource Procedures

Equally important in ensuring the efficiency and cost-effectiveness of the HR function is the recognition by human resource and strategic managers that the HR function is not merely the summation or aggregation of quasi-autonomous subfunctions: recruitment, selection, staffing, compensation, training, developing, succession planning, and the like. Each subfunction is necessarily linked to and will typically affect the need for and effectiveness of other HR activities. For maximum efficiency, implementation of HR activities must be better linked and integrated. For example, one strategy for linking the HR activities for positions at three levels of management across five separate job families (technical, support, operations, etc.) in an information services department (Mirabile, Caldwell, & O'Reilly, 1986) was to provide a common framework for the positions by developing a list of competencies required at different management levels and in different job families. Information concerning the overlap among the competencies was clearly applicable to such activities as selection and assessment, and career pathing and development.

The competencies were developed on the basis of information obtained from structured job analysis interviews and included both worker characteristics such as "analytical thinking," "persistence," and "tolerance for stress," and work characteristics or activities such as "developing others," "team building," and "delegation." In the STEP program, the worker characteristics are measured by the managerial and professional test battery. The work characteristics or job skills are derived from measures obtained from the standardized job analysis instrument (MP-JFI) mentioned earlier. It is the job analysis procedure that is the mechanism for linking the human resource procedures for the matrix of higher-level professional and managerial positions for which the STEP program was developed. It was demonstrated in Chapter 7 (see Figure 7.13) how a single administration of the Ability form of the MP-JFI together with an extended test battery can yield information concerning an employee's potential for successful performance and level of acquired skill in the important job functions for all of the horizontally and vertically linked positions in the job classification matrix. This information leads naturally to training and development programs and to succession planning. The obtained information also makes it possible to implement horizontal transfers (and thus the acquisition of general competencies) as efficiently and naturally as the traditional upward movement in organizations.

The job analysis instrument used in the STEP program is "generic" in the sense that it was developed for use across different organizational and institutional settings. The STEP procedure could be customized by developing a job analysis instrument to cover the key positions in a particular organization. This procedure requires the development of a single data base to implement human resource objectives. The multiplicity of specific tasks performed in lower-level jobs makes it unlikely that they could all be covered in a single task inventory or work-oriented analysis instrument. This suggests that the more feasible approach, often followed for other HR procedures such as wage and salary administration, would be to treat the higher-level (exempt) and lower-level (nonexempt) jobs separately. Not only are there likely to be more changes in higher-level positions, but the functions performed in these positions in larger organizations are generally fewer in number and more homogeneous in their underlying work behaviors.

The customization of a job instrument for a particular family of higher-level personnel represents a strong commitment of both managerial and a variety of professional/specialist personnel, but the advantages derived from its use in linking human resource management programs are clear and considerable. The organization will have specific information for career pathing and for the training required to develop general competencies in the work force. This, in turn, will provide maximum flexibility in the management of the work force to meet changing objectives or restructurings in the organization. The employees will acquire a broad array of competencies that, in turn, will provide a greater choice of career options and security for survival in a competitive and changing work environment. The challenges to HR professionals in the 1990s and beyond are clear, and the STEP program is one system that can help these professionals to meet these challenges successfully.

References

Alenderfer, M. S., & Blashfield, R. K. (1984). *Cluster analysis*. Sage University paper on Quantitative Applications in the Social Sciences, 07-044. Beverly Hills, CA: Sage Publications.

American Society for Personnel Administration. (1985). *Results of a resource survey on testing*. Arlington, VA: ASPA Information Services.

Andrews, J. R. (1987). Where doubts about the personnel role begin. *Personnel Journal*, 85–89.

Baehr, G. O. (1959/1987). *Emo questionnaire interpretation and research manual*. Park Ridge, IL: London House.

Baehr, G. O., & Baehr, M. E. (1958/1986). *Emo questionnaire*. Park Ridge, IL: London House.

Baehr, M. E. (in press). *Managerial and professional job functions inventory interpretation and research manual*. Park Ridge, IL: London House.

Baehr, M. E. (1991a). Job analysis procedures for higher-level executive and professional positions. In J. W. Jones, B. D. Steffy, & D. W. Bray (Eds.), *Applying psychology in business: The handbook for managers and human resource professionals*, 169–183. Lexington, MA: Lexington Books.

Baehr, M. E. (1991b). Identifying high-potential executive and professional personnel through psychological assessment. In J. W. Jones, B. D. Steffy, & D. W. Bray (Eds.), *Applying psychology in business: The handbook for managers and human resource professionals*, 345–356. Lexington, MA: Lexington Books.

Baehr, M. E. (1987a). The managerial and professional job functions inventory (MP-JFI). In S. Gael (Ed.), *Job analysis handbook*. New York: John Wiley & Sons.

Baehr, M. E. (1987b). A review of employee evaluation procedures and a description of "high potential" executives and professionals. *The Journal of Business and Psychology*, *1*, 172–202.

Baehr, M. E. (1986). *Validation of selection and placement procedures for the ordained ministry. Final report.* Chicago: The University of Chicago.

Baehr, M. E. (1984a). The empirical link between program development and performance needs of professionals and executives. *Continuum, 48,* 157–167.

Baehr, M. E. (1984b). *The development and validation of the estimates of potential for successful performance (PSP) of higher-level personnel.* Chicago: The University of Chicago, Office of Continuing Education.

Baehr, M. E. (1981). *A job-focussed approach to the validation of screening procedures for first line supervisory positions.* Chicago: The University of Chicago, Human Resources Center.

Baehr, M. E. (1979a). *Observational assessments of temperament.* Park Ridge, IL: London House

Baehr, M. E. (1979b). *A project to improve human resource planning and development in the sales division of NALCO chemical company.* Chicago: The University of Chicago, Human Resources Center.

Baehr, M. E. (1978). *A human resource planning and development project for The First National Bank of Pennsylvania.* Internal Research Report. Chicago: The University of Chicago, Human Resources Center.

Baehr, M. E. (1976). *National validation of a selection test battery for male transit bus operators* (UMTA-MA-06-0011-77-1). Chicago: The University of Chicago, Industrial Relations Center. (NTIS No. PB-283 709/AS).

Baehr, M. E. (1967). *A factorial framework for job description.* Paper presented at the meeting of the Industrial Section, Illinois Psychological Association, Springfield, IL.

Baehr, M. E. (1957/1985). *Temperament comparator.* Park Ridge, IL: London House.

Baehr, M. E. (1952). A factorial study of temperament. *Psychometrika, 17,* 107–126.

Baehr, M. E., & Corsini, R. J. (1957/1985). *The press test.* Park Ridge, IL: London House.

Baehr, M. E., & Froemel, E. C. (1980). *Experience and background inventory.* Park Ridge, IL: London House.

Baehr, M. E., Furcon, J. E., & Froemel, E. C. (1968). *Psychological assessment of patrolman qualifications in relation to field performance.* Washington, DC: U.S. Government Printing Office.

Baehr, M. E., Lonergan, W. G., & Hunt, B. A. (1978). *Managerial and professional job functions inventory.* Park Ridge, IL: London House.

Baehr, M. E., & Moretti, D. M. (1985). *System for testing and evaluation of potential (STEP) and legal compliance.* Park Ridge, IL: London House.

Baehr, M. E., & Orban, J. A. (1989). The role of intellectual abilities and personality characteristics in determining success in higher-level positions. *Journal of Vocational Behavior, 35,* 270–287.

Baehr, M. E., & Williams, G. B. (1968). Prediction of sales success from factorially determined dimensions of personal background data. *Journal of Applied Psychology, 52,* 98–103.

Bartlett, C. J., Bobko, P., & Pine, S. M. (1977). Single-group validity: Fallacy or the facts? *Journal of Applied Psychology, 62,* 155–157.

Bentz, V. J. (1983). Research findings from personality assessment of executives. *Sixth annual symposium on applied behavioral science,* at Virginia Polytechnic Institute and State University, Blacksburg, VA.

Binet, A. (1903). *Experimental studies of intelligence.* Paris: Schleicher.

Blanz, F., & Ghiselli, E. E. (1972). The mixed standard scale: A new rating system. *Personnel Psychology, 25,* 185–199.

Boehm, V. R. (1977). Differential prediction: A methodological artifact? *Journal of Applied Psychology, 62,* 146–154.

Bolen, L. M., & Torrance, E. P. (1978). The influence of creative thinking on locus of control, cooperation, and sex. *Journal of Clinical Psychology, 34,* 903–907.

Bonoma, T. V., & Johnston, W. V. (1979). Locus of control, trust, and decision making. *Decision Sciences, 10,* 39–55.

Borland, C. (1974). *Locus of control, need for achievement and entrepreneurship.* Doctoral dissertation. The University of Texas at Austin.

Borman, W. C. (1973). *First line supervisor validation study.* Minneapolis: Personnel Decisions, Inc.

Brady, K. R., Elliott, K. E., & Adams, E. A. (1990). *Validating STEP with performance ratings of theatre managers in the entertainment industry.* Technical Report No. S 21. Park Ridge, IL: London House.

Bray, D. W., & Campbell, R. J. (1968). Selection of salesmen by means of an assessment center. *Journal of Applied Psychology, 52,* 36–41.

Bray, D. W., Campbell, R. J., & Grant, D. L. (1974). *Formative years in business: A long-term AT&T study of managerial lives.* New York: Wiley-Interscience.

Bray, D. W., & Grant, D. L. (1966). The assessment center in the measurement of potential for business management. *Psychological Monographs, 80* (Serial No. 625).

Brockhaus, R. S. (1975). I-E locus of control scores of predictors of entrepreneurial intentions. *Proceedings of the Academy of Management,* 433–435.

Brown, S. H. (1978). Long-term validity of a personal history item scoring procedure. *Journal of Applied Psychology, 63,* 673–676.

Bruce, M. M. (1959). *Bruce vocabulary inventory.* New Rochellle, NY: Author.

Campbell, J. P., Dunnette, M. D., Arvey, R. D., & Hellervik, L. V. (1973). The development and evaluation of behaviorally based rating scales. *Journal of Applied Psychology, 57,* 15–22.

Campbell, D. T., & Fiske, D. W. (1959). Convergent and discriminant validation by the multitrait-multimethod matrix. *Psychological Bulletin, 56,* 81–105.

Chalupsky, A. B. (1962). Comparative factor analyses of clerical jobs. *Journal of Applied Psychology, 46,* 62–66.

Chusmir, L. H., & Koberg, C. S. (1986). Creativity differences among managers. *Journal of Vocational Behavior, 29,* 240–253.

Corsini, R. J. (1957/1985). *Non-verbal reasoning test.* Park Ridge, IL: London House.

Development Dimensions, Inc. (1975). *Catalog of assessment and development exercises.* Pittsburgh, PA: Author.

Dickinson, T. L. & Zellinger, P. M. (1980). A comparison of the behaviorally anchored rating and mixed standard scale formats. *Journal of Applied Psychology, 65,* 147–154.

Dictionary of occupational titles: Vol. I. Definition of titles; Vol. II. Occupational classification. (3rd ed.) (1965). U.S. Training and Employment Service. Washington, DC: U.S. Government Printing Office.

Dipboye, R. L., Fontenelle, G. A., and Garner, K. (1984). Effects of previewing the application on interview process and outcomes. *Journal of Applied Psychology, 69,* 118–128.

Doeringer, P. P., & Piore, M. J. (1971). *Internal labor markets and manpower analysis.* Lexington, MA: Heath.

Dunnette, M. D. (1976). Aptitudes, abilities, and skills. In M. D. Dunnette (Ed.), *Handbook of industrial-organizational psychology.* Chicago: Rand McNally.

Dunnette, M. D. (1962). Personnel management. *Annual Review of Psychology, 13,* 285–314.

Duval, S., & Wicklund, R. A. (Eds.) (1972). *A theory of objective self-awareness.* New York: Academic Press.

Dvorak, B. J. (1956). The general aptitude test battery. *Personnel and Guidance Journal, 35,* 145–154.

Edwards, A. L. (1959). *Manual for the Edwards personal preference schedule.* New York: Psychological Corporation.

Edwards, A. L. (1957). *Techniques of attitude scale construction.* New York: Appleton-Century-Crofts, Inc.

Elliott, K. E., Wilson, C. E., & Moretti, D. M. (1990). *Predicting performance and promotability of sales professionals in the petroleum industry.* Technical Report No. S 19. Park Ridge, IL: London House.

Eysenck, H. J. (1972). *Maudsley personality inventory.* San Diego, CA: Educational and Industrial Testing Service.

Eysenck, S.B.G., & Eysenck, H. J. (1970). Crime and personality: An empirical study of three factor theory. *British Journal of Psychology, 10,* 239–325.

Fine, S. A. (1974). Functional job analysis: An approach to a technology for manpower planning. *Personnel Journal,* 813–818.

Fine, S. A., & Wiley, W. W. (1971). *An introduction to functional job analysis.* Washington, DC: The W. E. Upjohn Institute for Employment Research.

Flanagan, J. C. (1954). The critical incident technique. *Psychological Bulletin, 51,* 327–358.

Frost, A. G., & Joy, D. S. (1987). *The use of the personnel selection inventory and the emo questionnaire in the selection of child care workers.* Technical Report Number 52. Park Ridge, IL: London House.

Furcon, J. E. (1965). *Creative personality: A factor analytic study.* Unpublished master's thesis, DePaul University, Chicago.

Ghiselli, E. E. (1971). *Explorations in managerial talent.* Pacific Palisades, CA: Goodyear Publishing Company, Inc.

Gilmour, P., & Lansbury, R. (1986). The first line supervisor and their managerial role. *Journal of Management Development, 5,* 59–72.

Goldstein, B. L., & Patterson, P. O. (1986). Can we count on muddling through the *g* crises in employment? *Journal of Vocational Behavior, 33,* 452–462.

Goldstein, M. L. (1988). Dual-career ladders. *Industry Week,* 57–60.

Gordon, L. V. (1960). *Manual for survey of international values.* Chicago: Science Research Associates.

Guilford, J. P. (1967). *The nature of human intelligence.* New York: McGraw-Hill.

Guilford, J. P. (1959). *Personality.* New York: McGraw-Hill.

Guilford, J. P. (1940). *Inventory of factors STDCR.* Beverly Hills, CA: Sheridan Supply Company.

Guilford, J. P., & Martin, H. G. (1943a). *Guilford-Martin inventory of factors GAMIN.* Beverly Hills, CA: Sheridan Supply Company.

Guilford, J. P., & Martin, H. G. (1943b). *Guilford-Martin personnel inventory O AG CO.* Beverly Hills, CA: Sheridan Supply Company.

Guion, R. M. (1976). Recruiting, selection, and job replacement. In M. D. Dunnette (Ed.), *Handbook of industrial-organizational psychology.* Chicago: Rand McNally.

Hambrick, D. C., Fredrickson, J. W., Korn, L. B., & Ferry, R. M. (1989). Preparing today's leaders for tomorrow's realities. *Personnel,* 23–26.

Hamner, W. C., Kim, J. S., Baird, L., & Bigoness, W. T. (1974). Race and sex as determinants of ratings by potential employees in a simulated work sampling task. *Journal of Applied Psychology, 59,* 705–711.

Handy, C. (1990). *The age of unreason.* Boston, MA: Harvard University Press.

Hathaway, S. R., & McKinley, J. C. (1943). *Minnesota multiphasic personality inventory.* New York: Psychological Corporation.

Hemphill, J. K. (1959). Job description for executives. *Harvard Business Review, 37,* 55–67.

Hendriksen, A. E., & White, P. O. (1964). Promax: A quick method of rotation to oblique structure. *British Journal of Statistical Psychology, 17,* 65–70.

Heneman, H. G., III, Schwab, D. P., Huett, D. L., & Ford, J. J. (1975). Interviewer validity as a function of interview structure, biographical data, and interviewee order. *Journal of Applied Psychology, 60,* 748–753.

Hilton, T. L., & Dill, W. R. (1962). Salary growth as a criterion of career progress. *Journal of Applied Psychology, 46,* 3, 153–158.

Hirsch, P. (1987). *Pack your own parachute.* Reading, MA: Addison-Wesley.

Holland, J. L., et al. (1970). *A psychological classification of occupations.* Baltimore: Center for Social Organization of Schools, Johns Hopkins University, Research Report No. 90.

Hornaday, J. A., & Aboud, J. (1971). Characteristics of successful entrepreneurs. *Personnel Psychology, 24,* 141–153.

Huck, J. R., & Bray, D. W. (1976). Management assessment center evaluations and subsequent job performance of white and black females. *Personnel Psychology, 29,* 13–20.

Hughes, J. F., Dunn, J. F., & Baxter, B. (1956). The validity of selection instruments under operating conditions. *Personnel Psychology, 9,* 321–324.

Human Resources Center, The University of Chicago. (1961). *Word fluency.* Park Ridge, IL: London House.

Hundall, P. S. (1971). A study of entrepreneurial motivation: Comparison of fast- and slow-progressing small scale industrial entrepreneurs in Punjab, India. *Journal of Applied Psychology, 55,* 317–323.

Hunter, J. E. (1986). Cognitive ability, cognitive aptitude, job knowledge and job performance. *Journal of Vocational Behavior, 29,* 340–362.

Hunter, J. E., & Schmidt, F. L. (1978). Differential and single-group validity of employment tests by race: A critical analysis of three recent studies. *Journal of Applied Psychology, 63,* 1–11.

Industrial Relations Center, The University of Chicago (1970). *Validation of a* sales selection test battery against paired comparison ratings of perfor-mance on the job. Chicago: Author.

Industrial Relations Center, The University of Chicago (1967). *Technical appen-dix to the validation of a sales selection test battery against paired com-parison ratings of performance on the job.* Chicago: Author.

Janz, T. (1982). Initial comparisons of patterned behavior description interviews versus unstructured interviews. *Journal of Applied Psychology, 67,* 577–580.

Jeanneret, P. J., & McCormick, E. J. (1969). *The job dimensions of "worker-ori-ented" job variables and of their attribute profiles as based on data from the position analysis questionnaire.* Lafayette, Indiana: Occupational Re-search Center, Purdue University, Report No. 2.

Jones, J. W. (1983). *The burnout syndrome: current research, theory, interven-tions.* Park Ridge, IL: London House Press.

Jones, J. W., Barge, B., Steffy, B. D., Fay, L., Kunz, L., & Wuebker, L. (1988). Stress and medical practices, organizational risk analysis and intervention. *Jour-nal of Applied Psychology, 73,* 727–735.

Jones, J. W., & Terris, W. (1991). A personnel selection approach to controlling employee theft and counterproductivity. In Jones, J. W., Steffy, B. D., & Bray, D. (Eds.), *Applying psychology in business: The handbook for man-agers and human resource professionals.* Lexington, MA: Lexington Books.

Katzell, R. A., & Dyer, F. J. (1977). Differential validity revived. *Journal of Applied Psychology, 62,* 137–145.

Kendall, M. J. (1955). *Rank correlation methods* (2nd Ed.) London: Charles Grif-fin.

Kets de Vries, M.F.R. (1977). The entrepreneurial personality: A person at the crossroads. *Journal of Management Studies, 14,* 34–57.

Kipper, D. A., & Baehr, M. E. (1988). Consistency as a moderating factor in self- and observational assessments of personality. *Perceptual and Motor Skills, 66,* 559–568.

Kobasa, S. C. (1979). Stressful life events, personality, and health: An enquiry into hardiness. *Journal of Personality and Social Psychology, 37,* 1–11.

Kogan, N. (1974). Creativity and sex differences. *Journal of Creative Behavior, 8,* 1–14.

Landy, F. J. & Farr, J. L. (1983). *The measurement of work performance: Methods, theory, and applications.* New York: Academic Press.

Ledvinka, J. (1982). *Federal regulation of personnel and human resource man-agement.* Boston, MA: Kent.

Lefcourt, H. M. (1981). *Research with the locus of control concept.* New York: Academic Press.

London House (1989). *Management styles questionnaire.* Park Ridge, IL: Author.

London House (1977). *Personnel selection inventory (PSI-5).* Park Ridge, IL: Au-thor.

MacKinnon, D. W. (1975). *An overview of assessment centers* (Technical Report). Greensboro, NC: Center for Creative Leadership.

Marquardt, D., & McCormick, E. J. (1974a). *The job dimensions underlying the job elements of the position analysis questionnaire (PAQ), form B.* La-fayette, IN: Occupational Research Center, Department of Psychological Sciences, Purdue University, Report No. 4.

Marquardt, L. D., & McCormick, E. J. (1974b). *The utility of job dimensions based on form B of the position analysis questionnaire (PAQ) in a job component validation model.* Lafayette, IN: Occupational Research Center, Department of Psychological Sciences, Purdue University, Report No. 5.

McClelland, D. C. (1978). *Guide to behavioral event interviewing.* Boston, Massachusetts: McBer and Company.

McClelland, D. C. (1961). *The achieving society.* Princeton: D. Van Nostrand.

McClelland, D., & Winter, D. G. (1969). *Motivating economic achievement.* New York: Free Press.

McCormick, E. J., DeNisi, A. S., & Shaw, J. B. (1979). Use of the position analysis questionnaire for establishing the job component validity of tests. *Journal of Applied Psychology, 64,* 51–56.

McCormick, E. J., Jeanneret, P. J., & Mecham, R. C. (1969). *Position analysis questionnaire.* West Lafayette, IN: Purdue University.

McDaniel, M. A., & Jones, J. W. (1988). Predicting employee theft: A quantitative review of the validity of a standardized measure of dishonesty. *Journal of Business and Psychology, 2,* 327–345.

McGregor, D. (1960). *The human side of enterprise.* New York: McGraw-Hill Book Company, Inc.

Mecham, R. C., & McCormick, E. J. (1969). *The use of data based on the position analysis questionnaire in developing synthetically derived attribute requirements of jobs.* Lafayette, IN: Purdue University, Occupational Research Center.

Mednick, S. A. (1962). The associative basis of the creative process. *Psychological Review, 69,* 220–232.

Meehl, P. E. (1954). *Clinical vs. statistical prediction.* Minneapolis: University of Minnesota Press.

Milkovich, T. T., & Newman, J. M. (1987). *Compensation,* Plano, Texas: Business Publications.

Mirable, R., Caldwell, D., & O'Reilly, C. (1986). Designing and linking human resource programs. *Training and Development Journal,* 60–65.

Moretti, D. M., & Allen, D. C. (1988). *Predicting performance of managers in a heavy industry organization.* Research Report No. S 17. Park Ridge, IL: London House.

Moretti, D. M., Morken, C. L., & Borkowski, J. M. (1989). *Profile of the American CEO: Comparing Inc. and Fortune executives.* Technical Report No. S 3. Park Ridge, IL: London House.

Morsh, J. E. (1964). Job analysis in the United States Air Force. *Personnel Psychology, 17,* 7–17.

Mosier, C. I. (1943). On the reliability of a weighted composite. *Psychometrika, 8,* 161–168.

Neiner, A. G., & Owens, W. A. (1985). Using biodata to predict job choice among college graduates. *Journal of Applied Psychology, 70,* 127–136.

Newmark, C. S. (1985). The MMPI. In C. S. Newmark (Ed.), *Major psychological assessment instruments.* Boston, MA: Allyn and Bacon.

Orban, J. A. (1984). *Profile analysis and comparison.* Internal Technical Report. Park Ridge, IL: London House, Research and Development Division.

OSS Assessment Staff (1948). *The assessment of men.* New York: Rinehart.

Ouchi, W. (1981). *Theory Z.* Reading, MA: Addison-Wesley.

Owens, W. A. (1976). Background data. In M. D. Dunnette (Ed.), *Handbook of industrial-organizational psychology.* Chicago: Rand McNally.

Owens, W. A. (1968). Toward one discipline of scientific psychology. *American Psychologist, 23,* 782–785.

Panel discussion on the changing role of the human resources executive (1985). *Personnel, 22–28.*

Perrow, C. (1986). *Complex organizations: A critical essay.* New York: Random House.

Personnel Research and Development Corporation (1960/1985). *Sales attitude check list.* Chicago: Science Research Associates, Inc.

Porter, L. W., & McKibbin, L. E. (1988). *Management education and development.* New York: McGraw-Hill Book Company, Inc.

Prediger, D. J. (1989). Ability differences across occupations: More than *g. Journal of Vocational Behavior, 34,* 1–27.

Prien, E. P. (1963). Development of a supervisor position description questionnaire. *Journal of Applied Psychology, 47,* 10–14.

Prien, E. P., & Ronan, W. W. (1971). Job analysis: Review of research findings. *Personnel Psychology, 24,* 371–396.

Primoff, E. S. (1972). *The job-element procedure in relation to employment procedures for the disadvantaged.* Washington, DC: U.S. Civil Service Commission, Bureau of Policies and Standards, Personnel Research and Development Center.

Primoff, E. S. (1969). *Use of measures of potential and motivation in a promotion examination from laborer-type positions to gardener-trainee park service.* Washington, DC: United States Civil Service Commission, Standards Division, Bureau of Policies and Standards, Personnel Measurement Research and Development Center.

Primoff, E. S. (1955). *Test selection by job analysis: The J-coefficient, what it is, how it works.* Washington, DC: U.S. Civil Service Commission, Standards Division, Test Development Section, Assembled Test Technical Series No. 20.

Pynes, J., Bernardin, H. J., Benton, A. L., & McEvoy, G. M. (1988). Should assessment center dimension ratings be mechanically derived? *Journal of Business and Psychology, 2,* 3, 217–227.

Raelin, J. (1987). Two-track plans for one-track careers. *Personnel Journal, 97–101.*

Rothstein, H. R., Schmidt, F. L., Erwin, F. W., Owens, W. A., & Sparks, C. P. (1990). Biographical data in employment selection: Can validities be made generalizable? *Journal of Applied Psychology, 75,* 175–184.

Rotter, J. B. (1990). Internal versus external control of reinforcement: A case history of a variable. *American Psychologist, 45,* 489–493.

Rotter, J. B. (1966). Generalized expectancies for internal versus external control of reinforcement. *Psychological Monographs: General and Applied, 80,* 1–28.

Runyon, K. E. (1973). Some interactions between personality variables and management styles. *Journal of Applied Psychology, 57,* 288–294.

Saal, F. E. (1979). Mixed standard rating scale: A consistent system for numerically coding inconsistent response combinations. *Journal of Applied Psychology, 64*, 422–428.

Sackett, P. R., Burris, L. R., & Collins, C. (1989). Integrity testing for personnel selection. *Personnel Psychology, 42*, 491–529.

Sackett, P. R., & Dreher, G. F. (1982). Constructs and assessment center dimensions: Some troubling empirical findings. *Journal of Applied Psychology, 4*, 401–410.

Sandroff, R. (1990). How ethical is American business? *Working Woman*, September, p. 113.

Saunders, D. R. (1962). Trans-varimax: Some properties of the ratiomax and equamax criteria for blind orthogonal rotation. *American Psychologist, 17*, 395–396.

Schmidt, F. L. (1988). The problem of group differences in ability test scores in employment selection. *Journal of Vocational Behavior, 33*, 272–292.

Schmidt, F. L., Berner, J. G., & Hunter, J. E. (1973). Racial differences in validity of employment tests: Reality or illusion? *Journal of Applied Psychology, 58*, 5–9.

Schmidt, F. L., & Hunter, J. E. (1977). Development of a general solution to the problem of validity generalization. *Journal of Applied Psychology, 62*, 529–540.

Schmidt, F. L., Hunter, J. E., Pearlman, K., & Shane, G. S. (1979). Further tests of the Schmidt-Hunter bayesian validity generalization procedure. *Personnel Psychology, 32*, 257–281.

Schmidt, F. L., Hunter, J. E., & Urry, V. W. (1976). Statistical power in criterion-related validation studies. *Journal of Applied Psychology, 61*, 473–485.

Schmidt, F. L., & Johnson, R. H. (1973). Effect of race on peer ratings in an industrial situation. *Journal of Applied Psychology, 57*, 237–241.

Schmitt, N., & Hill, T. E. (1977). Sex and race composition of assessment center groups as a determinant of peer and assessor ratings. *Journal of Applied Psychology, 62*, 261–264.

Scollay, R. W. (1957). Personal history data as a predictor of success. *Personnel Psychology, 10*, 23–26.

Seymour, R. T. (1986). Why plaintiffs' counsel challenge tests, and how they can successfully challenge the theory of "validity generalization." *Journal of Vocational Behavior, 33*, 331–364.

Singh, S. (1978). Achievement motivation and entrepreneurial success: A follow-up study. *Journal of Research in Psychology, 12*, 500–503.

Sparks, C. P. (1965). *Prediction of cognitive test scores by life history items: Comparison across two different ethnic groups*. Houston: Author.

Spearman, C. (1927). *The abilities of man*. New York: MacMillan.

Spector, P. E. (1982). Behavior in organizations as a function of employee's locus of control. *Psychological Bulletin, 91*, 482–497.

SRA/London House (1989). *Test catalog for business*. Park Ridge, IL: Author.

Srinivasan, T. (1984). Originality in relation to extraversion, introversion, neuroticism, and psychoticism. *Journal of Psychological Researches, 28*, 65–70.

Srivastva, S., and Associates (1988). *Executive integrity: The search for high human values in organizational life*. San Francisco, CA: Jossey-Bass.

Steffy, B. D., & Ledvinka, J. (1989). The impact of five definitions of fair employment selection on minority mobility and employee utility: A simulation model. *Organizational Behavior and Human Decision Process, 44,* 297–324.

Steffy, B. D., & Maurer, S. D. (1988). Conceptualizing and measuring the economic effectiveness of human resource activities. *Academy of Management Review, 13,* 271–286.

Strickland, B. R. (1978). Internal-external expectancies and health-related behaviors. *Journal of Consulting and Clinical Psychology, 46,* 1192–1211.

Stroop, J. R. (1935). Studies of interference in serial verbal reactions. *Journal of Experimental Psychology, 17,* 643–662.

Theologus, G. C., Romashko, T., & Fleishman, E. A. (1970). *Development of a taxonomy of human performance: A feasibility study of ability dimensions for classifying human tasks.* Washington, DC: American Institute for Research, AIR-7-26-1/70-TR-5.

Thurow, L. (1970). *Investment in human capital.* Belmont, CA: Wadsworth.

Thurstone, L. L. (1951). The dimensions of temperament. *Psychometrika, 15,* 11–20.

Thurstone, L. L. (1950). *Creative talent* (Report No. 61). Chicago: The University of Chicago, Psychometric Laboratory.

Thurstone, L. L. (1947). *Multiple factor analysis.* Chicago: The University of Chicago Press.

Thurstone, L. L. (1944). *A factorial study of perception* (Psychometric Monograph No. 4). Chicago: The University of Chicago Press.

Thurstone, L. L. (1938). *Primary mental abilities* (Psychometric Monograph No. 1). Chicago: The University of Chicago Press.

Thurstone, L. L., & Jeffrey, T. E. (1984). *Closure flexibility (concealed figures).* Park Ridge, IL: London House.

Thurstone, T. G., & Mellinger, J. J. (1957/1985). *Cree questionnaire.* Park Ridge, IL: London House.

Tornow, W. W., & Pinto, P. R. (1976). The development of a managerial job taxonomy: A system for describing, classifying, and evaluating executive positions. *Journal of Applied Psychology, 61,* 410–413.

Tucker, D. H., & Rowe, P. M. (1977). Consulting the application form prior to the interview: An essential step in the selection process. *Journal of Applied Psychology, 62,* 283–287.

Turnage, J. J., & Muchinsky, P. M. (1984). A comparison of the predictive validity of assessment center evaluations versus traditional measures in forecasting supervisory job performance: Interpretative implications of criterion distortion for the assessment paradigm. *Journal of Applied Psychology, 69,* 595–602.

Uniform guidelines on employee selection procedures (1978). Adopted by the Equal Employment Opportunity Commission, the Department of Labor, the Department of Justice, and the Civil Service Commission. *Federal Register, 43,* 38,290–38,315.

U.S. Equal Employment Opportunity Commission (1970). Guidelines on employee selection procedures. *Federal Register, 35,* 12,333–12,336. Republished *Federal Register,* 1976, *41,* 51,984–51,986.

U.S. Office of Federal Contract Compliance, Department of Labor (1974). Amendment to OFCC Order on Employee Testing Procedures, *Daily Labor Report*, 1/18/74, (No. 13), D-2. Washington, DC: The Bureau of National Affairs.

Wainer, H. A., & Rubin, I. M. (1969). Motivation of research and development entrepreneurs: Determinants of company success. *Journal of Applied Psychology, 53*, 178–184.

Ward, J. H., Jr., & Hook, M. E. (1963). Application of an hierarchical grouping procedure to a problem of grouping profiles. *Educational and Psychological Measurement, 23*, 69–82.

Watson, D., & Baumal, E. (1967). Effects of locus of control and expectation of future control upon present performance. *Journal of Personality and Social Psychology, 6*, 212–215.

Watson v. Fort Worth Bank & Trust (July 1988). *Labor Law Reports*, Report 332.

Webster, E. C. (1964). *Decision making in the employment interview.* Montreal: McGill University, Industrial Relations Center.

Wernimont, P. E. (1962). Re-evaluation of a weighted application blank for office personnel. *Journal of Applied Psychology, 46*, 416–419.

Wherry, R. J. (1955) *A review of the J-coefficient.* Washington, DC: U.S. Civil Service Commission, Test Development Section, Standards Division, Assembled Test Technical Series No. 26.

Zetlin, M. (1990). Is business ethics really an oxymoron? *Management Review*, June, 49.

Index

Performance evaluation (*continued*)
194–97. *See also* Career develop-
ment
Perrow, C., 242
Personal-emotional adjustment testing,
managerial and professional test
battery: descriptions of, 89–93, 124–
25, 127; studies using, 108, 109, 124–
25, 127, 141–42, 233–35
Personality testing. *See* Temperament
and personality testing, managerial
and professional test battery
Personnel Research and Development
Corporation, 84
Personnel Selection Inventory (PSI-5),
91
Pine, S. M., 76–77
Pinto, P. R., 25, 52
Piore, M. J., 240
Porter, L. W., 3
Position Analysis Questionnaire
(PAQ), 6, 23; description of, 20;
studies using, 20–21
Potential for Successful Performance
(PSP), 143, 144, 146, 178, 180, 187,
207, 209, 217; studies using, 149–50,
152, 157–61
Prediger, D. J., 83
Prenta, Ronald, 68
Press Test, The: definitions of variables in, 101; description of, 88–89;
studies using, 124
Prien, E. P., 24, 27
Primoff, E. S., 21–22
Professional hierarchy: abilities/skills/
attributes measurement, 107–11,
114–16, 118, 121–22, 124–25, 127–
30, 133–35, 138–40; analysis, job,
38–39, 44–47, 49, 52–55, 57–61, 63–
65; background of, 8–9, 134; career
development, 14–15, 179, 198–99,
201, 203, 209, 212–13, 217, 221–22,
225; earnings prediction, 154, 156–
57; executives, 9, 38–39, 44–47, 49,
52–55, 57–61, 63–65, 107–11, 114–
16, 118, 121–22, 124–25, 127–30,
139–40, 150, 154, 156–57, 159–60;
hiring of, 14, 132, 179; middle man-

agers, 8–9, 38–39, 44–47, 49, 52–55,
57–61, 63–65, 107–10, 114–16, 118,
121–22, 124, 127–30, 138–39, 150,
154, 156, 159–60, 209, 212–13, 217,
221–22, 225; nonmanagement professionals, 8–9, 11, 14–15, 38–39,
44–47, 49, 52–55, 58–61, 63–65, 107–
10, 114, 116, 118, 121–22, 124, 127–
28, 130, 133–35, 150, 154, 156, 179,
198–99, 201, 203, 209; performance
prediction, 149–50, 152, 154, 156–57,
159–60; training and, 61, 63–65,
212–13
Promotion. *See* Career development
PSI-5 (Personnel Selection Inventory),
91
PSP. *See* Potential for Successful Performance
Pynes, J., 75

Raelin, J., 243
Reassignment. *See* Career develop-
ment
Recruiting. *See* Hiring
Remote Associates Test (RAT), 120
"Review of Employee Evaluation Pro-
cedures and a Description of 'High
Potential' Executives and Profes-
sionals, A" (M. E. Baehr), 99
Romashko, T., 20
Ronan, W. W., 27
Rothstein, H. R., 80
Rotter, J. B., 93, 121
Rotter Scale, 93
Rowe, P. M., 71
Rubin, I. M., 121
Runyon, K. E., 93

Saal, F. E., 195
Sackett, P. R., 74
Sales Attitude Check List, 84; description of, 85; studies using, 108
Sales hierarchy: abilities/skills/ attributes measurement, 84, 85, 107–11,
114–16, 118, 121–22, 124–25, 127–
30, 135–36, 138–40; analysis, job,
38–39, 44–47, 49, 52–55, 57–61, 63–

About the Author

MELANY E. BAEHR is Senior Consultant to SRA/London House, a Macmillan/McGraw-Hill company, and also conducts a private practice in industrial-organizational psychology. She was previously the Associate Director, Research, of the Human Resources Center, and Associate Professor in the Social Science Division of The University of Chicago. Dr. Baehr has contributed chapters to a number of professional textbooks and has published widely in such journals as the *Journal of Applied Psychology*, *Psychometrika*, and the *Journal of Vocational Behavior*.